Everyday Literacy

Environmental Print Activities for Children 3 to 8

Stephanie Mueller
Illustrated by Kathy Dobbs

Dedication

To children everywhere who grow up starting their day reading the backs of cereal boxes just like I did.

To my friend, Ann, whose encouragement set me on this path.

To all those at Friends of Early Education whose impact on the world of children will live forever.

And especially to my dear family whose support and patience make it all possible.

Everyday Literacy

Environmental Print Activities for Children 3 to 8

Stephanie Mueller
Illustrations: Kathy Dobbs

gryphon house, inc.
Beltsville, MD

Bulk purchase

Gryphon House books are available for special premiums and sales promotions as well as for fund-raising use. Special editions or book excerpts also can be created to specification. For details, contact the Director of Marketing at Gryphon House.

Disclaimer

Copyright

Published by Gryphon House, Inc.
10726 Tucker Street, Beltsville, MD 20705
301.595.9500; 301.595.0051 (fax); 800.638.0928 (toll-free)

Visit us on the web at www.gryphonhouse.com

Library of Congress Cataloging-in-Publication Data

Mueller, Stephanie R.
Everyday literacy: environmental print activities for children 3-8 / by Stephanie Mueller.
    p. cm.
Includes bibliographical references and index.
ISBN13: 978-0-87659-286-1
ISBN10: 0-87659-286-8
1. Language arts (Early childhood) 2. Early childhood education—Activity programs. I. Wheeler, Ann E. II. Title.
LB1139.5.L35M84 2005
372.6—dc22   2004020394

Table of Contents

Chapter 5—Linking Environmental Print With Math

Chapter 6—Linking Environmental Print With Science

Chapter 7—Linking Environmental Print With Small Motor Skills and Creativity

Chapter 8—Linking Environmental Print With Dramatic Play

Chapter 9—Connecting Home and School With Environmental Print

Chapter 10—Linking Environmental Print With My Community

Introduction

Children develop a sense of the world around them early in life. From an early age they react to the sights, sounds, tastes, and smells of their environment. A young infant may cry in response to a loud sound, become alert in response to a particular image, and calm to a familiar voice reading a story. In infants, the brain is already at work taking in and processing information. In other words, the child is learning. Early childhood professionals know this learning and development is part of a continual process that builds throughout life. Part of the learning process in any society involves literacy. It is a process that culminates in understanding the language or symbols that society uses to communicate. As one's literacy experiences and opportunities build and expand, so does the ability to decipher the symbols, making them a meaningful and useful part of the child's or adult's world. Psychologist Jean Piaget points out that cognitive development moves from the concrete to the abstract. Such is the way of early literacy development, moving from the concrete, familiar print in a child's world of favorite toys, food signs, and picture books to the expanded world of reading.

Literacy development, especially in early childhood, is enhanced through experiences such as talking about the child's "print" world, being read to, drawing and writing, singing songs, reciting rhymes, asking questions, and interacting with others. Parents, teachers, caregivers, older siblings, and other caring adults can provide the interaction that is vital to building a literate person. The abundant tools used to develop literacy in early childhood include looking at books and being read to, doing fingerplays, singing songs, writing, painting, drawing, and being in a print-rich environment. Of these, one is readily available despite language, culture, or socio-economic status—the print in a child's environment (community).

What Is Environmental Print?

Environmental print consists of the symbols, letters, and words encountered in the places we live, shop, travel to, learn, work, and so on. It includes traffic signs, food labels, newspapers, menus, greeting cards, and any other print that is part of everyday living. In a school it may include the signs for the bathrooms, exits, and office. To a child it may include the labels on toys and games, a calendar, favorite restaurant signs, familiar books, and a favorite cereal box he or she "reads" in the morning. The print in communities varies. In one community, much of the print may be in Spanish, while in another it may contain symbols and signs related to seed and farm equipment companies.

How Can Environmental Print Help in Literacy Development?

Environmental print as a tool in literacy development has the potential to be a motivating force in creating enthusiasm toward reading and using language with young children and developmentally delayed children. It can serve as a tool in language development. The benefit of using environmental print in literacy development has been shown in some studies to be directly related to the amount of guidance a caring adult provides in using it, and emphasizing the relationships it has to alphabet letters, words, and messages. It can be as simple as reading newspaper comics out loud to a toddler or engaging a preschooler in "reading" familiar signs while on a trip.

Adult interaction is vital to achieve the maximum benefit of using environmental print as a tool in literacy development. It involves gradually moving from using context clues (pictures, cartoon characters, colors, shapes, photos, and so on) to the printed letters and words themselves. Teachers and caregivers can enhance the application of print as a teaching tool by addressing it in a variety of contexts, settings, and uses. This involves establishing literacy connections between the print a child sees in his or her home environment and how he or she can use it to learn through interaction with caring adults. Using this readily available tool has the potential to motivate and encourage involvement from parents and caregivers who might otherwise be reluctant or intimidated by the literacy process.

Selecting Environmental Print

When collecting environmental print, it is important to give children the opportunity to help gather and use it. When selecting material to use in activities, it is important to consider the socio-economic groups, genders, cultures, and languages represented in the early childhood learning setting. Mainstream culture or a single culture should not be assumed to represent all children in a given setting. Environmental print is going to vary for each group of learners. Rural communities may be different from urban areas; monolingual communities may be different from multi-lingual environments. Teachers and caregivers need to be aware that some environmental print may be offensive or unidentifiable to a particular group of children. If the children are

involved in gathering the items, and the items are carefully selected to meet objectives, the activities have the potential to become accurate representations of children's environment while expanding their understanding of new vocabulary, other cultures, communities, genders, and languages.

Enlist the help of local area businesses, organizations, and parents to obtain print material and to schedule field trip opportunities.

Environmental print items to save and collect include:
✦ newspapers
✦ newspaper inserts, advertisements, and circulars
✦ coupons
✦ magazines and catalogs
✦ food product boxes, packages, and labels
✦ signs
✦ menus
✦ toy labels and packaging
✦ recipes
✦ greeting cards
✦ travel brochures
✦ restaurant take-home containers, placemats, and posters
✦ movie posters and flyers
✦ business letterhead, cards, forms, envelopes, and magnets

Things to Consider When Selecting and Using Environmental Print

The labels on generic or store brands of food often contain clearer and larger print than name-brand items. For example, a store-brand label may have "green beans" in large letters and "Max's Foods" in small letters, while a name-brand label may have "Marie's French Cut" in large letters and "green beans" in small letters. The first label would be more applicable to use in activities involving discussion about color words or words that begin with "g" or "b". The second label may be useful as an example of words that begin with "m". An item's print and context clues (pictures) need to be considered to determine its usefulness in meeting specific objectives. The intention a child might have in selecting a piece of environmental print also needs to be taken into account. For example, a child may bring in a container of frosting as an example of something that begins with a letter "f". However, the largest word on the container might be "chocolate." The connection with the print can by made by asking the child to find the word "frosting," which begins with the letter "f". Another option would be to identify the word for the children and underline it or re-write it somewhere on the container or blank label to emphasize it.

It is important to consider the font (or type) of printed letters and/or numbers on environmental print when making selections for a particular activity. For example, using a cereal box with the name in large print, cursive letters will not work well for an activity involving sewing through the letters to practice printed letter formation. Look at the print in terms of size, shape, and readability for a given activity.

When copying or using words from environmental print, make sure you and the child are referring to the same print. For example, if a child brings a can of green beans for a sharing opportunity involving color words and "green" is one of the smallest words in print on the label, take the time to underline or emphasize to the child where the word is on the label.

"Identifying words" is a term used in the book to describe the prominent words on the environmental print and can, in many instances, include a brand name. When copying identifying words from a label, it is important to reflect the lettering (upper- and lowercase) that is present, especially for activities using one-to-one correspondence with young children.

Organizing the collected print for various activities can be a big task. Use the objectives to help determine specific needs for environmental print. Sort environmental print as it is gathered by:

✦ subject matter or theme (apple products for an apple unit, business print for a community unit)
✦ type (cereal boxes, soup labels)
✦ literacy skill (print examples for letters and letter sounds, rhyming word examples, color word examples)
✦ specific activity (recipe books, travel, dramatic play)

Safety is another thing to keep in mind when collecting and selecting environmental print. Avoid using packaging or items that may be sharp, breakable, or hazardous. If metal cans are used, try using just the labels or unopened cans. Clean any items that may need disinfecting with a light bleach solution, and seal shut if possible before using them with children. Be aware of any allergies children may have when using environmental print of certain food products, such as peanuts, foods made with wheat, and so on.

Visual media on logos, labels, and signage can be a powerful tool in attracting attention and interest to building literacy skills. However, a lot of environmental print is created with the purpose of advertising products and businesses. Teachers and caregivers need to be aware of the powerful influence of advertising, especially toward children. Communication with parents as to the value, objectives, and reasoning behind the use of environmental print is vital. Careful and well-balanced choices in environmental print selection are important. Adult interaction will provide opportunities for discussion about the print and what it represents. Use of environmental print has the potential to include topics of discussion such as nutrition, safety, new vocabulary, and use of products without focusing on a particular brand name. For example, using print from fast-food restaurants in activities provides an avenue to talk about making balanced and healthy food choices.

Why I Wrote This Book

I wrote this book to provide a resource for teachers, caregivers, and parents to expand the already prevalent notion of using environmental print in the early childhood setting to encompass specific skills needed along the early literacy development process. The activities invite guiding adults to interact with the children at their level along the literacy development continuum. The purpose of the interaction is to build the bridge between seeing the print as a whole in context, and viewing it in the form of its function, letters, symbols, words and/or word meanings.

This book provides activity ideas using environmental print that can be used in the early childhood learning curriculum as well as at a child's home and community. Most of the activities are generically designed so that they can be adapted to use print materials that directly relate to the community that surrounds the child. The environmental print activities were designed keeping in mind they are only one of the tools needed for ongoing literacy development in an early childhood curriculum. Certainly, an ample supply of wonderful books, rhymes, and songs to listen to, read, explore, and act out are critical to the early childhood literacy curriculum.

This literacy tool can hold meaning for children and show the useful nature of print. Young children see and react to symbols that have meaning to them. Over time, they use the familiar context clues of such things as a favorite restaurant or toy label to decipher meaning and, in turn, see themselves as readers. When children think of themselves as readers, they become more involved or motivated to decipher words.

See the appendix for a complete list of definitions of terms used throughout the book.

Parts of the Book

The chapters encompass many areas of the early childhood curriculum. Literacy goals are provided in each chapter to show how concepts of print, letters, and words can be integrated in learning opportunities throughout the curriculum.

The chapters are divided into linking environmental print with: literacy skills; books and stories; building, blocks, and bulletin boards; group time; movement and music; math; science; small motor and creativity; dramatic play; connecting home and school; and being outside in the community.

Activities Layout

The Activity

Specifies the basic objective for the prepared materials and/or a brief description of how the children will use the activity.

Objectives

The objectives listed for each activity represent some of the literacy and language skills that can be addressed through using environmental print. Each one can be considered as part of introducing, reviewing, or practicing a skill in an existing sequence or curriculum. The objectives correspond to literacy interaction choices, which, in turn reflect varied levels of literacy/language skill development for each activity. For example, at a beginning preschool level, a literacy interaction may meet the objective of Print Awareness, while another literacy interaction in the same activity may meet the objective of Beginning Reading for children in kindergarten or early elementary ages. When doing an activity you can choose to concentrate on one or more of the objectives, depending on how they support the needs of the children. The important thing is that the chosen literacy interactions and corresponding objectives should match the development needs of the children and the overall goals of the curriculum in the learning environment. The listed objectives do not include all of the possible objectives for a given activity and can be added to or changed to fit the developmental needs of the children in your class.

Following are the objectives listed in this book.

Print Awareness: Children learn about the rules of written language, including:
- ✦ identifying the front and back of a book
- ✦ following print from left to right and top to bottom on a page
- ✦ distinguishing between print and pictures in having meaning in the classroom, home, and community

- following print as it is read aloud
- distinguishing letters from words
- recognizing that sentences are made up of separate words
- understanding that print and writing carries a message by recognizing labels, signs, and other print forms
- developing understanding of functions of forms of print such as lists, signs, and labels

Oral Language/Speaking and Listening: Children listen for information and pleasure and also verbally express ideas, share stories, and opinions. Specific skills include:

- listening to stories read aloud
- listening to and following oral directions
- sharing information about stories, artwork, and events
- participating in discussions and conversations
- retelling or reciting simple poems, rhymes, and songs

Phonics: Children demonstrate the ability to apply sound to alphabet symbols, including:

- identifying alphabet letters, especially those in their own name
- recognizing their name in print
- recognizing matching sounds associated with letters

Phonological/Phonemic Awareness: Children develop the ability to hear, identify, and manipulate individual sounds (phonemes) in spoken words and large parts of spoken language such as syllables, rhymes, words, onsets, and rimes. Specific skills include:

- discriminating individual phonemes in spoken words (the first sound in "pig" is /p/)
- recognizing which words in a set begin or end with the same sound ("sun," "snap," and "sink" all have /s/ at the beginning)
- hearing, identifying, and making oral rhymes
- hearing, identifying, counting, and working with syllables in spoken words
- distinguishing rimes (/at/ in "cat") and onsets (/c/ in "cat") in simple words
- blending phonemes to sound out words (/d/ /o/ /g/ = "dog")
- segmenting phonemes of simple words ("mat" = /m/ /a/ /t/)

Vocabulary: Children develop and expand knowledge of words and word meanings, including:

- increasing listening and speaking vocabulary
- understanding positional and directional vocabulary
- linking new experiences and words to prior knowledge
- using new words and language in writing and dictating experiences

Comprehension: Children pull meaning and understanding from spoken and written words. Specific skills include:

✦ using pre-reading skills to develop understanding (predicting, using picture context, and connecting to prior knowledge or experiences)

✦ retelling, reenacting, or dramatizing a familiar story, sequence, or event

✦ drawing meaning from a picture

✦ answering questions about a story or events

Writing Process: Children use writing, dictating, and/or drawing to express thoughts and feelings. Specific skills include:

✦ developing understanding of writing and drawing as a way of communicating

✦ progressing from drawing symbols and pictures to using letters to write name and other words

✦ participating in drawing, writing, and dictating stories, experiences, and recollections

✦ using letter and letter sound knowledge to write/spell words emergently

✦ tracing, copying, and writing alphabet letters, name, or words

Beginning Reading: Children identify words in text precisely or emergently, including:

✦ identifying and reading their own name in text

✦ reading familiar texts emergently, not necessarily from print alone

✦ recognizing some sight words

✦ reading simple sentences

Materials

Most of the material lists involve gathering environmental print. Consider alternatives when necessary to make the activity work for your setting. Ask businesses and parents to collect and donate materials. Some businesses have a lot of print available to give away, others will save discarded displays, posters, brochures, and so on if you request ahead of time. Look at websites of businesses and organizations for free print items and activities for educators. The other materials to complete the activities include those that are easy to find or readily available (see list on page 11 in introduction).

Theme Connections

Thematic units are used in many early childhood curriculum settings. Each activity in the book lends itself to several subjects or topics depending on the environmental print selected or used. Many activities can also be adjusted to fit a specific subject by the way it is presented. Listed in this section are several ideas for themes or subject areas that complement the activity.

Preparation

This is the area where adult preparation is described and specific instructions for children gathering and working with the environmental print are stated. Not all activities have this separate section. Some activities involve a lot of preparation before using the materials with the children, and some involve simply setting out the materials for the children to use. Adjust the amount of child involvement in any activity to relate to their development. For example, young preschool children may have little or no involvement in preparation that requires cutting out environmental print from cereal boxes while older preschool, kindergarten, and early elementary children may be able to do most of the preparation.

Literacy Interactions

This area offers one or more alternatives for using the activity based on the literacy development level of the children. (In chapter 9, "Connecting Home and School," "time together" activities are listed as part of the literacy interactions and are provided as options to send home with children to involve family and friends.) Most of the ideas are linked to the literacy objectives. The opportunities can be used as needed in isolation, or as a series of activities that build and expand the activity over time. It is important to know the literacy needs of the children that are using the activity and select the alternatives in this section to fit those needs. This will enable the children to achieve the maximum benefit from the activity. Some additions and changes are offered in this section to adjust the activity to meet a specific skill.

Things to Make

This section is included in the "Dramatic Play" chapter to provide ideas of things to make to enhance or include in a specific literacy interaction.

Linking With Books

Some of the activities or chapters contain a list of children's literature that may connect with or expand the concepts in the activity. Gathering and reading the suggested books will expand vocabulary and connections with the environmental print used in the activity. Many of the books listed incorporate environmental print into their illustrations.

Children's Literacy Development: A Continuum

The activities and objectives in this book primarily meet the needs of children ages three to eight, but with an understanding that literacy development can vary widely within an age group. A child's literacy development is a continual progression that can vary at any age depending on his or her social, physical, mental, and cultural circumstances. Even though each child may develop literacy skills differently and at different levels, research and patterns have emerged that show tendencies or goals in literacy development in particular age groups. Keeping in mind that literacy development is a continual progression, general literacy skills that are usually present in an age grouping are listed here to provide assistance in planning activities and selecting objectives.

Preschool

Preschoolers may:

+ listen to and discuss favorite storybooks read to them
+ tell about artwork
+ dictate messages, some in complete sentences
+ have some awareness of the function of print and writing in communication
+ distinguish between print and pictures in carrying meaning
+ engage in reading and writing attempts emergently or through role play
+ identify labels and signs in their environments
+ hear and identify some rhyming words in songs and rhymes
+ identify some letters
+ match some letters to sounds
+ use letters to represent written language such as their names, invented spelling
+ learn new vocabulary related to experiences
+ increase ability to hear, identify, and work with syllables in words

Kindergarten

Children in kindergarten may:

+ read favorite books, predictable books, and dictated stories emergently
+ listen to stories and retell familiar texts
+ use descriptive vocabulary to explain and explore
+ recognize letters
+ match letters to sounds
+ rhyme words
+ match and recognize beginning sounds and some ending sounds
+ understand concepts of print: left to right and top to bottom
+ match spoken words with written words
+ sound out some words (blending phonemes)
+ identify some sight words such as their names
+ write some alphabet letters
+ write some words including their names, maybe with spaces in between

- ✦ identify and count some syllables in spoken words
- ✦ predict, retell, and dramatize stories and events

Early Elementary

Children in first, second, and third grades may:

- ✦ read and retell familiar stories and rhymes
- ✦ read and write stories, lists, notes, and so on
- ✦ use reading strategies such as predicting, questioning, and rereading to understand text
- ✦ read some text orally
- ✦ decipher new words by using letter-sound associations, word parts, and context
- ✦ develop sight word vocabulary
- ✦ spell some words by sounding out or segmenting sounds
- ✦ work on sentence tools such as capitalization and punctuation

Linking Environmental Print With Literacy Skills

✦ In each activity in this chapter, the **objectives** are listed in order of difficulty—use them according to the skill level of the children in your class.

✦ In each activity in this chapter, the **literacy interactions** are listed in order of difficulty; use them according to the abilities and interests of the children.

Coupon Pocket Sort

Children sort coupons into pockets that contain matching products.

Objectives

Print Awareness: Children will use print clues to match coupons to environmental print pictures using one-to-one correspondence.

Phonics: Children will practice recognizing letters and letter sounds by using coupons in a sorting activity.

Materials

newspaper coupon inserts
library pockets or envelopes
scissors
poster board
glue
clothespins (optional)

Theme Connections

Alphabet
Community Helpers
Farms
Food and Nutrition
Gardening and Plants
Grocery Store
Health and Safety
Holidays

Preparation

1. Cut out product pictures and corresponding coupons from newspaper inserts.
2. Glue the product picture to the front of a library pocket or envelope.
3. Glue the envelopes in rows on a large piece of poster board, or glue clothespins to the poster board and clip on envelopes to create a versatile board.

Literacy Interactions

✦ Explain to the children what coupons are used for. Show a few examples of product pictures and corresponding coupons. Give coupons to the children and invite them to sort them into the pockets as you read each product name. Encourage them to use context clues or read the words to locate the correct pocket. Increase the level of one-to-one correspondence by using one type of environmental print (such as all toothpaste or all juice) or print the identifying name of the item on a pocket without the picture.

✦ Print letters or beginning letter sounds on the pockets with the product pictures. Say the sound or letter and invite the children to find the coupon that matches the picture and letter and/or sound. Invite the children to play the game with each other.

French Fry Word Match

Children identify letters or words on paper strips and match them to those on french fry containers.

Objectives

Print Awareness: Children will distinguish among words or letters on paper strips to locate the matching fry container.

Materials

clean french fry
     containers/envelopes
heavy paper or poster board
scissors
glue
marker

Theme Connections

Our Community
Restaurant

Preparation

1. Cut paper or poster board into 5–6" strips, approximately four or five per fry container.
2. Print the name of each restaurant on a set of strips ("fries"). For those containers that do not have words, print an identifying word such as a restaurant name somewhere on the front of each.
3. If desired, glue the fry containers on a large piece of poster board to create pockets.

Literacy Interactions

✦ Drop the "fries" on the floor. Read and identify a word or words on a fry container pocket. Let the children take turns picking up the fries and putting them in the correct container. Repeat for other pockets. Ask them what clues the letters provide to help them match them to the correct pocket. Use this activity as an opportunity to review names of letters.

✦ Teach the children how to play "Old Maid" using the fry containers as cardholders and the paper fries as cards. Draw a funny face on a blank strip and write "funny fry" on it. Give each child a cardholder (fry container) from a different restaurant. Shuffle the cards, deal them to the children, and ask them to put them in their holder with the words facing them. The children remove the cards that match their fry container and lay them next to them (these have been "eaten"). Let them take turns drawing fries from each other, adding matches to their pile until only the funny face card remains. The child who has it makes a funny face.

Box Front Memory

Children use box fronts containing print to play a memory game.

Objectives

Print Awareness: Children will attend to environmental print and use one-to-one correspondence to play the game of memory.

Beginning Reading: Children will use identifying words on environmental print to build sight word lists.

Materials

empty food boxes
    (two of each item)
scissors
permanent marker
poster board or index cards
glue

Theme Connections

Alphabet
Colors
Food and Nutrition
Grocery Store
Recycling

Literacy Interactions

✦ Collect boxes of one type of product, such as all juice boxes, flavored gelatin, or cereal boxes. Make sure there are two of each flavor or other distinguishing characteristic. The number of boxes you use depends on the level of the children. Cut off the front of each box so that they are all the same size. Show the children the box front cards and invite them to identify and discuss what is different and similar about the words and context clues on each. As you introduce each box front, write the word ("apple," "grape," "strawberry" or whatever is on the box) someplace where the children can see it, such as the blackboard. To attract further attention to the print on each card, write the identifying word on a small blank address label or piece of masking tape and adhere it to the front of the card. Include the children in this process as you introduce each identifying word by asking which word(s) are unique to each pair of cards.

✦ Play a game by putting the box front cards face down. Let them take turns turning over two at a time. Encourage them to look for matching pairs using their memory and one-to-one correspondence. Emphasize that they will need to attend to identifying words on the cards to find exact matches.

✦ Play the game as "Go Fish." Divide the cards equally among the children. Direct them to ask each other for cards using the products' identifying names to complete a match.

✦ Cut poster board into pieces the size of the box labels, or use index cards. Glue a box front to one and on the other, write the name of the product and identifying word. The children can use them to play a memory game, or "Go Fish" to practice sight word matching.

Variation

✦ Use other types of packages to make cards, such as small chip bags, vegetable labels, or seed packages. Glue to poster board or index cards.

Label Word Match

Children match sets of environmental print using context clues and/or letter or word recognition.

Objectives

Print Awareness: Children will play a game matching environmental print to identical print and identifying words.

Phonics: Children will identify letters of the alphabet and match them with words that start with those letters.

Phonological/Phonemic Awareness: Children will identify words that rhyme with environmental print words and use them to create and play a matching game.

Materials

newspaper inserts or magazines
scissors
index cards or 3" x 5" heavy
    paper or cardstock
glue
markers

Theme Connections

Community Helpers
Food and Nutrition
Health and Safety
Holidays

Preparation

1. Find two identical pictures of familiar products or places that contain print. Cut out pictures of objects or places starting with each letter of the alphabet (for example, a picture of apple juice, a baby, and so on).
2. Glue the pictures to index cards.
3. Print the identifying word or words on each card under the picture or logo.
4. On another index card, glue the identical picture (with identifying word) or choose one of the literacy interactions below.

Literacy Interactions

✦ Show the children one of each of the sets and encourage them to identify them by name. Place one of each set of matching picture cards on the floor or a table. Put the other cards in a bag. Encourage the children to select cards from the bag and match them to the identical pictures on the floor using context clues and/or letter or word knowledge.

✦ Write each letter of the alphabet on separate index cards. Ask the children to identify the letters and lay them out in order. Put the picture cards in a basket or bag. Let children take turns pulling them out. Identify the beginning letter together or individually and have a child place it under the matching letter card.

Variation

✦ Cut out and use coupons as matching cards for each product.

Learning With Lotto

Children match pictures and words on cards to matching spaces on a lotto game card.

Objectives

Print Awareness: Children will use environmental print words to find identical print in a matching game.

Phonics: Children will use what they know about letters and letter sounds to find matching environmental print words.

Phonological/Phonemic Awareness: Children will identify the rhyming word or picture that matches the environmental print on the lotto card.

Materials

poster board, large blank index cards, or cardstock

scissors

marker

ruler

small pictures from newspaper inserts

glue

Theme Connections

Alphabet

Community Helpers

Food and Nutrition

Gardening and Plants

Health and Safety

Holidays

Preparation

1. Create lotto game boards by cutting poster board, index cards, or cardstock into squares or rectangles, 8 ½" x 11" or smaller. (See page 244 for a blank bingo or lotto board.)

2. Draw a grid on each game board with approximately 6 to 12 boxes, depending on the developmental level of the children.

3. Cut out lotto cards from cardstock or other heavy paper the same size as the game board squares.

4. Cut out identical environmental print pictures (small pictures from newspaper inserts), two of each, to fit in the squares. Make sure the pictures have identifying print on them.

5. Glue one picture to a game board square and the other to a card. (Also see additional ideas in the literacy interactions below.)

6. Print the identifying name of the item on each card underneath the picture.

Literacy Interactions

✦ Introduce the game by pointing out the words below the picture on each card. Ask the children to find the same word on the environmental print picture. Encourage them to put the card on the matching picture on the lotto game board. To increase level of one-to-one correspondence, print the identifying word for each picture on a blank card and encourage the children to match the letters and sounds.

✦ Make matching cards containing only beginning or ending letter(s). Say the letter sound(s) and ask children to put the card on the matching space on the game board.

✦ Let children find and cut out items that pertain to a particular letter or letter sound they are working on. They can use them to make their own lotto games to take home.

✦ Find environmental print pictures that contain a clearly printed easy-to-rhyme word. Glue pictures on game board squares and print identifying words underneath. Print words or glue pictures on the cards that rhyme with the environmental print on the lotto game board. Hold up a card, read it out loud, and have children locate the match on the game board.

Variations

✦ Make cards with a unifying theme, such as a set of food group cards (one bread/cereal, one fruit, one dairy, and so on). Create a lotto game with one theme, such as cereal, gelatin, candy, restaurants, community helpers, signs, and so on.

✦ Make a grid on the floor using masking tape or colored tape. Tape large print, such as box fronts, signs, and so on in the grid squares. Make large cards to match with such things as beginning letter, identifying word, or matching picture. Play lotto.

Alphabet Picture Bingo

Children identify items on bingo game boards that match environmental print.

Objectives

Print Awareness: Children will distinguish among letters in environmental print words and use one-to-one correspondence to find identical letters, words, or pictures in a bingo game.

Phonics: Children will apply knowledge of alphabet letters, words, and so on to find matching environmental print words in a bingo game.

Phonological/Phonemic Awareness: Children will identify the syllables in environmental print by identifying the matching number on their bingo game board.

Materials

small pictures from newspaper inserts, coupons, and magazines
poster board, large blank index cards, or cardstock
markers and ruler
glue and scissors
bingo markers (chips, pieces of paper, buttons, and so on)

Theme Connections

Alphabet
Community Helpers
Food and Nutrition
Gardening and Plants
Health and Safety
Holidays

Preparation

1. Cut poster board, index cards, or cardstock into same size squares or rectangles (8 ½" x 11" or smaller).

2. Create bingo game boards by drawing a grid of approximately six to twelve squares on each card, depending on the developmental level of the children. (See page 244 for a blank bingo or lotto board.)

3. Put a word, letter, or picture in each square, depending on which Literacy Interaction you choose to do (see below for specific instructions). Create cards with a variety of arrangements.

4. Make bingo cards from cardstock or other heavy paper. Select pictures from environmental print that correspond to the words, letters, or pictures on the game boards and cut them to fit the bingo cards. Print the distinguishing characteristic such as name, beginning letter, and so on underneath the picture.

5. Explain how to play bingo. Tell the children that you will hold up a bingo card and they check their game boards for a match. If they have a match, they place a marker on the square.

Literacy Interactions

✦ Create a one-to-one matching picture bingo game by gluing small pictures from newspaper inserts, coupons, and magazines to two or three grid cards. Photocopy the cards using the photo setting on a copy machine. Cut apart the rows of the original cards. Rearrange the rows on another piece of paper and photocopy again. Do this several times to produce variations. Use the photocopied grids as bingo game boards. Cut the remaining original individual sections into bingo cards to use for the game. To play the game, hold up each card and say the name of the environmental print. When the children become familiar with the game, encourage them to play on their own.

✦ Choose a literacy skill on which the children are working, such as beginning letters, vowels, or identifying words. Write letters or words in the squares on the bingo game boards. Locate environmental print that relates to the letters or words in the squares. Cut out the print and glue to paper or cards to make bingo cards. As you hold up each card, read the name of the print. Encourage the children to listen carefully in order to identify where to place their bingo markers.

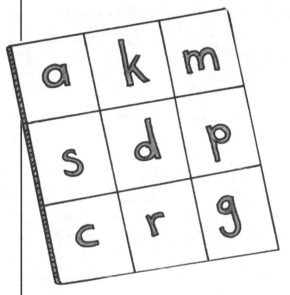

✦ Play "syllable count bingo." Find pictures that contain identifying words with a variety of syllables. Glue each picture to paper or cards to create bingo cards. Print the identifying word underneath, using a "-" to divide it into syllables as needed (for example, "pop-corn" and "dog-food"). Print numbers in the squares on the bingo game boards that correspond to the number of syllables represented (1, 2, 3, and so on). Create a variety of game boards. There can be duplicates of each number on the board but in a varied sequence. There are two ways to play:

Option 1: Clap or invite the children to clap the number of syllables on the cards as they are read. Direct the children to place a marker on a number that contains the same number of syllables on their bingo card.

Option 2: Hold up a bingo card, read the word, and have the children place a marker on a number that matches the number of syllables.

Variation

✦ Use the picture version of bingo when teaching children a new language. Find environmental print related to foods, signs, and other words children are learning. Say the word in the language the children are learning. Give them a chance to locate the matching picture, and then show them the picture on the card.

Labels on Lids Memory

Children use environmental print on lids to play various memory games.

Objectives

Print Awareness: Children will identify environmental print and use it to find identical print in a memory game.

Phonics/Decoding: Children will identify letters and/or sounds and find environmental print that contains matching letters and/or sounds.

Phonological/Phonemic Awareness: Children will identify environmental print and find words containing the same characteristic (such as beginning letter sounds, word families, or rimes).

Materials

newspaper inserts, small environmental print from businesses or products, stickers of signs, and so on

identical lids, at least 10 (such as film canister lids, juice can lids, plastic cup lids, or milk lids)

scissors and glue

permanent marker

Theme Connections

Alphabet
Community Helpers
Food and Nutrition
Health and Safety
Transportation

Literacy Interactions

✦ Cut environmental print (newspaper inserts, small environmental print from businesses or products, and stickers) to fit on the underside of lids and glue in place. Make matching pairs by gluing identical print in the same size lids. Turn over all the lids and explain how to play memory. Let children take turns picking up two at a time to reveal the environmental print underneath. Direct the children to replace those that do not match in the same spots and keep those lids that do match. Provide opportunities for them to play the game in small groups.

✦ Word-to-word match: Identify the clues that help distinguish the print on each lid. Make lid sets that include one lid with the environmental print in context (text with picture or symbol) and one lid with only the printed identifying word or words. Encourage the children to play the memory game using context clues and letter/word recognition to locate matching lids.

✦ Word-to-letter match: Choose environmental print that corresponds to letters or letter sounds children are learning. On one lid, glue the picture and print and on the matching lid, print the identifying letter(s). For example, one lid could have environmental print containing the word "spaghetti" and the other could have the printed letters "sp". Review the letters and/or letter sounds with the children before they play the game.

✦ Same sound/different word match: Locate environmental print that has the same sounds, such as beginning letters, word families, or ending letter, but are different words (for example, "butter" and "biscuit"). Together, identify the sounds and words on the lids before playing the game. Encourage children to identify sound similarities in the print verbally as they play the game.

Variation

✦ Help children make their own memory game using environmental print that emphasizes a literacy objective. Encourage them to bring home the game to play with their families.

Rhyme Time

Children identify words that rhyme with various products.

Objectives

Phonemic/Phonological Awareness: Children will hear and identify rhyming words.

Beginning Reading: Children will have the opportunity to add to sight word recognition using environmental print and the words that rhyme with it.

Materials

10–15 product containers with visible easy-to-rhyme names

large box or child-size shopping cart

chart paper, calculator tape, or other writing surface

marker

Theme Connections

Colors

Food and Nutrition

Grocery Store

Literacy Interactions

✦ Gather product containers that contain easy-to-rhyme words, such as "pop" tart, "red" licorice, and so on. Put the containers in a large box or child-size shopping cart. Use this activity to review or introduce rhyming words. Feature a word from one of the containers each day. Invite the children to generate rhyming words. Make a list of their words and display it next to or on the environmental print. Encourage the children to add to the list as they think of new words. Use the lists as an opportunity to demonstrate how sounds within a word can sound the same but look different ("pie" and "fly").

✦ Encourage the children to bring in product items from home to add to the collection of environmental print rhyming words. Sort the print into rhyming pairs to play a matching game (for example, "trail *mix*" and "potato *stix*").

✦ Use the rhyming word lists to build sight-word identification. Guide children in finding word families within the lists and environmental print. Use these words to create rhymes. Make books of rhyming words for children to read (using the environmental print for the cover). Encourage the children to use the rhyming words from a product in a dictated group story or poem.

Variation

✦ Use this activity as an opportunity to introduce *homophones* (words that sound the same but look different), for example, "flower" and "flour." Find examples of homophones on product containers.

Pick a Product

Children select environmental print that best corresponds to sentences on a recorded tape.

Objectives

Phonics: Children will listen and select environmental print associated with letter names and/or sounds.

Oral Language/Speaking and Listening: Children will use listening skills to identify environmental print and follow directions.

Phonemic/Phonological Awareness: Children will select environmental print that matches rhyming words.

Materials

environmental print that contains clear identifying words, such as product boxes, signs, and business cards
tape recorder
blank tape

Theme Connections

Community Helpers
Food and Nutrition
Grocery Store
Nursery Rhymes
Our Community

Preparation

1. For each piece of environmental print you choose, compose a sentence using the brand name, related letters, phonetic sounds, or whatever you desire.

2. Tape record a sentence for each piece of print. For example, "This food starts with a /p/ sound, like the word 'pig'."

3. Tape record each sentence again and include the answer for self-checking. ("This food starts with a /p/ sound like the word 'pig'." "Popcorn.")

4. Put the tape, tape recorder, and environmental print in the Listening Center for children to use, or use it as a large-group activity.

Literacy Interactions

✦ Create sentences that invite children to review letter recognition. For example, "Hold up the item that begins with the letter 'b' (beans)." Be sure to use environmental print that contains clearly printed words. Underline letter(s) you want the children to attend to (beans).

✦ Use the identifying business name on the environmental print in a sentence to reinforce listening skills. For example, "I drove to the (insert business name) yesterday." At the end of the sentences, repeat the names used. The children then select the environmental print used in the sentence.

✦ Choose beginning or ending letters or letter sounds to identify in sentences. For example, "Put the item that begins with the sound /i/ on your leg," or "Remove the item that has the same sound as in bike, ball, and bat." Let children listen to the tape and select print that best fits each sentence.

✦ Use words that rhyme with the environmental print in sentences. For example, "Shake the item that rhymes with the word 'nice'" (answer: "rice"). Have the children listen to the tape and select print that rhymes with the key word in each sentence.

Variation

✦ Make up sentences without using the tape recorder. Encourage children to make up their own sentences to challenge others.

What's in a Name?

Children explain why pieces of environmental print are labeled a certain way.

Objectives

Print Awareness: Children will learn the function of print in providing meaning about contents, services, and so on.

Vocabulary: Children will expand understanding of concepts and words using environmental print.

Oral Language/Speaking and Listening: Children will verbalize ideas and share knowledge about the meaning of words within environmental print.

Materials

a variety of environmental print, such as product containers, packaging, signage, and business print

paper or other writing surface

marker, pencil, or pen

Theme Connections

Babies

Colors

Community Helpers

Cultural Awareness

Food and Nutrition

Gardening and Plants

Health and Safety

Holidays

Shapes

Literacy Interactions

✦ Gather items with words that provide clues or descriptions for what it is, what it is used for, what is in it, and so on. For example, "peanut butter" contains peanuts, "chunk pineapple" has large pieces of pineapple, and "crispy rice" cereal makes a crunchy noise. Choose several examples and read the labels or names on each piece of print. Ask the children to provide ideas as to how the words describe or relate to the product or service. Document responses for each item, and use the responses to develop and broaden vocabulary and word usage. If possible, let them see the contents of the product, read ingredients, and so on to check their responses.

✦ Use environmental print that contains specific descriptive words to introduce concepts and vocabulary (for example, a product with the word "loop" in it to describe its circle shape, or a restaurant with the name "fiesta" in it to introduce the concept of feast or celebration). Invite children to bring in examples of environmental print that relate to a concept, such as "potato rounds" and "cereal squares" for shape vocabulary.

✦ Find environmental print that contains similar words or phrases, such as a few products that all have the word "green" in their name or on the label. Ask the children to guess what is alike and different among the print. Does the word or phrase represent the same thing on each piece of print? For example, is "green" the color of the items or is "Green" a person's name? What are some clues that help give the meaning?

Variations

✦ For older children, use the activity to introduce word origins and definitions.

✦ Incorporate the activity as part of expanding understanding of another language or culture by using labels of various ethnic foods.

Ch, Ch, Cheese Train

Children gather and sort environmental print into "train cars" (boxes) using what they know about letter sounds.

Objectives

Phonics: Children will practice recognizing various letter sounds using environmental print.

Writing Process: Children will use environmental print words representative of a phonetic sound to express and dictate or write a story.

Phonological/Phonemic Awareness: Children will have an opportunity to locate, identify, and sort environmental print by letter sounds on train car boxes.

Materials

boxes with lids, such as
    shoeboxes
paint, construction paper and
    tape, or contact paper
scissors
marker
product containers and
    wrappers, print from
    newspaper inserts, or
    magazines
yarn or heavy string
stapler or tape

Theme Connections

All About Me
Alphabet
Community Helpers
Food and Nutrition
Holidays
Our Community

Preparation

1. Remove and save lids from boxes.
2. Cover box sides and lids with paint, construction paper, or contact paper. Make each box a different color.
3. Cut out circles or draw circles on box sides to make wheels to create train cars.
4. Label each train car with a different phonetic sound, such as consonants, vowels, consonant blends ("bl", "pl", "gl'), digraphs, and so on as appropriate to literacy objectives.
5. Gather environmental print (product containers and wrappers, print from newspaper inserts, or magazines) that contains identifying words relating to the phonetic sounds on the train cars. For example, if the blend "ch" is printed on one of the boxes, you could use a cheese wrapper and chocolate wrapper.

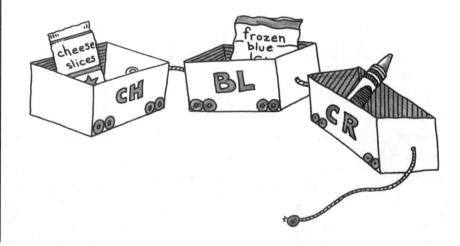

Literacy Interactions

✦ Introduce the phonetic sound and invite the children to repeat the sound specified on the train car. Make the letter sound(s) as you place environmental print item(s) in the car. Add more cars and sounds as they are introduced in study.

✦ Connect the train cars together by stapling or taping yarn to each box. Invite the children to pull the train around the room and put in items from different learning centers (crayons, glue, and so on) that contain the same beginning sounds identified by letters or words on the side of each car.

✦ Gather the items collected for a train car. Print the words related to the specific sounds on a writing surface for children to view. Invite the children to assist in creating a silly story incorporating all the environmental print words in the train car. Compile the stories into books and place in the cars for children to read.

Variation

✦ Let each child take a train car home to add items and return as a sharing activity. (See "Looking Out for Letters" on page 198 for ideas.)

✦ Use plastic ice cream tubs with lids instead of boxes.

Word Connections

Children match labels to complete words.

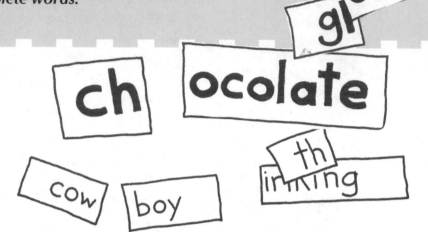

Objectives

Phonological/Phonemic Awareness: Children will identify and isolate letter(s) sounds using environmental print words.

Beginning Reading: Children will practice recognizing sight words and have an opportunity to use them to create compound words.

Materials

labels or pictures of labels that contain blends, digraphs, compound words, and so on

scissors

cards or heavy paper for mounting

glue

Theme Connections

Grocery Store

Newspapers

Preparation

1. Cut apart labels or pictures of labels to isolate individual words or sounds.
2. Glue each word or segment to a card.
3. On the back of each card write or type the corresponding word sections.

Literacy Interactions

✦ Begin the activity with the word pieces together. Say a sound such as /gl/ and invite the children to locate the environmental print that contains that sound ("glue"). Instruct them to pull the word apart to isolate the letters and put it back again.

✦ This is a great activity to introduce or review beginning sounds, such as consonant blends ("gl", "pl") or consonant digraphs ("th", "ch"). A consonant blend is a combination of two or more consonants blended together where all the letters are sounded and maintain their identity ("gl" in "glue"). A consonant digraph is two letters representing one sound ("th" in "thin"). Cut apart labels to isolate blends or digraphs. Say each sound and ask the children to complete a word that represents that sound (for example, "ch" cut from the word "chocolate"). Invite them to find the card with the rest of the word using context clues or by reading the word that needs to be completed. Guide them to put the pieces together to make the word. Read it together.

✦ Use the activity to introduce or review sight words located in compound words. Cut apart labels containing compound words to isolate the two words. Invite children to read each word separately, and then match the pieces to create a compound word. Encourage them to practice reading them together. Or, play a game by giving each child a piece of several sets. Help them identify the isolated sight words, and then locate the child with the word that creates the compound. Let them make new compound words by mixing the sets.

Word Parts Puzzles

Children put segmented words together to complete a word.

Objectives

Phonological/Phonemic Awareness: Children will learn about various sounds of spoken words (syllables, digraphs, and compound words, and so on) by putting segmented environmental print words back together.

Materials

small pieces from labels, newspaper inserts, packaging, and so on
scissors
envelopes
glue
index cards or strips of poster board
marker

Theme Connections

Community Helpers
Food and Nutrition
Gardening and Plants
Grocery Store

Preparation

1. Gather and cut out environmental print (small pieces from labels, newspaper inserts, packaging, and so on) according to a specific skill (for example, words with various syllables, consonant blends, digraphs, or compound words). Syllable examples include "chick-en" and "but-ter," consonant blends include "/bl/ueberry" and "/sp/lash," and consonant digraph examples include "/ch/eese" and "/ch/ocolate." (See the first Literacy Interaction below for more information.)
2. Glue each piece to an envelope.
3. Add the identifying word under the picture.
4. Write the same word on an index card, and cut apart each card according to the objective (by syllables, consonant blends, or whatever you choose).

Literacy Interactions

✦ Explain the literacy skill on which you want to focus and provide examples. When preparing the activity, engage children in locating environmental print that meets the literacy skill. Ask them to share their collections, and then use them to make the game.

✦ Use sound segment cards as a way to introduce letter sounds and combinations. Point to and read the identifying word on the envelope and ask the children to find the index cards that make the word when put together. Indicate how the words will be segmented. For example, "chicken" could be divided into digraph ("ch" and "icken") or by syllable ("chick" and "en"). Read the segmented sounds as each card is put back together. Mix up the cards and encourage the children to put them back together and place them in the correct envelope.

Coaster Characters in Cups

Children match plastic or foam letters to letters in words on restaurant drink coasters.

Objectives

Phonics: Children will identify letters and letter sounds and match them to environmental print.

Phonemic/Phonological Awareness: Children will demonstrate recognition of isolated sounds in environmental print by listening and matching them to representative letter(s).

Writing Process: Children will have the opportunity to practice the process of spelling words using one-to-one correspondence or by phonetic spelling.

Materials

4–8 restaurant drink coasters
plastic or foam letters, letter
     tiles, or paper squares
marker
small plastic pitcher or large cup
plastic cups

Theme Connections

Alphabet
Our Community
Restaurant

Literacy Interactions

✦ Gather appropriate imprinted drink coasters from several different restaurants, and plastic or foam alphabet letters that spell the brand name on each coaster. (If these are not available, make letters by printing on paper and cutting into squares.) Put the beginning or ending alphabet letter for each restaurant name in a pitcher. Pull out one letter at a time and say the letter or letter sound. Ask the children to find the coaster with the name that begins or ends with the letter. Read the coaster names as needed to help them locate the match. When the match is found, they drop the letter in a cup and set it on the coaster. As you play the game, ask the children to think of other words that contain the same letter or letter sound.

✦ Point to a coaster. Read the word(s) or invite children to use picture clues to read it (for example, a picture of a chicken on "Max's Chicken"). Ask them to listen and identify the beginning, middle, or ending sound of the word(s). Have children locate the represented sound using the letter or letter combinations in the pitcher and place them in the cup.

✦ Put the exact amount of letters needed to spell out each identifying word on the coasters in the pitcher. As children become familiar with the words on the coaster, encourage them to spell out the words using one-to-one correspondence. As they spell each word, they can dump the letters into the cup.

Variation

✦ Use purchased, plastic, linking letter cubes to spell out words on the coasters. They look like ice cubes and add interest to the activity!

Missing Letter Labels

Children complete words by identifying missing letter(s) and placing them on sentence strips where they belong.

Objectives

Phonics: Children will identify the letter and sound missing in environmental print word(s) on sentence strips.

Phonological/Phonemic Awareness: Children will identify beginning sounds, ending sounds, or vowel sounds missing in environmental print words.

Materials

product labels, print from businesses, newspaper inserts, and so on
sentence strips or strips of paper
scissors
plastic or wooden alphabet letters
glue

Theme Connections

Alphabet
Food and Nutrition
Gardening and Plants
Grocery Store

Preparation

1. Cut out familiar environmental print (product labels, print from businesses, newspaper inserts, and so on) to fit on sentence strips or paper strips.

2. Glue to the left end of the paper.

3. Print the identifying word next to the picture, leaving out a letter that represents a sound (for example, beginning letters, ending letters, or vowels). For example, if the environmental print word is "chocolate," the missing letters may be "ch" (__ocolate).

Literacy Interactions

✦ Review parts of language or sounds that are represented on the missing letter labels. For example, list words that have examples of the missing sounds (for the "ch" sound, children may say "checkers," "cheat," "church," and so on). Proceed with other sounds represented on other labels. Show them the sentence strips and encourage them to practice identifying sounds by inserting appropriate plastic or wooden alphabet letters into the blanks. Encourage them to use the clues on the environmental print picture.

✦ Cover the letter or letters on the picture that have been omitted on the sentence strip. Read the word(s) or encourage the children to "read" the word. Encourage them to listen and identify the letter that belongs in the word by selecting appropriate letter(s). Can they identify other words that have the same sound?

Variation

✦ Encourage the children to experiment with sounds by substituting letters in the blanks to create new, silly words. Ask, "What happens if we put a new letter in this word?" For example, putting a "sh" in "__ocolate" would make "shocolate." Read the word together and encourage them to come up with meanings for these silly words.

What's Missing on the Cereal Box?

Children find and match missing letters on cereal boxes with letters in cereal bowls.

Objectives

Phonics: Children will practice identifying letter(s) and their sounds.

Phonological/Phonemic Awareness: Children will listen to identify missing sounds in names of cereals.

Materials

cereal boxes or other
    environmental print with
    large print

scissors

tape

paper squares

plastic, wood, or foam alphabet
    letters (optional)

cereal bowls

Theme Connections

Alphabet

Food and Nutrition

Recycling

Preparation

1. Collect a variety of cereal boxes. Select cereal boxes that contain names with letters or sounds that the children are practicing (beginning letter sounds, consonant blends, consonant digraphs, vowels, and so on). A digraph is two letters representing one sound ("ch" in "chunky oats"), a consonant blend is a combination of two or more consonants blended together and each letter is sounded ("bl" in "blueberry").

2. On each box, block out one or more letters of the cereal name by taping paper squares over them to create a flap.

3. Type or print the missing letters on paper squares, or use plastic or foam letters.

4. Put letters into cereal bowls.

Literacy Interactions

✦ Use this activity to review alphabet letters, letter sounds, or sounds of letter combinations. Point to beginning letters on each cereal box and ask children to identify them by name. Cover letters in each cereal name (for example, "c" in "corn" and "p" in "puffs" or "ch" in "chunky oats"). Read the name of each cereal, emphasizing the sound(s) of the covered letters. For example, hold up a cereal box and read the name ("<u>ch</u>unky oats") with the emphasis on the beginning sound (/ch/). Ask the children to listen and identify which letter or letters are missing to make the sound, such as /ch/. Ask a child to select the missing letter or letters covered on the cereal box from the cereal bowl and put it on the box above the flap. The child can lift the flap(s) to check his or her answer.

Alliteration Advertisements

Children use environmental print to learn about and create alliterative phrases.

Objectives

Phonics: The children will use environmental print in letter and letter sound recognition activities.

Oral Language/Speaking and Listening: Children will have the opportunity to listen to and recite alliterative phrases.

Vocabulary: Children will use new words and knowledge about beginning letter sounds to produce descriptive alliteration.

Phonological/Phonemic Awareness: Children will practice isolating, identifying, and categorizing the same sounds in different words through alliteration activities.

Materials

newspaper inserts, product
    labels, magazines, and so on
scissors
paper (8 ½" x 11" or larger)
glue
markers, crayons, and pencils

Theme Connections

All About Me
Alphabet
Community Helpers
Food and Nutrition

Literacy Interactions

✦ Talk about alliterative phrases. Explain to the children that *alliteration* is the repetition of the same initial sound. Use environmental print (newspaper inserts, product labels, magazines, and so on) to give examples of a few. For example, an advertisement for toothpaste could contain the words "tingly" and "tasty." Read the words together. Ask what the words have in common. "What letters and/or letter sounds are the same?"

✦ Gather or have the children locate print that begins with the same sounds as the beginning of their names. Invite the children to to write or dictate on paper other words that begin with the same sound. Combine the print and other words to create a silly poem.

✦ Gather environmental print representative of beginning consonant sounds the children are learning. Trim it to a size smaller than the paper. Present a few to introduce discussion about words that have the same sound. Let each child choose a piece of environmental print and glue it on paper. Encourage the children to provide words that begin with the same sound. Write the alliterative words next to the environmental print for each child. Ask the children to add illustrations to their pages. Display the descriptive alliteration creations or compile them into a book. Read them together.

✦ Read the alliterative phrases and poems children have created. Ask the children to stand up, clap, jump, and so on when they hear words that start with a specified letter or sound. Or, glue pairs of matching print to cards. Invite the children to identify the one that matches as they listen to the alliterative phrases or poems.

Variation

✦ Do the literacy interactions above, substituting rhyming words or word families for alliteration.

Linking Environmental Print With Books and Stories

✦ In each activity in this chapter, the **objectives** are listed in order of difficulty—use them according to the skill level of the children in your class.

✦ In each activity in this chapter, the **literacy interactions** are listed in order of difficulty; use them according to the abilities and interests of the children.

Favorite Products or Places Books

Children share and read about their favorite products, foods, or places in a book they create.

Objectives

Print Awareness: Children will learn about the function of print while making product or places books.

Oral Language/Speaking and Listening: Children will have opportunities to share information about their favorite products, foods, or places.

Writing Process: Children will dictate written stories about their favorite products or places.

Beginning Reading: Children will expand sight words using environmental print.

Materials

labels, pictures, or packaging from similar items, such as all gelatin boxes, all crackers, all soups, and so on

self-adhesive address labels (as needed)

paper, glue, scissors, string, marker and hole punch

laminate or clear contact paper

Theme Connections

All About Me

Farms

Food and Nutrition

Gardening and Plants

Holidays

Our Community

Preparation

1. Collect environmental print (label pictures or packaging) from similar items. Cut off fronts of food boxes and packaging.
2. If using cardboard box fronts, print the identifying name of each item on a blank label and place it somewhere on the item where it will not cover the print.
3. If using paper or soft plastic labels, glue each to a piece of paper. Print the identifying name for each item directly on the paper.
4. If desired, laminate or cover with contact paper.
5. Attach pages together by punching holes and adding string.

Literacy Interactions

✦ Ask each child to contribute one page to a collective book on favorites in one area, such as restaurants or cereals (see Ideas for "Favorites" Books, below). Encourage them to bring in print associated with their favorite, share information about it, and add it to the book.

✦ Compile books of favorites. Sit with one or two children and look through their books. Discuss what they see, the flavors, shapes, and so on. Invite them to tell about their favorites as you point to the identifying words.

✦ Discuss the similarities and differences in the environmental print the children put in the books. Ask questions such as, "Which is different? What do the pictures tell us? What do the words tell us?"

✦ Use the compiled books as story or poem starters. Incorporate words into a story that the children dictate, for example, "Cracker Caper" or "Soup Shop."

✦ Use identifying words from product books to teach beginning sight words. For example, in a favorite vegetable book made from can labels, key words could include "peas," "corn," and "beets."

Ideas for "Favorites" Books

Canned fruit	Gelatin	Soup
Canned vegetables	Jelly	Toothpaste
Cereal	Pasta	Yogurt
Crackers	Places	
Fruit juice	Restaurant	

Cereal Book

Children help make a book of cereal box fronts and use it to identify parts of words.

Objectives

Print Awareness: Children will have an opportunity to share and learn about the function of print on cereal boxes.

Oral Language/Speaking and Listening: Children will share what they know about cereals.

Phonics: Children will identify letters and sounds in the cereal names, and use them to put the pages in order.

Phonological/Phonemic Awareness: Children will learn how cereal names can be segmented into individual sounds.

Materials

cereal boxes
scissors
hole punch
book rings or string
permanent marker

Theme Connections

Alphabet
Food and Nutrition
Grocery Store
Recycling

Literacy Interactions

✦ Before making the books, involve the children in a Show and Tell activity. Encourage the children to bring an empty cereal box from home to create the book. As you collect the boxes, give them an opportunity to share about their box. Ask questions, such as "What does the cereal look like? What shape is it? What does it taste like? What do you see on the box?"

✦ Cut off fronts of cereal boxes. Assist the children as they place the cereal box fronts on the floor in order of the alphabet. Discuss the letters that each of the cereals begin with. Emphasize the sounds these letters make. Punch holes along the left edge of each front, making sure that the holes line up. Attach the pages together with book rings or string to make a book. Put the book in an area where it can be "read" by the children.

✦ Use the cereal book to identify, introduce, and segment such parts of words as syllables, compound words, onsets and rimes, or word families. Use a permanent marker to draw attention to the word parts in each cereal name and emphasize the sounds, words, or syllables as you read each name. Look for similarities among the cereal names, for example, three of the cereals might have the word "nuts" in their name.

Variation

✦ Collect several different kinds of cereals to create books. Save the contents for a taste-testing party or snack. Create a graph of favorites. **Safety Note**: Be aware of any food allergies and plan accordingly.

Seed Packet Pocket Books

Children match cards to seed packets by examining the letters or words.

Objectives

Print Awareness: Children will recognize the function of print by matching word cards to seed packets using one-to-one correspondence.

Phonics: Children will identify letters and beginning letter sounds on seed packets.

Phonological/Phonemic Awareness: Children will use what they know about beginning letter sounds on the seed packets to identify other words with the same sound. They will practice identifying syllables using the seed names.

Materials

clean, empty seed packets
paper or index cards
scissors
hole punch
book rings or string
foam, wooden, or cutout
    alphabet letters (optional)

Theme Connections

Food and Nutrition
Gardening and Plants
Seasons

Preparation

1. Cut paper or index cards slightly smaller than seed packets so that they can fit inside the packet.
2. Print the beginning alphabet letter or name of each item on a card, such as "p," "b," "pumpkin," "bean," and so on. (Option: Use foam, wooden, or cutout letters instead of cards.)
3. Punch a hole in the upper right-hand corner of each pocket.
4. Put letter or word cards inside matching seed packets.
5. Attach the pockets together using book rings or string.

Literacy Interactions

✦ Read the seed packets with the children, pointing to each identifying word. Talk about the letter the plant starts with and others in each word on the packet and card. Give each child a seed letter or word card (from inside seed packets). As you read each packet, allow the children to identify and insert the matching card.

✦ Discuss characteristics of each plant using the seed packets. Ask questions such as, "What type of plant will it grow into?" "Is it something we eat?" "What beginning letter is the same in some of the seed packets?" "What sound does the word start or end with?" "Can you think of other plants that start with the same sound?" List their responses on chart paper (for example, pumpkins, peas, and parsley begin with the letter "p").

✦ Introduce and identify syllables by clapping the parts in each word as you read the word card and add it to the matching seed packet.

Alphabet Scrapbook

Children sort, read, and use environmental print to make an alphabet scrapbook.

Objectives

Print Awareness: Children will gather and sort print by similar characteristics such as theme of study or beginning letter.

Phonics: Children will have opportunities to practice letter and corresponding beginning sound recognition by creating a book.

Beginning Reading: Children will practice identifying beginning sight words.

Materials

construction paper or white paper
clear page protectors
three-ring binder
hole punch
product labels, photos, and newspaper inserts
glue
scissors
poster board
craft sticks

Theme Connections

Alphabet
Community Helpers
Food and Nutrition
Gardening and Plants
Holidays
Zoo

Literacy Interactions

✦ Create pages for a book by writing a letter of the alphabet in the upper right-hand corner on each piece of paper. Put each completed page in a clear page protector and place in alphabetical order in a three-ring binder. Collect environmental print, such as product labels, photos, and newspaper inserts. Show the children the blank alphabet book. Review one or more letters of the alphabet and talk about different words that start with each letter. Encourage children to cut out words beginning with the letters and glue to the corresponding pages. Invite them to look for similarities and differences among the print that begins with the same letters. (For example, on the "g" page ask, "Which letters are the same?" Answer: *grape* jelly and *granola*—both start with the letter "g.") Add pages as existing pages become full. Place the book in an area where the children can read it as they wish.

✦ Encourage children to find and cut out items that begin with a specific letter or words that coordinate with a particular unit or curriculum study. Discuss and identify the varied sounds that beginning letters and letter combinations can make as they appear on each page. If desired, place items that begin with other letters in a box to add later as they are introduced. Add one or a few letters to the book each week. Another option is to make a book related to a theme of study and find things associated with it for each letter (for example, Thanksgiving: apple pie, bread, cornucopia, and so on).

✦ As children select items to add to the book, ask them to identify which word on the label they would like to use to categorize the item alphabetically. Talk about the letter and the beginning sound they hear. Print the word under the label as it is added to the page. If an identifying word is not available for a label or picture, ask the child to dictate or write one.

✦ Play "I Spy" with a small group of children by removing a page from the book. Select an item and use the identifying word, shown separately, to distinguish which item to locate. Make "I Spy" paddles by cutting out various shapes, such as a circle and rectangle, from poster board or construction paper. Cut out a

center viewing hole or shape and attach a craft stick handle. As children become familiar with the book, invite them to use the paddles to look for specific print, letters, words, and so on. The paddles can be stored in the binder page pockets to use again.

Variations

✦ Provide materials for each child to make his or her own book. Use spiral notebooks or pages stapled together instead of a binder.

✦ Create a book of examples of vowel sounds or blends.

"It's in the Bag" Book

Children participate in matching games, and "read" and add environmental print to bag books.

Objectives

Print Awareness: Children will attend to and match print in a one-to-one correspondence activity.

Phonics: Children will use beginning letter sounds to match products to letter pockets.

Phonological/Phonemic Awareness: Children will locate environmental print that represents a letter or letter sound combinations.

Beginning Reading: Children will "read" familiar environmental print by sight or in context.

Materials

front labels of products or
    pictures from newspaper
    inserts
zipper-closure plastic bags
    (small or large)
index cards or construction
    paper
glue
permanent markers
yarn or rings
hole punch

Theme Connections

Bakery
Grocery Store
Restaurant
Transportation

Preparation

1. Cut environmental print labels (front labels of products or pictures from newspaper inserts) to fit inside plastic bags. Slide one into each bag. If the label is thin, glue it to a sturdy index card or construction paper (cut to fit bag) before placing it in the bag.

2. Using a permanent marker, print either the product name (as it appears on the label) or the product's beginning letter on the bottom portion of the bag ("rice" or "r"). Another option is to write the name of the label on colored tape and adhere it to the bag.

3. Punch holes through the upper left corner of each bag. Secure bags together using ring clasps or yarn.

Literacy Interactions

◆ Print the beginning letter or identifying words on the plastic bag pages. Talk with the children about the print on each piece of matching environmental print. Ask questions such as, "Where do you see letters or words that tell what it is? Which letters, letter combinations, or words do you recognize that can help to identify where it belongs in the book?" Encourage them to use this knowledge to find the matching page for each piece of print.

◆ Print sound combinations such as those found in consonant digraphs (such as "**sh**aving cream" or "**sh**ampoo") or word families on the bags and have the children identify and cut out print from newspaper inserts to put in each bag page that represent the sounds. For example, the "_at" family may include "*cat* litter," "party *hat*," and "plastic *bat*." Use the books to review new sounds and words.

◆ Let each child make his or her own bag book using labels brought from home. Incorporate them into a theme or unit of study. Provide opportunities for children to "read" their books.

Our Community Book

Children share in small or large groups what they know about the places in their community.

Objectives

Oral language/Listening and Speaking: Children will share their knowledge about their community in a book they create.

Writing Process: Children will dictate stories or write about places in their community.

Print Awareness: Children will follow the left to right, top to bottom reading process as dictated experiences are read.

Vocabulary: Children will learn new words related to their community.

Materials

environmental print from the
    community, such as
    business cards, carry-out
    menus, imprinted napkins,
    maps, photos, newspaper
    inserts, and so on
paper
glue
scissors
markers
hole punch
three-ring binder

Theme Connections

All About Me
Community Helpers
Families
Our Community

Literacy Interactions

✦ Encourage children to collect imprinted items from businesses they visit or identify in their community (grocery store, barber, dentist, and so on) and places where family and friends work. Let them share their contributions during Show and Tell. Sort and glue items from each place in the community or type of business on separate pieces of paper (restaurants, retail stores, schools, doctors, and so on). Print the name or type of business on each page, leaving plenty of space on each page for children to write (or dictate) experiences. Invite each child to make a collection and tell stories about their favorite places in the community. Put the pages in a three-ring binder so that additional pages can be added easily.

✦ Ask children to dictate or write stories about the places in the community they visit or see. Ask questions, such as "What do you do at this place? What kinds of things are sold there? Where is it located? What happens when you go there?"

✦ Follow the print with a finger while reading back the written accounts the children contribute. Provide opportunities for them to look at it and discuss it in terms of their own experiences. Use the activity as an opportunity to talk about and expand their understanding of unfamiliar words or places, such as "optometrist."

Variations

✦ Invite community workers to come and share what they do with the children. Ask them to bring print items related to their business to add to the book.

✦ Graph the places on a chart by type, such as grocery stores, gas stations, doctors, and so on.

Hungry Animal Story

Children create a story using environmental print and move a puppet through the pages as the story is read.

Objectives

Oral Language Development/ Speaking and Listening: Children will dictate, listen to, and read an interactive story using familiar print.

Print Awareness: Children will learn about parts of a story, following print from left to right, and beginning, middle, and end.

Writing Process: Children will learn about letter formation, words, and sentence and story structure while observing the writing of their dictated stories.

Materials

heavy paper or poster board
scissors
tube sock
collage materials (yarn, felt, stickers, fabric scraps, pompoms, and so on)
glue and markers
food labels or pictures from newspaper inserts
yarn or metal rings
hole punch

Theme Connections

Fairy Tales
Food and Nutrition
Gardening and Plants
Nursery Rhymes
Pets
Science and Nature
Zoo

Preparation

1. Cut heavy paper or poster board so that it is 8 ½" x 11" (about 5–15 pieces).
2. Cut out a circle from the middle of each piece large enough for an arm to fit through.
3. Punch holes on the left side of each page. Attach pages together using yarn or metal rings.
4. Choose an animal or create an imaginary creature to be the character that eats the food in the story. Use a tube sock, glue, markers, and collage materials to create the puppet. Involve the children in making the puppets.

(continued on the next page)

Literacy Interactions

✦ Read the book *The Very Hungry Caterpillar* by Eric Carle to the children. Talk about the foods that the caterpillar eats. Tell the children that they will be making their own book similar to this one.

✦ Introduce the puppet (or puppets) that will be the main character(s) in the story. Encourage the children to bring in one environmental print item (food labels or pictures from newspaper inserts) from home for the puppet to "eat." Encourage them to select the identifying word or words on the print to use in the story. As you glue each item to a different page, invite each child to contribute to the story by dictating a sentence about his or her item. Highlight the identifying word in each sentence. For example, "The whale was so hungry it ate a box of <u>Fruity O's cereal</u>." (This is a good time to remind children not to feed animals at the zoo.)

✦ Introduce or review the progression of a story as part of the activity. Read several stories that have a distinct beginning, middle, and end. Identify those that have predictable text. Encourage the children to develop a beginning to their "Hungry Animal" story, and write down their contributions for them. Discuss how predictable words can be incorporated on each page. What will happen in the middle when the animal eats the food? What will happen at the end when the animal is finished?

✦ Let children listen to or re-read the story using the puppet. Point to the words as you read them to enhance their awareness of the print, and left to right progression.

Variation

✦ Provide materials for children to create their own book and puppet.

Recipe Books

Children use a recipe book to make food or use in dramatic play.

Objectives

Writing Process: Children will copy or dictate a list of ingredients needed for a recipe by looking at environmental print.

Print Awareness: Children will focus on context clues in environmental print to discuss similarities and differences among the ingredient names and labels.

Vocabulary: Children will learn measurement, cooking, and ingredient terms.

Beginning Reading: Children will "read" words and use context clues to follow a sequence of steps in a recipe.

Materials

recipe
ingredient labels, package
    fronts, or pictures from
    newspaper inserts
8 ½" x 11" paper
glue, scissors, marker
laminate or clear contact paper
hole punch
book rings or string

Theme Connections

Bakery
Food and Nutrition
Gardening and Plants
Health and Safety
Holidays

Preparation

1. Choose a recipe to make with the children.
2. Gather the ingredient labels or package fronts of each ingredient and glue each to a piece of paper.
3. Print the name of the item and amount needed for the recipe on each page. Include specific instructions on how to combine ingredients where appropriate.
4. Laminate or cover with contact paper to protect.
5. Attach the pages together in order of the recipe.

Literacy Interactions

✦ Read the recipe together with the children before making the item. Together, make a shopping list of ingredients needed to complete the recipe (see page 204). If desired, have the children use picture and word clues to identify and find each ingredient as it is added in the recipe.

✦ Ask children to identify and find the ingredients as they appear in the book. Identify similarities and differences on the packages between those in the book and those used to make the recipe (for example, fruity cereal rings from two different brands).

✦ Discuss vocabulary words in the book that are new or that re-appear several times, such as cup, teaspoon, or sift. Find the tools that match the print or symbols. Demonstrate how to measure and count using the tools.

✦ Collect ingredients and make books for single-serving recipes. Encourage beginning readers to follow the recipe to make their own item.

Variations

✦ Create the recipe on cards. Place the cards, in order, on an easel or by hanging from a string for children to follow when making the recipe.

✦ Send single-serving recipe books home with ingredients so the children can cook with their families at home (see "Cook Together" on pages 208).

Silly Stories

Children use environmental print cards as part of developing stories.

Objectives

Oral Language/Speaking and Listening: Children will use environmental print to generate, share, and express ideas and stories.

Writing Process: Children will observe the process of story structure and revision by dictating a story.

Vocabulary: Children will review word meanings using environmental print and other new vocabulary in stories and sentences.

Comprehension: Children will demonstrate understanding of environmental print by creating stories with it and answering questions about parts of a story.

Beginning Reading: Children will use sight words and environmental print to create and then recognize the words in a story.

Materials

environmental print from
    businesses and products
index cards or paper
scissors
glue
marker
bag or box

Theme Connections

Alphabet
Babies
Community Helpers
Health and Safety

Holidays
Our Community
Transportation

Literacy Interactions

✦ Cut out environmental print to fit on index cards or paper (cut to size of index cards). Glue in place and print the distinguishing name under each item. Place the cards in a bag or box. Discuss the parts of a story, such as beginning, middle (climax), end, and characters. Explain to the children that they will be writing their own stories using print from products. Invite them to pull out cards, one at a time, from the box or bag. As each card is drawn, engage the children in adding it to a story. Write down each story as children add to it. Underline all the words in the story from the word cards. Encourage the children to illustrate their stories. Read the stories together. Ask questions about what happens in each story. If the children find parts are missing, invite them to add to and change the story. Use this opportunity to talk about how writers use "revision" to create a final story.

✦ Gather environmental print to create cards relating to your current theme or unit of study. For example, for a unit on Dental Health, create cards for "toothpaste," "milk," "candy," "floss," "local dentist's name," and so on. Add other vocabulary words that have been introduced by writing the words on blank cards or paper. Have children select card(s) and share or dictate a written fact or story using the word(s) on the card. Use the interaction to assess comprehension about the topic, review a field trip, or create a silly story. Underline all the words from word cards as they are used in a dictated story.

✦ Print beginning sight words (such as "pop," "cat," "man," "the," "and") on blank cards and put them in a box or bag. Add familiar environmental print cards to the bag. Encourage the children to take turns pulling out the cards, reading them, and using them in a sentence or silly story. Record their dictated phrases. Invite the children to read portions of their completed phrases or stories.

What Happens Next?

Children use comic strip sequences to generate or complete stories.

Objectives

Oral Language: Children will verbalize ideas to continue and create an ending for a story in a comic strip.

Writing Process: Children will observe and/or participate in writing as they complete stories using comic strips.

Comprehension: Children will demonstrate understanding of a story sequence by adding to a comic strip and/or creating a logical ending.

Materials

comic strips from newspapers and magazines
scissors
photocopy machine (optional)
construction paper or cardstock
glue
chart paper
marker

Theme Connections

Community Helpers
Newspaper
Recycling
Storytelling

Preparation

1. Find and cut out comic strips with and without words.
2. If possible, enlarge comic sequences on a photocopy machine.
3. Glue each comic strip to a piece of paper or cardstock.
   Note: Be aware of any copyrighted material use.

Literacy Interactions

✦ Invite children to choose a comic strip that interests them. Remove or cover the last frame before reading the story. Invite the children to continue the story and formulate an ending. Record their story on chart paper. Transfer segments of their story to paper and invite them to illustrate their frames. Compile the comic strips and added frames into a book. Read together. Use the opportunity to discuss cartooning methods and illustrations.

✦ Cut off or black out words from comic strips that have easy-to-sequence picture clues and keep intact. Encourage children to look at the comic strips and come up with their own narrative. Record each child's narrative on chart paper, or invite the children to write their own narrative on enlarged versions of a comic strip. Read them together. Invite the children to act out the sequences. (See "Sequence Cartoons" on page 56 for other ways to use comic strips.)

Sequence Cartoons

Children put comic strips in order using context clues and/or words in each frame.

Objectives

Print Awareness: Children will use context clues and print to understand the stories in comic strips.

Oral Language/Speaking and Listening: Children will listen as comic strip stories are read to them.

Comprehension: Children will demonstrate their understanding of the comic strip stories by putting them in order and retelling the story, using listening skills and picture and word clues.

Materials

comic strips from newspapers
    and magazines
scissors
construction paper or cardstock
glue

Theme Connections

Newspaper
Recycling
Storytelling

Literacy Interactions

✦ Find comic strips that reflect the comprehension ability of the children. For example, pre-readers might have more success with a wordless or simple comic sequence containing three frames. Beginning readers may be challenged more from complex comics with some wording and more frames in the sequence. Cut each comic strip into separate frames as indicated by the dividing lines. Glue each frame to a piece of construction paper or cardstock cut slightly larger than the frame. Give each child a frame. Encourage them to look at it, read it, or use context clues to identify what is happening. Ask questions such as, "What do you see in the pictures? When we read it, what do the words tell us has happened?" Encourage them to move around and put the frames in order. Let each child share what is happening in the frame he or she is holding. (See "What Happens Next?" on page 55 for another way to use comic strips.)

✦ Read a copy of the comic strip to small groups or individual children. Invite them to retell what happened. Write the sequence in order on chart paper and read it to the children. Then ask them to put the separate frames in order and retell the story again.

Tale of the Colorful Food

Children listen to or read a repetitive story and match environmental print to the corresponding print on each page.

Objectives

Oral Language/Speaking and Listening: The children will listen to a story containing environmental print.

Phonological/Phonemic Awareness: The children will identify rhyming words in a story.

Beginning Reading: The children will recognize color words and other sight words in environmental print.

Materials

product pictures from
    newspaper inserts or food
    labels with a color word,
    such as flavored gelatin,
    juice boxes, and cake mix
construction paper
scissors
glue
Velcro or magnet tape
marker
laminate or clear contact paper
    (optional)

Theme Connections

Community Helpers
Food and Nutrition
Holidays
Restaurant

Preparation

1. Ask children to collect environmental print (labels or pictures of food products) that contain a color word.

2. Designate a page for each label or picture containing a color word. Glue each label or picture to a piece of paper, or make the item removable by using Velcro or magnet tape. (Be sure to add Velcro or magnet tape after laminating or covering pages if this option is used.)

3. Write a sentence on each page similar to the patterning in *Brown Bear, Brown Bear, What Do You See?* by Bill Martin, Jr. Leave blanks for product name and color (see "Rhyme Idea" below). On the first page print or type the first line of the rhyme, inserting the color word and brand name in the blanks. (For example, Brown gravy, brown gravy, what should I munch?)

4. On the next page insert the next product color and name into the rhyme (For example, Eat some yummy Green beans with your lunch. Green beans, green beans, what should I munch?)

5. Continue through the subsequent pages, each time entering the color and product name in the blanks.

6. On the last page, list all of the food products and their colors.

7. If desired, laminate or cover with contact paper to protect pages and/or removable pieces. Add Velcro or magnet tape to any removable pieces.

8. Attach pages together by stapling or using a hole punch and string.

Rhyme Idea

Page 1: (1st color word) (1st food product), *what should I munch?*
Page 2: *Eat some yummy* (2nd color word) (2nd food product) *with your lunch.* (2nd color word) (2nd food product), *what should I munch?*
Page 3: *Eat some yummy* (3rd color word) (3rd food product) *with your lunch.* (3rd color word) (3rd food product), what should I munch?

(continued on the next page)

Continue pattern on subsequent pages. On the last page, write: *I will eat* (1st color word) (1st food product), (2nd color word) (2nd food product), (3rd color word) (3rd food product) …*for my lunch.*

Literacy Interactions

✦ Read the story to the children. Discuss rhyming words and patterns. Ask questions, such as "What words rhyme in the story? Which part sounds the same on every page?" Identify the words that are the same or have letters and sounds that are the same.

✦ After reading the story several times, encourage the children to read the color words together or independently. Give each child one of the removable environmental print pieces, a piece of colored paper, or a piece of paper with a color word written on it to hold up and match as the color words are read.

Variation

✦ Write color and product names on index cards instead of in the blanks on the pages. Laminate or cover with contact paper. Adhere self-adhesive Velcro on the back of each card and above each blank on each page. Encourage children to put the correct color and product name in the blanks using the product picture glued on each page to match.

Building a Sandwich Story

Children make a book, "read" it, and use it to learn about parts of a story.

Objectives

Print Awareness: Children will learn about the parts of a story, such as following the print from left to right; climax; and beginning, middle, and end.

Phonics: Children will practice letter and letter sound recognition by locating representative print or listing words to include in a story.

Oral Language/Listening and Speaking: Children will dictate a story incorporating environmental print.

Beginning Reading: Children will practice reading beginning sight words using the food names included in the book.

Materials

brown construction paper, paper bag, or cardboard
scissors
food labels or pictures cut from newspaper inserts
white paper or assorted colored construction paper
glue
markers

Theme Connections

Fairy Tales
Food and Nutrition
Gardening and Plants
Restaurant

Literacy Interactions

✦ Cut out two "bread" slice shapes from construction paper, paper bags, or cardboard for each child. These will be the front and back cover of the book. Gather food labels or pictures of different foods from newspaper inserts. Talk to the children about what kind of sandwiches they like to eat. Ask them to collect labels of items that they would put in a sandwich. Help them glue each item on its own page cut slightly smaller than the bread shapes. If desired, cut and shape pages like the item (for example, bologna on a circle shape). Label each page with the identifying name of the product. Attach the pages together to create a book.

◆ Talk about the beginning, middle, and end parts of stories using the sandwich book. Put a silly surprise in the middle, such as a picture of an unusual food item to find in a sandwich, such as a cookie, to incorporate discussion about the climax of a story.

◆ Find other foods that start with the same letter sound as each item in the sandwich, for example, pickle, pizza, peanut butter, and popcorn. Create a list or make silly sandwich books using food environmental print all beginning with the same letter.

◆ Add dictated or child-written information to each page, including such information as the written name of the pictured item and child's name. Story-starter ideas for a group or individuals include:

   ◆ How did the sandwich come together? What happened first? Second?

   ◆ Where do you think each ingredient comes from?

   ◆ Incorporate color words. How did each ingredient get its color?

   ◆ What food group does each item in the sandwich belong to?

◆ Invite the children to share and "read" their books. Create a visual graph using identifying ingredient names, and then count and compare ingredients among the books.

Variation

◆ In conjunction with creating the books, have a sandwich-making day. Provide ingredients or ask children to bring in favorite ingredients (in unique containers, if possible, to incorporate into discussion). **Safety Note**: Be aware of any food allergies and plan accordingly.

Trip Through Town Rebus

Children help create a "Trip Through Town" rebus story from their travel logs (see page 216).

Objectives

Oral Language/Speaking and Listening: Children will share information about their observations made on the field trip.

Writing Process: Children will dictate a story about the trip using environmental print and their travel logs.

Vocabulary: Children will expand vocabulary through discussion about environmental print used in the rebus story.

Beginning Reading: Children will identify familiar words to add to sight word knowledge.

Materials

children's notebooks containing recorded observations from "Trip Through Town Travel Log" (see page 216)

large writing surface, such as chart paper or dry-erase board

markers

pictures or photos from places in the community

clear tape

Theme Connections

Community Helpers

Maps

Our Community

Transportation

Literacy Interactions

✦ Gather recorded observations from "Trip Through Town Travel Log" activity (see page 216). Position a dry-erase board or chart paper so children can observe as you record a sequential description of what they noticed on the trip. Collect environmental print (pictures or photos from places in the community) or create pictures that correspond to the places recorded. Talk to the children about their travel logs. Encourage them to dictate what they saw in the community while en route, including signs, businesses, and so on. Together refer to the travel logs to add observations to the story. Ask questions such as, "What colors, pictures, and letters did you see?"

✦ If children do not have any environmental print in their travel log, encourage them to locate and cut out logos and labels that correspond to the places mentioned in their logs. Record dictated observations or sequences on chart paper. Demonstrate how to use clear tape to adhere the collected environmental print over the matching written word on their dictated observations to form a flap that can be lifted easily. These become the rebus pictures.

(continued on the next page)

If children are unable to find some of the logos or labels, provide slips of paper so they can design a visual representation, such as a mailbox to symbolize the post office. Read the rebus story aloud with the children several times. Encourage them to read the words and places they recognize as they appear in the story.

◆ Expand children's vocabulary by discussing other words used to describe the same place as they appear in the travel logs or dictated story (such as "grocery" and "market"). Invite them to look at environmental print and find examples in the story.

◆ After creating the rebus story and after the children have had the opportunity to listen to it several times, lift the rebus flaps while reading. Point out similarities among the written words used to describe some of the places, such as "grocery" or "gas station." Have them find where words like these are repeated in the story. Ask them to identify similarities among words. Use this opportunity to review or add to sight words.

Variations

◆ Write observations on sentence strips or long strips of paper and then arrange in order.

◆ Find or draw a simple map of the route and area of the field trip to plot the places the children saw. Use environmental print to create markers.

My Name in Products Acrostic

Children collect environmental print that starts with the same letters as the letters in their names and add the print to their own books.

Objectives

Print Awareness: Children will identify and match letters in their names with other print.

Phonics: Children will identify environmental print words that begin with the same letters and letter sounds as those in their names.

Writing Process: Children will practice writing their name and environmental print words that begin with the same letters.

Materials

paper
stapler
markers or crayons
newspaper inserts, coupons,
    business envelopes,
    and so on
scissors
glue

Theme Connections

All About Me
Alphabet

Literacy Interactions

✦ Help the children identify and count the letters that are in their names. Staple the same amount of pages together and one for a cover to form a book for each child (for example, a child named John would have a five-page book). Write each child's name on the front page of his or her book. In order, write or have the child write one letter of the child's name in the upper right-hand corner of each page. Encourage them to find and cut out environmental print that begins with the same letters of their names. For example, a child named Pat may find words such as "peanut butter," "applesauce," and "toothpaste." Direct the children to glue each item to the corresponding letter page in their books. Talk about the letter sounds and words they place on the pages. Discuss the similarities and differences the same letter can have in various words as you read the pages together.

✦ Show the children how to create an acrostic by using their name on the front cover. Invite them to select names on the environmental print in their book that represent each letter in their name. Write the acrostic on the front cover. Have the children share the words they have found when they are finished with their book. For example:

    *P*eanut butter
    *A*pplesauce
    *T*oothpaste

✦ Encourage the children to write or dictate the letters of their names on the front cover of their books. Guide them to write, in order, one letter of their name in the upper right-hand corner of each page. As the print is added, print or have the child copy the identifying name of each item underneath.

Hunting for Ingredients Cookbook

Children listen to or read each ingredient description and select the matching ingredient card.

Objectives

Oral Language Development/ Speaking and Listening: Children will verbalize descriptions of recipe ingredients using information from print clues and prior knowledge.

Vocabulary: Children will encounter new words and gain understanding of their meanings by using recipe ingredients in interaction activities.

Comprehension: Children will confirm understanding of ingredients and recipe sequence using environmental print.

Beginning Reading: Children will practice sight word identification as words are used in ingredient descriptions, for example, "brown" or "nuts."

Materials

recipe, ingredients, and cooking utensils

paper, pen or marker

glue, scissors

library pockets or envelopes

index cards

pictures or labels of ingredients for a recipe

Theme Connections

Bakery

Cooking

Cultural Awareness

Holidays

Senses

Literacy Interactions

✦ Before starting this activity, have a discussion about recipes and ingredients. Ask the children if they know what a recipe is and what ingredients are. Ask if they have ever used a recipe to make something. Provide opportunities for children to assist in following a recipe, such as making playdough or no-bake cookies.

✦ Choose a recipe and introduce each ingredient in its original packaging. Engage the children in creating descriptions for each ingredient (such as where the item comes from, what letters it starts with, rhyming words, food group, color, and taste) based on their prior knowledge, or ask them to describe ingredients after experiencing them in a cooking project. Use one- or two-word phrases in each description that beginning readers could identify (for example, "nuts," "brown," and "p" for peanut butter). Write each ingredient and its description on a piece of paper and glue pockets or envelopes to each page. Attach the pages together in order of the recipe. Glue environmental print related to each ingredient on separate index cards, and print the identifying word or words underneath. Encourage children to match ingredient labels with their descriptions as they are read by placing the cards in the pocket.

✦ Write the amount of each ingredient needed for the recipe on a corresponding index card. Help the children follow the sequence and use these cards when cooking.

✦ Place ingredients for the recipe (in original containers) around the room. Read the descriptions from the book, and have children find the items to gather for cooking.

Magnet Strip Rebus Stories

Children use magnetic words to build sight words, sentences, and stories.

Objectives

Writing Process: Children will participate in building and dictating a story using magnetic sight words and environmental print.

Oral Language/Speaking and Listening: Children will listen to and follow directions using environmental print.

Beginning Reading: Children will practice reading and using sight words by including environmental print in sentences and stories.

Comprehension: Children will retell, dramatize, or illustrate a story created with environmental print.

Materials

small pieces from magazines or
　　　newspaper inserts
scissors
paper
glue
marker
laminate or clear contact paper
magnet tape
index cards
cake pan or other magnetic
　　　surface

Theme Connections

Families
Food and Nutrition
Gardening and Plants
Grocery Store
Health and Safety
Our Community
Restaurant

Preparation

1. Cut paper into 1" to 2" wide strips, or use index cards to create larger print cards.

2. Cut environmental print (small pieces from magazines or newspaper inserts) to fit and glue one piece onto each paper strip. Print the distinguishing word to the left of each piece.

3. Print sight words such as "I," "go," "and," "or," "not," and "on" on remaining blank strips and cut apart. If desired, add punctuation to strips as appropriate.

4. Another option is to type sight words and words from environmental print on paper, allowing space for pictures. Cut the words apart and glue environmental print in front of each distinguishing name.

5. Laminate or cover with clear contact paper.

(continued on the next page)

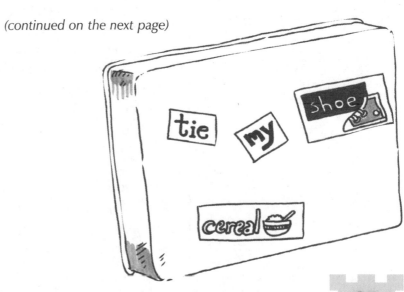

6. Adhere magnet tape to each piece to create a magnetic word.
7. Use a cake pan or other magnetic surface to place the magnetic words.

Literacy Interactions

✦ Collect environmental print related to dramatic play subjects (see pages 166-192) and create magnetic words. Introduce them as part of the imaginative play area (for example, restaurant magnetic boards). Invite children to create sentences and phrases during play.

✦ Use magnetic words to give simple directions involving day-to-day activities in the learning area. Incorporate signs, children's photos and names, games, toys, writing and art equipment, and so on. For example, "The (brand name) blocks are ready for use," or "Pick up (brand-name) crayons."

✦ Use magnetic word strips to introduce or review beginning sight words. Read the words together with the children. Provide environmental print words and magnets obtained from places and businesses to encourage children to build simple sentences and phrases. Use this opportunity to talk about parts of a sentence.

✦ Create a short story together using the magnetic words. Work with the children to create a beginning, middle, and end. Invite them to read the story or fill in the words they recognize as it is read together. Copy the story onto paper. Create several stories to have available to read again and again. Invite the children to retell, illustrate, or dramatize the story.

Variation

✦ Use pre-purchased magnetic words and add environmental print words to motivate children to build sentences and stories.

Linking Environmental Print With Building, Blocks, and Bulletin Boards

◆ In each activity in this chapter, the **objectives** are listed in order of difficulty—use them according to the skill level of the children in your class.

◆ In each activity in this chapter, the **literacy interactions** are listed in order of difficulty; use them according to the abilities and interests of the children.

Box Blocks

Children use box blocks and tube tunnels (made from product containers) for construction play.

Objectives

Print Awareness: Children will be exposed to environmental print using boxes and containers during building play.

Vocabulary: Children will practice new vocabulary (positional words and shapes) using box blocks.

Materials

boxes (juice, gelatin, pasta, tissue) and cylinder-shaped containers and lids with environmental print (tennis ball, chips, juice)

newspaper or scrap paper

clear packing tape

box knife (adult only)

Theme Connections

Bakery
Food and Nutrition
Opposites
Recycling
Shapes

Literacy Interactions

◆ Encourage children to help collect clean boxes and containers to make blocks. Stuff boxes and containers with newspaper or scrap paper, secure lids, and tape shut. Cut off ends of some of the cylinder-shaped containers to form tube tunnels. Invite the children to share what they know about the words on the boxes and cylinders. Show them how to label structures using the identifying words on the containers and boxes (for example, "brand name" oatmeal factory or toothpaste tower).

◆ Spend some time building with the children. Draw attention to the print and context clues on the blocks by asking questions and making comments about them. For example, "Can you pass me the *apple juice* block for the tower?" or "Sam, did you find the tunnel that starts with the letter 'o'? What color is it?" Introduce and incorporate vocabulary including positional words ("under," "top," "beside") and shapes ("cube," "rectangle," "cylinder") during play with blocks and containers.

Stuffed and Rolled Construction

Children roll newspapers and stuff bags to create blocks to use in building.

Objectives

Print Awareness: Children will identify environmental print used in newspapers and on printed paper bags.

Phonics: Children will recognize and name alphabet letters in environmental print and associate them with letters in their names.

Beginning Reading: Children will "read" familiar environmental print as they use it in construction activities.

Materials

imprinted paper bags from
    supermarkets, restaurants,
    and department stores
newspapers and inserts
tape

Theme Connections

Construction
Grocery Store
Our Community
Newspaper
Recycling

Literacy Interactions

✦ Gather imprinted bags from department stores and grocery stores. Collect newspapers to use to roll and stuff into bags. Create signs using newspaper inserts. Demonstrate how to roll up the insert so that the name of the business remains visible. Secure the tube with tape. Encourage the children to use these to label buildings. Ask if they can think of other ways to use newspapers for building. For example, cut it into wide strips and tape together to produce a "Letter Lane" for toy cars to drive on, squish up newspaper to use in trucks to load and dump, and so on.

✦ Involve the children in stuffing printed paper bags (restaurant and supermarket bags) half full with newspaper or scrap paper. Fold the top closed and tape shut. As the children build with the blocks, encourage them to identify letters and familiar print they can "read." Draw attention to those that begin with the same letters as those in their names.

✦ Encourage the children to roll newspaper into tubes and tape to maintain the form. Demonstrate how to roll newspaper loosely to create tunnels, and how to roll tightly and tape together to make columns, arches, frames, and so on. As the children roll the newspaper, engage them in conversation about the letters and words they can identify.

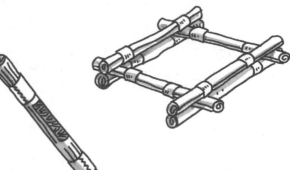

Simple Signs

Children create and use print on signs in building activities.

Objectives

Print Awareness: Children will use print on signs to identify places and to provide information.

Vocabulary: Children will learn about safety words and symbols used on signs in their environment.

Phonics: Children will identify letters in signs.

Phonological/Phonemic Awareness: Children will practice identifying rhyming words, letter sounds, and phonemes using signs.

Materials

business logos from packaging, envelopes, and newspaper inserts

poster board or heavy paper cut to size

glue

clear packing tape

empty film canister

wooden dowels or straws (about 6" long)

Theme Connections

All About Me
Community Helpers
Health and Safety
Our Community

Preparation

1. Trim business logos and adhere to poster board cut slightly larger than the logo.
2. Attach each logo to the top of a wooden dowel or straw using clear packing tape.
3. Wrap tape completely around each logo to protect it.
4. Poke a hole in the bottoms of empty film canisters.
5. Push the dowel through the hole to secure the sign in a standing position.

Literacy Interactions

✦ Encourage children to save and bring in environmental print (business logos from packaging, envelopes, and newspaper inserts) from their favorite places in the community. Have materials available for them to make their own signs (see "My Own Signs" on page 199). Make street name signs using familiar roads and the names of streets the children live on. Use these signs in building activities and when children are learning their addresses.

✦ Make street safety signs (see page 240). Discuss meanings of the signs during play. Add vehicles, toy people, blocks, and so on for the children to use with the signs.

✦ Invite the children to sort signs by type of business or service offered (such as restaurants, grocery stores, schools, and gas stations). Encourage them to sort the signs by beginning letter.

✦ Play "Guess the Sign." Put signs where children can see them. Choose one and describe it, providing clues such as beginning letter sounds, rhyming words, and phonemes, along with characteristics about the sign. For example, "The word on this sign has one syllable, rhymes with 'hop', and is red." (Answer: stop sign) Let children guess which one is being described.

Building Billboards

Children use and "read" billboard signs in block play.

Objectives

Print Awareness: Children will learn about the use of print in signs to identify places and provide information.

Vocabulary: Children will expand understanding of words they see in their community.

Writing Process: Children will use writing materials to produce their own signs.

Materials

large environmental print labels, such as pizza boxes and paper bags from restaurants

scissors

paper towel tubes

masking tape or glue

Styrofoam cups or bowls or round plastic tubs

large note cards or poster board cut to size

Theme Connections

Alphabet

Community Helpers

Our Community

Transportation

Literacy Interactions

✦ Cut labels from pizza boxes, food boxes, and paper bags. Adhere the labels to the top end of paper towel tubes. Cut a small hole in the bottom of Styrofoam cups or bowls. Turn over cups or bowls and slide in the bottom end of the paper towel tube to form a stand. Explain what billboards are used for and ask children if they can describe any they have seen. Encourage them to use the billboard signs in block and vehicle play. Engage them in conversations about where their vehicles are going, the letters in the signs, and so on.

✦ Remove Styrofoam bases and make up rhymes involving the signs. For example:

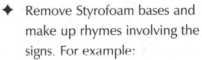

Doo dee doo dee dee dibble dibble dee
It says (sign name),
It has a (alphabet letter) like me.
Have a parade using the signs.

✦ Use signs to introduce vocabulary about places in the community the children see. Ask questions about what they are, what happens there, and what services they provide.

✦ Create billboards as a follow-up activity to looking for them while on a field trip or a walk. Provide note cards or pieces of poster board, markers, and scissors for children to create their own billboards or large signs for play. Provide environmental print for them to add to what they have created.

Variation

✦ Make large signs by punching holes into the bottoms of large plastic containers. Stick dowels or yardsticks into the holes in inverted large plastic containers to use in outdoor play.

Brainstorming With Boxes

Children build permanent constructions using product boxes.

Objectives

Print Awareness: Children will use boxes containing environmental print when building and interacting.

Vocabulary: Children will learn and use vocabulary such as positional words and words identified on environmental print.

Writing Process: Children will write or dictate descriptions of their box creations.

Phonics: Children will identify and sort environmental print boxes by letter and letter sounds.

Materials

boxes from various items, such as food products, toys, and shoes

large pieces of cardboard from cut-up boxes

tape

glue

scissors

marker

Theme Connections

Alphabet

Construction

Opposites

Our Community

Recycling

Shoes

Literacy Interactions

✦ Provide a variety of product boxes and engage children as they build and stack with them. Make verbal observations as they build by drawing attention to and using identifying words on the product boxes. Incorporate positional words such as "up," "under," "beside," and "over." Invite them to find letter similarities with words such as their names and words on the boxes and to identify familiar print. Ask questions about the boxes they are using. Encourage them to think of a name or dictate a story about the buildings they create, for example, "Adventures at Taco Box Palace."

✦ Invite children to bring in boxes starting with different letters. Gather product boxes that begin with every letter of the alphabet. Work with the children to stack the boxes in order of the alphabet to create a tower or train. Talk about the words and letters on each box. Distinguish the beginning letter by underlining or circling with a marker. Provide opportunities for children to take apart and create the tower or train again.

✦ Invite children to bring in boxes that contain a specific beginning letter. For example, boxes containing the beginning letter "p" might include "popcorn," "peppermint candy," and "paper clips." Let children build with all the boxes after they are introduced to the group. Use the activity as an opportunity to introduce or review letter names and sounds.

Box Businesses

Children create businesses and places in the community using boxes and environmental print.

Objectives

Print Awareness: Children will recognize, sort, and use environmental print to create a business in their community.

Writing Process: Children will use drawing and writing skills to create signs, products, and other items pertaining to a business. Children will dictate written lists about things located in community businesses.

Oral Language/Speaking and Listening: Children will share what they know about different businesses.

Materials

boxes, shoebox size or larger
    box knife (adult only)
newspaper inserts, catalogs,
    magazines, and business-
    related print
scissors
glue
markers or crayons

Theme Connections

Community Helpers
Maps
Our Community
Restaurant
Transportation

Literacy Interactions

✦ Cut doors and windows in boxes to create buildings. Gather newspaper inserts and other environmental print for children to use to create businesses. Talk about different businesses. Ask children questions about what kinds of places they visit in their community. Talk about what goes on in different businesses and stores. Explain that they will be making their own businesses using environmental print.

✦ Encourage the children to find environmental print associated with one type of business at a time, such as a grocery store or bookstore. Direct them to cut out and glue environmental print into the "business" (box) it is associated with, such as toys for a toy store. Provide markers or crayons to add details, signs, and so on.

✦ Encourage the children to dictate a list of items found in specific places in the community. Let them search through environmental print, select, and cut out items using the list. Sort them by business and category (for example, milk and fruit for a grocery store, or books and videos for a book store). Identify and label "departments" in boxes using a marker, and let children glue items into the matching areas.

✦ Put the completed box businesses in the Block Area. Observe how children interact using the buildings. Ask questions about the businesses and places they have in their "community." "What kind of service does it provide?" "What do they sell there?" Add vehicles, toy people and animals, and signs for the children to use with the box buildings.

Variations

✦ Create large box buildings out of appliance boxes to use in the Dramatic Play area. Make a set of box buildings for children to crawl or walk through.

✦ After a field trip, invite the children to recreate the place they visited and things found there using a box building and environmental print gathered from the trip.

Pile-Up Print Plans

Children build a structure by following directions on "plans" containing environmental print or corresponding words.

Objectives

Print Awareness: Children will learn about the use of print in building plans.

Vocabulary: Children will learn about words associated with building and construction.

Comprehension: Children will demonstrate understanding of directions by building a structure.

Writing Process: Children will use environmental print and writing instruments to generate building "plans."

Materials

boxes, cans, or plastic
    containers with print, and
    corresponding coupons or
    pictures from newspaper
    inserts

blueprints from building projects
    (if available)

newspaper or other scrap paper

tape, scissors

markers, glue

large note cards or construction
    paper

Theme Connections

Boxes

Community Helpers

Construction

Transportation

Preparation

1. Gather stackable containers that contain environmental print. Make sure none of the cans have sharp edges.

2. Stuff any boxes with paper and tape shut.

3. Locate coupons or other pictures identical to each piece of environmental print.

4. Option 1: Cut out and glue matching pictures from coupons or other sources to note cards or paper. "Stack" the pictures on the card or paper (3–8 items per card) and glue in place (for example, glue a picture of a cereal box on the bottom, a picture of a cracker box in the middle, and a picture of a toothpaste box on top).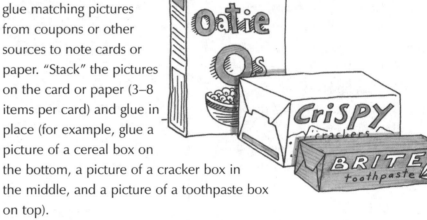

5. Option 2: Draw the shape of each container in its "stack" position on a note card or construction paper (for example, a large rectangle on the bottom, a smaller rectangle in the middle, and a narrow rectangle on top). Print the corresponding brand name as it appears on the print inside each shape.

Literacy Interactions

✦ Gather the "blocks" and invite the children to assist in reading them. Give them time to explore and experiment with them in building activities. Talk about words such as "contractors," "builders," "plans," and "blueprints," and how the latter two are used as "recipes" to construct buildings. Provide examples of blueprints, if available. Show them the "plans" created using environmental print (see option #1 in Preparation) or identifying words (see option #2 in Preparation). Challenge them to follow the plans to build a tower or building using the matching print containers.

✦ Provide cards, paper, environmental print, markers, scissors, and glue for the children to create their own "plans" for building structures, bridges, trains, and so on.

Town Map

Children use a map containing environmental print in building and play activities.

Objectives

Print Awareness: Children will recognize and understand the function of print on a map through play.

Vocabulary: Children will demonstrate understanding of positional words using a map.

Oral language/Speaking and Listening: Children will practice following oral directions by moving objects around the map. Children will share narratives of what is happening by referring to print on the map.

Writing Process: Children will dictate or write a story about an imaginary trip using environmental print on a map.

Comprehension: Children will demonstrate comprehension of a story by acting out its sequence using a map.

Materials

solid-colored shower curtain or vinyl tablecloth

permanent markers

logos and names of community businesses and places

photos of community businesses and places

clear packing tape or clear contact paper

scissors

Theme Connections

Community Helpers

Maps

Transportation

Literacy Interactions

✦ Talk about maps as a representation of an area. Show or draw a simple map of a room, school, or home. (It doesn't have to be a true scale map, just a simple representation of places in the community that are important to the children.) Invite the children to identify where windows, doorways, and furniture are located.

✦ Draw roads on a shower curtain or tablecloth using a permanent marker. Cut out and place environmental print (logos and names of community businesses and places) and photos from the community along the roads. Print the name of each place under the picture using a permanent marker. Secure in place by covering with

(continued on the next page)

contact paper or tape. Encourage the children to identify familiar places, streets, and so on. Let them bring in or create other representative print from their community. Be sure to include the learning environment or school.

◆ Create a matching game using toy vehicle shapes cut from paper. Print the name of each business or place on a vehicle shape. Ask the children to match the name on the shape to the place on the map by placing the vehicle on the business.

◆ Use the map as a direction-following activity by incorporating toy people, cars, or bingo chips. Tell the children where to place the objects in reference to the print, introducing and using positional vocabulary such as "left," "right," "up," and "beside."

◆ Use the map to create stories. Write or ask children to dictate an imaginary story about a trip on chart paper using the businesses, places, and additional items on the map. Read the story to the whole group. Read it again to small groups of children and have them move toy cars or people to act out the story. Encourage them to verbalize what is happening as they move items around the map.

Around Town Block Center

Children use blocks and vehicles labeled with environmental print when building or playing in the sensory table.

Objectives

Print Awareness: Children will understand the various functions of print through play activities using vehicles and blocks labeled with environmental print.

Phonics: Children will use letter recognition to sort and match letters and words using the environmental print labels on vehicles and blocks.

Writing Process: Children will use writing/drawing materials to create their own print for buildings and vehicles.

Materials

small labels or logos from
    community businesses or
    places
scissors
smooth wood or plastic blocks
toy vehicles
clear book or packing tape
colored or masking tape
markers

Theme Connections

All About Me
Community Helpers
Maps
Our Community
Tools and Machines
Transportation

Literacy Interactions

✦ Cut out labels from environmental print (small labels or logos from community businesses or places) to fit on blocks, boxes, and sides of toy vehicles and attach using book tape or packing tape. Tape over the labels. Write the name of each place on a piece of colored tape to fit on the same item as the label. Secure this label on an opposite side of the block or vehicle. Provide label blocks, boxes, and vehicles in the Block Area for children to build with. Interact with the children as they build. Ask them about the places they visit in their community. Ask questions such as, "What clues are on the vehicle or block that identify the name?" "What is the story about your construction?" Observe the interaction and listen to the children's conversations as they use the materials. Use this information to generate discussion about the use of print in their play.

✦ Invite the children to identify the similarities and differences among the labeled items they are using. Encourage them to categorize them, for example, putting all the same types (such as grocery stores), colors, or shapes together, or sorting them by beginning letters on the print.

✦ Let the children create their own vehicle labels or block signs for familiar locations such as stores, businesses, and homes using blank stickers or tape and markers. Encourage the children to draw pictures and write or dictate words on the labels to represent places from their community.

Note: Use the vehicles with Box Businesses (see page 73). Remove the environmental print labels and encourage the children to identify the words and letters on the tape and match them with letters and words on the box. Encourage them to "drive" the vehicle to the matching business. Add items created in Billboard and Town Map activity (see page 75).

"I Spy" Bulletin Board

Children select and find items on an "I Spy" board using various criteria, such as description or name.

Objectives

Print Awareness: Children will learn how environmental print can be used to provide information.

Phonics: Children will locate and identify environmental print on an "I Spy" bulletin board that relates to specific alphabet letters or sounds.

Phonological/Phonemic Awareness: Children will listen to and identify sounds in word examples, and locate environmental print according to a literacy skill (letter sound, onsets, rimes, and so on).

Beginning Reading: Children will locate and learn new sight words using environmental print on an "I Spy" bulletin board.

Materials

newspaper inserts, product packaging, and business brochures
bulletin board or large poster board
tape or stapler
dry-erase board or chart paper
marker
magnifying glasses (optional)

Theme Connections

Alphabet
Camping
Community Helpers
Families

Farms
Food and Nutrition
Gardening and Plants
Health and Safety

Literacy Interactions

✦ Invite the children to bring in environmental print (newspaper inserts, product packaging, and business brochures) from home to create an "I Spy" bulletin board. Let them put the print on the bulletin board or large piece of poster board to create a display. Add items until the area is full. Say an alphabet letter and invite the children to find as many pieces of environmental print as possible on the "I Spy" board that start with or contain that letter. Create a list of the words as they are found. (This is a great activity to do when children must wait for something or to go somewhere.)

✦ Encourage children to use the "I Spy" bulletin board as an interaction activity with each other. Add magnifying glasses or paper towel tubes to use in locating items.

✦ Identify a piece of environmental print by name. Invite the children to find it on the "I Spy" bulletin board. Write the identifying words on a dry-erase board or chart paper to highlight. Ask them, "What clues did you use to find the item?" Point out the clues that the word gives or review new letters or sounds.

✦ Gather environmental print that contains beginning sight words to create a word wall (color words, numbers). Put them on the "I Spy" board. Ask the children to locate various words on the board. As they become familiar with the board, remove a few pieces and, in its place, put the identifying word on a piece of paper. Play "I Spy." Continue to do this as the children are able to read new words.

Variation

✦ Let children make their own version to take home in a folder. Or use laminated supermarket newspaper inserts to play "I Spy" (see "I Spy Search" on page 209).

Special Events Board

Children collect and share environmental print that pertains to important events in their lives such as awards, birthdays, and so on.

Objectives

Print Awareness: Children will collect, create, and learn about print that documents special events in their lives.

Oral Language/Speaking and Listening: Children will listen to and tell about special events in their lives using environmental print.

Writing Process: Children will write, draw, and dictate about special events in their lives.

Beginning Reading: Children will have opportunity to "read" about special events in their lives.

Materials

a variety of environmental print, such as newspapers, magazine clippings, business cards, ribbons, greeting cards, and so on
bulletin board or poster board
tape or stapler
scissors
pencils, markers, and paper

Theme Connections

All About Me
Families
Holidays
Our Community

Literacy Interactions

✦ Create a place such as a bulletin board, wall area, or poster board where children can display environmental print relating to special events in their lives. Introduce the "special events" board as a place for the children to bring in and share print items that tell about or represent special things in their lives. Ask children about things and events that are special to them, such as birthdays, holidays, and family time. Talk about print associated with these events that they could bring in, such as special greeting cards, parent business cards, wedding or birth announcements, sports summaries, dance programs, and award ribbons. Provide examples for children to see and invite them to bring in items as the events occur. Encourage children to look at the board to share and "read" the special events.

✦ Provide paper, markers, and pencils for the children to draw pictures and dictate or write about important events to add to the board if other print is not available. As an alternative, invite them to bring in photos and add text about the special event depicted.

✦ As the board fills, children can remove items and paste them into individual or group scrapbooks. Provide notebooks or stapled pieces of paper for them to glue items. Keep the books in a location where they can add to and re-read them frequently. Offer markers, crayons, and pencils for them to write, draw, or dictate additional information about the special event in the scrapbook.

Big Letter Pocket Match

Children sort environmental print into pockets using letter and letter sound recognition.

Objectives

Phonics: Children will sort environmental print by identifying beginning letters or letter sounds and putting it into a pocket.

Phonological/Phonemic Awareness: Children will listen to an environmental print word as it is read and identify the beginning sound or sounds.

Beginning Reading: Children will "read" environmental print they bring from home.

Materials

26 clear page covers or pockets
permanent marker or solid-
    colored contact paper and
    scissors
yarn or string
newspaper inserts, magazines,
    and catalogs

Theme Connections

Alphabet
Community Helpers
Farms
Food and Nutrition
Gardening and Plants
Grocery Store
Holidays
Our Community

Literacy Interactions

✦ Print one large alphabet letter on each clear page cover using a permanent marker, or cut out letters from colored contact paper and adhere one to each cover. String covers from yarn or string by running it through the pre-punched holes. Hang from a wall or other flat surface at children's level. As each new letter is introduced, add that letter pocket to the string. Encourage children to locate and cut out environmental print (from newspaper inserts, magazines, and catalogs) that begins with that letter or letter sound and add it to the pocket.

✦ After several letter pockets have been added to the string, remove some of the print from each pocket and read it. As you read each piece, ask the children to listen for the beginning letter sound to determine in which pocket it belongs. Let them play this on their own in small groups.

✦ As each pocket is added to the string, encourage the children to "read" their contributions. Write the words on chart paper or a dry-erase board to create a list of words that begin with each letter or letter sound represented. Underline the beginning letter as each word is added. Invite the children to continue to add to and read the list as they find relevant environmental print.

Bag It Bulletin Board

Children sort environmental print into labeled bags on a bulletin board.

Objectives

Print Awareness: Children will match pictures, letters, and words on environmental print using one-to-one correspondence.

Phonics: Children will demonstrate understanding of sound and/or letter symbol relationship by matching environmental print to an alphabet letter.

Phonological/Phonemic Awareness: Children will match environmental print words to other words by rhyming and isolating letter sounds.

Materials

large, zipper-closure plastic bags
cut-out alphabet letters,
    alphabet stickers, or thick
    permanent marker
product labels, newspaper
    inserts, and catalogs
stapler or tape
bulletin board or other large
    surface
index cards

Theme Connections

Alphabet
Camping
Community Helpers
Farms
Gardening and Plants
Grocery Store

Literacy Interactions

✦ Create a one-to-one correspondence activity by locating pairs of product brands or labels. Tape one of each pair on a plastic bag and staple to a bulletin board. Ask the children to find the matching pictures and glue to index cards to make environmental print cards. Print the identifying word or words on the bag and underline it on the card. Show the children that things that look the same may be different because of the letters and words on the picture (for example, various flavors of gelatin or assorted soup labels). Invite the children to match the print by sorting the cards into the labeled bags.

✦ Adhere or print upper- and/or lowercase letters to each plastic bag. Staple the bags to a bulletin board. Give each child a card that contains a word. Ask the children to put their cards into the bags marked with the appropriate beginning alphabet letter. Read the word or encourage them to use clues to "read" the word before putting it in the bag.

✦ Focus on letter sounds that are part of your literacy objectives, such as "b," "d," and "p" or "ch," "sh," and "th". Put the bags labeled with those letters on the bulletin board. Invite the children to locate and sort environmental print items and items from their learning environment that begin with those letters. Or, read a piece of environmental print and ask the children to listen and select the bag that contains the letters that represent beginning letter sounds, such as those in consonant blends, vowels, and so on. For example, put environmental print such as "*Glad* wrap," "vanilla *glaze*," "*glue*," and "*glide*-on deodorant" in a bag containing the letter "g" or the consonant blend "gl." Add more bags as new letters and/or letter sounds are introduced.

✦ Put a picture or print a rhyming word on the outside of each bag. Locate print that rhymes with each word. For example, print the word "snake" on a bag and find a picture of a cake on a cake mix label. Say the word represented on the bag ("snake") and invite the children to find the piece(s) of environmental print that rhymes with it ("cake"). Read the pieces of environmental print together to help make the selection. Point out similarities in letters of words that rhyme.

In the Box Bulletin Board

Children sort various items into boxes using letters, pictures, word clues, and so on.

Objectives

Print Awareness: Children will use context clues, letters, and words to match environmental print.

Phonics: Children will demonstrate sound and/or letter-symbol relationships by matching alphabet letters to environmental print.

Phonological/Phonemic Awareness: Children will demonstrate understanding of word families using environmental print.

Beginning Reading: Children will read and match sight words to environmental print using one-to-one correspondence.

Materials

empty product boxes
scissors
bulletin board or other large
 surface
stapler or tape
index cards and markers or
 plastic letters

Theme Connections

Alphabet
Camping
Community Helpers
Farms
Gardening and Plants
Grocery Store

Literacy Interactions

✦ Gather a variety of environmental print boxes, such as cracker, shoe, and toothpaste boxes. Cut off the top flaps of each box. Attach the back side of each box to the bulletin board using a stapler or strong tape. Create a one-to-one correspondence activity by locating a picture or coupon associated with each product box. Ask the children to match the picture with the appropriate box on the board by looking at the printed letters and words.

✦ As a letter recognition review, give each child an alphabet letter (plastic letter or written on an index card) to put into a box that begins with or contains that letter. Call out the letter together or have the child identify it before putting it in the appropriate box.

✦ Collect boxes that contain beginning sight words, such as color words. Underline or circle the words using a dark marker. Print the words on index cards. Ask the children to put the word cards inside the box that contains the same word (for example, the "red" card would go into a box of "Red Hots"). Add colored items (blocks, cars, buttons, and so on) or other environmental print containing color words ("red cherries") to sort into the boxes.

✦ Introduce or review word families with children. Collect product boxes that contain words that are a part of word families, such as "pop," "cat," and "man." For example, a box with the words "shake and bake" would be in the family of words containing "_ake." Change the beginning letter(s) and make new words in the family. Print words in each word family on index cards (for example, "cake," "rake," and "stake") for children to sort into the boxes as they read them or hear them read. An alternative could be to ask the children to think of words to add to the family. Use these as sight words for children to identify.

Chapter 4

Linking Environmental Print With Group Time, Movement, and Music

✦ In each activity in this chapter, the **objectives** are listed in order of difficulty—use them according to the skill level of the children in your class.

✦ In each activity in this chapter, the **literacy interactions** are listed in order of difficulty; use them according to the abilities and interests of the children.

Cereal Box Royalty

Children help make or choose cereal box crowns to wear.

Objectives

Oral Language/Speaking and Listening: Children will recite a rhyme and tell stories about their cereal box adventures.

Writing Process: Children will dictate or write a "cereal box kingdom" story.

Phonics: Children will use cereal box crowns to review alphabet letter recognition and letter sound identification.

Materials

cereal boxes
scissors
hole punch
elastic

Theme Connections

All About Me
Alphabet
Grocery Store

Literacy Interactions

✦ Ask children to bring in several empty cereal boxes. Cut off each box front and cut the top edges to look like a crown. Punch holes in the bottom two corners of the "crown." Thread elastic through and tie. If possible, let children help make the crowns. If not, make the crowns beforehand and let each child select a crown to wear. Invite each child to give a dictated declaration of what he or she would do as king or queen of a "cereal kingdom." Put these into book form for children to illustrate. Use cereal box fronts as covers. Read and invite children to retell their stories.

✦ Ask children to identify the beginning letter of the name on their cereal box crown. Ask the children to put on their crowns and sit down. Sing an alphabet song and invite them to pop up out of their "thrones" as they sing the letter that their cereal crown starts with.

✦ Direct the children to locate other environmental print or things ("treasures") in their "kingdom" that start with the same letter as their cereal box crown. Provide opportunities for them to share their findings.

✦ Use a chant to review letter sounds associated with a cereal name. For example:
King/queen of (cereal name) is who you see.
(letter sound) is the sound of me.

Variations

✦ Make cereal box crowns while doing other activities involving cereal boxes.

✦ Use other environmental print to make crowns, such as signs, soup labels, restaurant products, and so on.

Cereal Box Hopscotch

Children take turns throwing a beanbag, hopping onto a cereal box hopscotch grid, and identifying cereal box front squares.

Objectives

Print Awareness: Children will develop awareness of letters and print on cereal boxes.

Phonics: Children will identify letter sounds and words using cereal boxes.

Phonological/Phonemic Awareness: Children will use cereal boxes to practice pre-reading skills, such as syllable recognition or rhyming words.

Materials

cereal box fronts
masking tape or clear packing tape
beanbag
list paper or chart paper
marker

Theme Connections

Alphabet
Community Helpers
Food and Nutrition
Grocery Store
Holidays

Literacy Interactions

✦ Collect a variety of cereal boxes and cut off the fronts of each. Invite the children to identify each cereal and talk about their favorites. Arrange cereal box fronts on the floor like a hopscotch grid and tape together using masking tape or clear packing tape. As the children play the game, ask them to throw the beanbag and say the name of the cereal it lands on. Encourage them to identify the beginning letter and whether it is upper- or lowercase.

✦ As the game is played, ask the children to think of other words that start with the same letter as the cereal where the beanbag lands. Make a list and add to it for each cereal. Use the lists for reviewing letter sounds.

✦ Play the game when introducing or reviewing syllables. Children take turns throwing a beanbag on one of the cereal box fronts. The child hops on the box fronts a number equal to the number of syllables in the cereal name. For example, if the cereal name is "Crispy O's" the child hops three times.

✦ Use the game to introduce or review rhyming words. Ask the children to think of and share words that rhyme with the cereal the beanbag lands on.

Variation

✦ Use other environmental print to make a hopscotch grid.

Sharing Time Favorites

Children collect and share information about environmental print.

Objectives

Print Awareness: Children will discover uses of environmental print in their classroom, home, and community.

Oral Language/Speaking and Listening: Children will share their observations and knowledge about environmental print they find.

Phonics: Children will associate alphabet letters or letter sounds in their name with those that appear on environmental print.

Materials

a variety of environmental print, such as packaging, newspaper inserts, coupons, brochures, and letterhead stationery

brown paper bags

Theme Connections

All About Me
Colors
Families
Farms
Grocery Store
Health and Safety
Holidays
Sports

Literacy Interactions

✦ Encourage the children to look for print in their learning environment (crayons, markers, books, tissue boxes). Ask them to share what they know about these items. Use this as an opportunity to show how print offers information.

✦ Use this activity as part of a unit, such as apples, holidays, sports, dental health, and so on. Write a note on paper bags explaining what type of environmental print children should bring in. Give each child a brown paper bag (with note) to bring home. Ask them to collect environmental print related to the unit of study, put it in the bag, and bring it back in. Provide extra print for children who do not find any. Invite them to share what they know about their print and what the clues (pictures, symbols, colors, photos) represent.

✦ Invite the children to find environmental print that starts with the same letter as their name, or letter(s) of study. Ask them, "Where did you find this item?" "What is it?" "How is the print (letters) the same or different than how you write?" Look at the letters and discuss what the print looks like. Use these items to make a book, such as an alphabet scrapbook (see "Alphabet Scrapbook" on page 47).

Musical Cereal Go-Round

Children walk on or dance around cereal box fronts as music plays, then stop and identify the one they are standing on as directed.

Objectives

Print Awareness: Children will use print and picture clues to identify names of cereals.

Oral Language/Speaking and Listening: Children will listen to a rhyme in order to locate environmental print identified by name.

Phonics: Children will identify alphabet letters and sounds using cereal boxes.

Beginning Reading: Children will identify names of cereals by sight.

Materials

cereal boxes
markers
music (CD or cassette player or radio)
8 ½" x 11" paper or large chart paper
drawing tools or camera
glue

Theme Connections

All About Me
Food and Nutrition
Grocery Store

Literacy Interactions

✦ Cut off front panels of cereal boxes. On the back of each cereal box panel, use a marker to clearly print the name of the cereal that appears on the front. Prior to starting the game, show the cereal panels to the children. Discuss the words on each, the letters the words start with, and clues they can use to identify each.

✦ Place the panels on the floor in a circle or randomly. Before playing the game, explain to the children how they can share panels by touching the shoulder of others who have a foot or hand touching a box front. Play music and encourage the children to walk on the panels or dance around them. When the music stops, direct each child to touch or share a cereal box front using their foot or hand. Call out a cereal name by saying:

"Good morning, everybody, rise and shine. I'm eating (say a cereal name) for breakfast and I'm feeling fine."

Guide the children to look at the cereal panels they are touching. Ask the child(ren) who is touching the panel used in the rhyme to bring it forward. Continue to play music, stop it, and say the rhyme until all the cereal panels are gone.

✦ Reinforce letter recognition or sounds. As you recite the rhyme, insert a letter of the alphabet or its sound instead of the name of the cereal. Encourage children to find the cereal(s) associated with the letter.

✦ After playing the game, use the panels to create a group book. Ask each child to pick his or her favorite cereal. Write the "Good Morning" rhyme on separate pieces of smaller paper. Insert the name of each child's favorite cereal in the blank. Let the children add illustrations to the rhymes or take photos of them holding their favorite cereal panel and insert into the story. Compile the book version.

✦ Use the back of the cereal box panels (with the identifying words printed on it) after playing the game several times or at the point where many have mastered the game to challenge them in recognizing some of the words by sight. Read together.

Cube Orders

Children toss an environmental print-covered cube to reveal a place where they can obtain a product or service, and then list things found there.

Objectives

Oral language/Speaking and Listening: Children will practice expressing their thoughts and information related to environmental print using complete sentences.

Writing Process: Children will use the writing process to record information about places represented by environmental print.

Vocabulary: Children will use vocabulary associated with familiar places depicted by environmental print.

Materials

small cube-shaped carton
    or box
paper
restaurant and/or business logos
scissors
glue
clear packing tape or contact
    paper

Theme Connections

Careers
Community Helpers
Our Community

Preparation

1. Cover a cube with contact paper or regular paper.
2. Cut out environmental print (restaurant and/or business logos) with similar characteristics, such as all places in the community, all restaurants, or all stores.
3. Glue one piece of environmental print one each side. Print the name of the place under each piece.
4. Wrap the cube in clear packing tape or clear contact paper.

Literacy Interactions

✦ Use as a transitional activity. Have children take turns tossing the cube. After a child tosses the cube, ask him to point to and identify the environmental print facing up. Invite the children to use the word in a sentence about what they would do or get at the place, how they would get there, who they would go with, and so on. Provide several examples of sentences before beginning. For example, "I will go to Taylor's Toy Store and buy a truck."

✦ Show the cube to the children and talk about the places on each side. Ask the children to choose a restaurant (or store or place) on the cube and tell what they would order (or purchase or do there). Document their responses next to their name on a piece of paper. Count and compare similar responses for each place.

✦ Gather various items, including environmental print, associated with places in the community represented on the cube. Toss the cube to reveal a place and invite the children to identify the environmental print or other items that belong there.

✦ Use the cube to review vocabulary about places in the community. Cover the cube with print from places around the community, such as a store, restaurant, and service station. As the cube is tossed, invite the children to share what they know about each place. Use this activity to introduce or review community helpers.

What's Missing?

Children study environmental print and identify the one that is missing.

Objectives

Print Awareness: Children will recognize and recall environmental print as it is associated with their names or other literacy-related skill.

Vocabulary: Children will learn new words and meanings using environmental print.

Oral Language/Speaking and Listening: Children will share information about environmental print in a group setting.

Comprehension: Children will discuss similarities and recall relationships between environmental print items and a unit of study.

Materials

a variety of environmental print, such as child photos, product packaging, brochures, newspaper inserts, business logos, and so on to fit literacy interaction choice below
plastic tray
piece of fabric or towel
writing surface
marker
magnet tape (optional)

Theme Connections

All About Me
Babies
Camping
Colors
Community Helpers
Farms
Food and Nutrition

Gardening and Plants
Grocery Store
Health and Safety
Holidays
Picnic
Sports

Literacy Interactions

✦ Use this activity for a transition activity on name recognition. Write each child's name on a card and attach his or her photo to it (or use the name with no photo). Place photos on a tray or put a piece of magnet tape on the back of each card and use them with a magnetic board or metal tray. Cover and remove one or two names. Ask children to guess who is missing. Let those children with names missing transition to the next activity as they are discovered.

✦ Gather environmental print associated with a unit of study or literacy-related skill. For example, for a farm unit, collect food packaging, seed packets, and miniatures of farm equipment. Arrange items on a tray. Show the tray to the children and talk about each item. Cover the items and remove one or two (without children seeing). Remove the fabric and ask the children to guess which item(s) are missing. Review or introduce how this item is associated with the unit. Ask questions such as, "What do these things have in common?" "How are they different?" "What do you know about this?" Draw attention to corresponding print by writing the names of items on a writing surface as they are mentioned.

The Sandwich Song

Children use sandwich ingredient word cards to insert into blanks to complete the song.

Objectives

Print Awareness: Children will understand the function of print as it is used in a song.

Phonics: Children will identify familiar letters and sounds in environmental print as it is used in the song.

Phonological/Phonemic Awareness: Children will identify and repeat individual sounds that make up an ingredient name as it is introduced in the song.

Beginning Reading: Children will practice reading sight words by repeating words to the song.

Materials

pictures of food or fronts of
    food packaging
scissors
sentence strips
glue
marker
large piece of paper or poster
    board

Theme Connections

Alphabet
Cooking
Picnic

Preparation

1. Encourage children to find and cut out pictures of food they would put in a sandwich.
2. Create word cards by gluing each food picture on the left edge of sentence strips. Print the identifying words to the right of the environmental print. If desired, use strips of paper or index cards instead of sentence strips.
3. Cut sandwich ingredient word cards to size.

4. Write each line of the following song on sentence strips, or write the entire song on a large piece of paper or poster board. Make sure to provide enough space in the blanks to insert sandwich ingredient word cards.

The _____ in the store, the _____ in the store.
Hi ho, did you know, there's _____ in the store?
The _____ takes some _____.
The _____ takes some _____.
Hi ho, did you know, there's _____ in the store?

Literacy Interactions

✦ Invite each child to choose a sandwich ingredient word card to fill in the blanks. You will need two word cards for the first verse, then a new word card for each additional verse. Sing the song with the children (tune: "Farmer in the Dell"). For example:

The cheese in the store, the cheese in the store.
Hi ho, did you know, there's cheese in the store?
The cheese takes some bologna.
The cheese takes some bologna.
Hi ho, did you know, there's bologna in the store.

The bologna in the store…
Ask the children to identify each ingredient as it is added to the song. Hold up the cards or hold and move them through the blanks as they are used in the song.

✦ Talk about the context and picture clues and letters and letter sounds in the ingredient word cards before they are used in the song. Ask, "What clues can you use to help you read this ingredient as it is added to the song?"

✦ Keep ingredient sentence strips in order as they are added to the song. Encourage the children to recall the order when the song is finished.

✦ Use this song to practice using beginning sight words ("in," "the," "did," "and," "you"). Add some of the ingredient words to the list.

Variations

✦ Encourage the children to create actions or sounds to correspond with each ingredient and use them when singing the song. (For example, make a sour face for "pickle.")

✦ Collect real ingredients used in the song and have a sandwich-making party and picnic.

E-I-E-I-O We Go to the Store

Children insert sensory words into a song to describe a product.

Objectives

Oral Language/Speaking and Listening: Children will learn and sing a song that incorporates environmental print.

Vocabulary: Children will use environmental print to generate and understand sensory words.

Print Awareness: Children will follow printed words to a song from right to left.

Beginning Reading: Children will add to or review sight words by following along to words in a song.

Materials

product packaging or pictures of environmental print
index cards and glue (optional)
large paper, sentence strips, or other writing surface
marker

Theme Connections

Colors
Grocery Store
Holidays
Senses

Literacy Interactions

✦ Collect packaging from grocery or department store products. If using pictures of environmental print, glue to index cards. Print the words of the following song on chart paper or other large writing surface where children can see. Leave blanks (as indicated by parentheses) to insert product names and sensory words later. Examples of sensory words include "sweet," "buttery," "blue," "warm," "spicy," and "loud. "

E-I-E-I-O We Go to the Store (sung to tune of "Old MacDonald Had a Farm")
Old Miss Sam she had a store, E-I-E-I-O
And in this store she had some (product name, such as "apples")
    E-I-E-I-O
With a (sensory word to describe smell, sound, taste, or sight, such as "crisp" or "sweet" or "red"), (sensory word) *here,*
And a (sensory word), (sensory word) *there,*
Here a (sensory word),
There a (sensory word),
Everywhere a (sensory word), (sensory word).
Old Miss Sam she had a store, E-I-E-I-O!

Change the name of the storeowner to your name or children's names as they select and insert environmental print.

✦ Let children take turns choosing a piece of familiar environmental print to insert in the song. Invite them to think of a sensory word to describe one characteristic of the product. For example, a sensory word for cookie could be "sweet" or "crunchy." Sing the song with the children.

✦ Make environmental print cards to insert into the song. This works well using sentence strips and a pocket chart. Print sensory words on cards or sentence strips to insert in the blanks as the children think of them. Use these cards for reviewing beginning sight words or new vocabulary.

✦ As children become familiar with the song, invite them to take turns tracking the printed words for the group.

Up and Over: Following Directions

Children listen to and follow directions using environmental print.

Objectives

Print Awareness: Children will focus on print and context clues as they follow directions using environmental print.

Oral Language/Speaking and Listening: Children will understand, follow, and give oral directions using environmental print.

Vocabulary: Children will use environmental print to learn and understand positional words.

Materials

markers
index cards
pictures from newspapers, catalogs, and magazines and/or product packaging
sentence strips
scissors
glue
dry-erase board or chart paper

Theme Connections

Food and Nutrition
Grocery Store

Literacy Interactions

✦ Compile a list of positional vocabulary words, such as "up," "over," "in," "out," "under," and "over." Print each positional word on separate index cards. Collect environmental print (product packaging and/or matching product pictures). Cut out environmental print pictures that match the packaging or containers, and glue it to index cards. Write the identifying words under each picture. Introduce or review the positional words. Encourage children to act out examples of each as you read the cards. Give each child a product container. The containers can be all different, or some or all can be the same. Use positional words and words from collected product containers to give directions. Adjust the directions to fit the variations among the print. For example, "Sam, put the (brand-name) cracker box *over* your head," or "Everyone who has apple juice, put it *on top of* your foot."

✦ Write the name of a product ("candy") and positional vocabulary word ("up") on chart paper or use the cards created for previous interaction. As you read the words and point to them, invite a child to locate the product from a grouping and act out a direction using the positional vocabulary word. For example, "Jackie, find the bag of *candy* and hold it *up*." Allow each child a turn using various combinations of environmental print and positional words. Introduce positional words as beginning sight words using the card set. Encourage children to read these and environmental print cards as they give directions for others to follow.

Variation

✦ Collect containers of one type of product with varied flavors or colors (for example, pudding or gelatin boxes). Give each child a box. Vary directions based on flavor or color. For example, "If you are holding a box of grape gelatin, put it above your head; if you are holding cherry gelatin, put it under your chin."

Sign Signals

Children "read" traffic and safety signs and demonstrate understanding through movement or action.

Objectives

Print Awareness: Children will identify and recall traffic and safety print in their community.

Vocabulary: Children will learn and demonstrate meaning of words related to traffic and safety signs.

Oral Language/Speaking and Listening: Children will follow oral and written directions using traffic and safety signs.

Comprehension: Children will demonstrate understanding of traffic and safety signs by performing a related action.

Materials

traffic and safety signs, made or purchased paper in a variety of colors
markers

Theme Connections

Health and Safety
Our Community
Transportation

Literacy Interactions

✦ Create traffic and safety signs (see patterns on page 240). Make large signs such as "Stop," "One Way," "Walk," and "Don't Walk." (You can also purchase signs, if desired.) For signs that do not contain words, write the implied words underneath or on a separate piece of paper and attach (for example, write "Railroad Crossing" for underneath the symbol). Introduce or review traffic and safety signs and the words that coincide with each. Discuss and act out the meanings. ("Show me how to stop.") Encourage children to share where they have seen these signs in their own community.

✦ Hold up signs, one at a time. Encourage the children to read each one out loud and then imitate the action associated with its meaning (see sample sign signal actions below).

Variation

✦ Go on a walk in your community or look for and read the same signs while on a field trip. Review their meaning.

Sample Sign Signal Actions:

✦ Do Not Enter—stop and turn around
✦ Railroad Crossing—stop and make a train sound
✦ Danger—run in opposite direction
✦ Rest Area—lie down and snore
✦ Stop—freeze in place
✦ One Way—go right or left as directed by arrow
✦ No Passing—proceed walking forward without passing anyone
✦ Walk—walk forward
✦ Don't Walk—freeze in place
✦ Exit—go to a door
✦ Caution—tiptoe
✦ Speed Limit 55—run
✦ School Zone—walk in slow motion

Stroll to the Store

Children follow directions to move from place to place along an environmental print path.

Objectives

Print Awareness: Children will focus on environmental print as part of following oral directions.

Vocabulary: Children will demonstrate understanding of positional or directional words through movement.

Oral Language/Speaking and Listening: Children will follow and give oral directions using an environmental print path.

Comprehension: Children will dramatize and retell a story using an environmental print path.

Materials

business logos from packaging, such as pizza boxes and shopping bags, or related print from newspaper inserts

scissors

construction paper

glue

markers

traffic and safety signs (see page 240)

long piece of clear vinyl table covering

tape

Theme Connections

Community Helpers

Health and Safety

Our Community

Preparation

1. Cut out large pieces of environmental print and glue each to a piece of construction paper. Print the identifying word(s) under each.

2. Make or copy traffic and safety signs (see page 240). Glue to construction paper and print identifying word(s) under each.

3. Position environmental print underneath a clear vinyl table covering, alternating between traffic/safety signs and environmental print, to make a path. Tape in place.

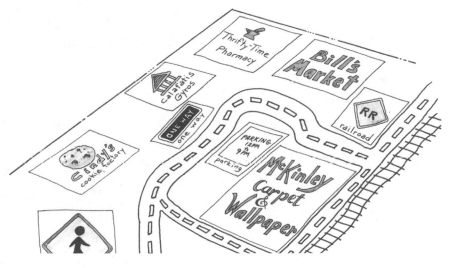

Literacy Interactions

✦ Introduce or review positional words ("right," "left," "back," "front"). Give small groups of children directions for using the path. For example, "Susan, turn right and walk to the stop sign," or "John, walk backward to the restaurant sign." Draw attention to identifying words for each sign by writing each on chart paper or other writing surface as they are introduced in the directions.

✦ Encourage children to give each other directions or make up a story for others to act out using the path and environmental print signs.

✦ Make up an oral story using the path. Let several children act out the story as you tell it. Enlist other children to recall what happened in the story. Ask questions such as, "What happened first?" "Next?" "How did the story end?"

Picture This

Children use environmental print to draw, write, or share descriptions of the product or business it represents.

Objectives

Print Awareness: Children will study word and picture clues to identify what they represent.

Vocabulary: Children will learn about and share new vocabulary using environmental print related to the unit of study.

Writing Process: Children will write and draw representations of environmental print words and encourage others to identify the matching picture.

Oral Language/Speaking and Listening: Children will share and listen to descriptions of environmental print.

Materials

a variety of environmental print, such as product packaging, newspaper inserts, and business stationery or packaging)

scissors

glue

index cards

markers

paper or dry-erase board

pencils or dry-erase markers

Theme Connections

Alphabet	Farms
Babies	Food and Nutrition
Camping	Gardening and Plants
Colors	Health and Safety
Community Helpers	Holidays

Literacy Interactions

✦ Gather environmental print relating to a unit of study. Cut out pictures and glue one on each index card. Print identifying word(s) under each picture ("yellow corn"). Make a set of about 15–20 cards. Encourage the children to share what they know about each card. Record children's responses on chart paper or a dry-erase board. Ask them what the clues on the print or picture tell them about the item.

✦ Provide environmental print cards that each contain a color word or other beginning sight word. Read the cards several times. On separate sets of cards, draw pictures or invite the children to draw pictures that represent the identifying words and encourage the others to guess which print matches the picture. Let children use the cards to play a guessing game.

✦ Invite the children to bring environmental print from home hidden in a bag. Encourage the children to create picture and word clues on a piece of paper about what they brought to share with others. Explain that they can share these clues with others, and invite them to guess the item in the bag.

Logo Card Game

Children identify similarities and differences among sets of environmental print.

Objectives

Print Awareness: Children will use visual and print clues on environmental print to identify similarities and differences.

Vocabulary: Children will use understanding of word meanings and context clues to identify environmental print that has similar characteristics.

Phonics: Children will distinguish between letters using environmental print.

Phonological/Phonemic Awareness: Children will identify similarities among environmental print using literacy skills such as rhyming, word families, syllable segmentation, and so on.

Comprehension: Children will demonstrate understanding of concepts or unit of study by identifying related environmental print.

Materials

large index cards (4" x 6")
    or cardstock cut to size
glue
product labels or pictures of
    products from newspaper
    inserts

Theme Connections

Camping

Community Helpers

Cultural Awareness

Farms

Food and Nutrition

Gardening and Plants

Grocery Store

Health and Safety

Holidays

Sports

Transportation

Preparation

1. Select product pictures or labels that have similar characteristics (for example, all soups or all toothpastes) in sets of three (for example, three different soup labels or three different toothpaste boxes). Then select one label that is dissimilar for each set, such as one candy bar wrapper.

2. Trim product labels or cut out pictures of products to fit on index cards.

3. Glue one label on each card to complete sets of four cards. For example, one set could contain three different soup labels and one canned fruit label. Or, mix and match sets of three by adding one dissimilar item from another set.

4. Print the identifying word of each product below the label on each card ("chicken soup").

(continued on the next page)

Literacy Interactions

✦ After creating sets, talk to the children about sets. Discuss similarities and differences between a few product examples. Introduce the sets of cards and ask the children to identify the products by type (three toy cards and one food card), by properties (three liquids and one solid), or by brand name (three juices from one company and one juice from another company). Invite the children to explain why they think the selected three belong together.

✦ For each set, collect three pieces of environmental print that begin with the same alphabet letter and one piece that does not. Ask the children to identify the beginning letter of the item that does not belong. Invite them to think of something that starts with the same letter as the others in the set. Create sets using environmental print with word families, ending sounds, or rhyming words. Ask the children if they recognize the word with the different sound in a sequence as you read them out loud.

✦ Incorporate the cards into a unit of study. For each set include environmental print associated with the unit and one or more that do not. Ask questions such as, "What makes the item that doesn't belong different from the others?" "What clues did you use to decide which card was different?" "What is similar about the other cards?"

Variation

✦ After doing the activity, put the sets of cards in the Games Area or Language Center for children to play with and mix to make their own sets.

Things That Go Together

Children put puzzle pairs back together using unifying characteristics.

Objectives

Vocabulary: Children will demonstrate understanding of word meanings by listing uses for each word, and then grouping the words into pairs.

Phonics/Decoding: Children will put together puzzles by identifying matching letter sounds.

Phonological/Phonemic Awareness: Children will recognize the same sounds in different words to put together puzzle pieces.

Materials

magazines and newspaper inserts
scissors
glue
large index cards or rectangular pieces of poster board
marker
chart paper

Theme Connections

Alphabet
Camping
Community Helpers
Food and Nutrition
Gardening and Plants
Grocery Store
Holidays

Preparation

1. Find and cut out pictures from environmental print of pairs of things with a unifying characteristic or that are used together (for example, peanut butter and bread, toothpaste and floss, and bakery and donuts).

2. Glue the pairs on opposite ends of a large index card, leaving a space between them.

3. Write the identifying words under the pictures.

4. Make puzzles of each card by cutting them in two in a way that no two sets of cards are alike (use zigzag lines, curved lines, and so on).

Literacy interactions

✦ Introduce the cards to the children and draw their attention to identifying words and context clues. Ask questions such as, "What is this item?" "What is it used for?" "Which items can be or are used together?" Make a list of their responses for each word. Encourage them to test their responses by putting the cards together.

✦ Create "go-together" cards for items that have similar characteristics, such as beginning with the same letter sound, containing the same vowel sound, or rhyming. Review these characteristics before playing the game. Divide the pairs among the children and challenge them to find the person that has the matching card.

Grocery Cart Rhyme Time

Children use environmental print to identify rhyming words, create lists of rhyming words, and compose rhymes.

Objectives

Phonological/Phonemic Awareness: Children will recognize, match, and list rhyming words using environmental print.

Materials

product packaging
child-size grocery cart or other
    large container
paper and marker

Theme Connections

Food and Nutrition
Grocery Store
Nursery Rhymes

Literacy Interactions

✦ Collect environmental print packaging with print that rhymes ("yummy in your tummy") or that easily rhymes with other words. Sort into rhyming pairs ("chocolate chips" and "veggie dip" or "cake mix" and "Kix cereal") and put in a small shopping cart. Introduce each piece by name so that the children hear the word sounds. Ask them to help you find the rhyming match for each piece. Hand out one of each pair to each child. Emphasize the rhyming word as you read each one. Encourage the children to find the match to their piece and put it in the cart.

✦ Have a rhyming "special of the week." Preview one item in the cart that contains an easy-to-rhyme word, for example, cat food or popcorn. Encourage the children to load the cart with items or other environmental print that rhymes with the "special." Create a list for children to use later to make up their own rhyming chants.

Trash to Treasure Hunt

Children use clues to find environmental print related to a cooking activity or theme.

Objectives

Print Awareness: Children will use knowledge of print and pictures to identify ingredients.

Oral Language/Speaking and Listening: Children will share and listen to descriptions of environmental print.

Vocabulary: Children will learn new word meanings related to cooking or a unit of study through experiences with environmental print.

Comprehension: Children will make predictions and recall a sequence using environmental print.

Materials

environmental print related to a theme or cooking activity (see literacy interactions below)

chart paper or other writing surface

marker

Theme Connections

All About Me	Farms
Alphabet	Food and Nutrition
Colors	Gardening and Plants
Community Helpers	Grocery Store
Cooking	Health and Safety
Cultural Awareness	Our Community

Literacy interactions

✦ Choose a recipe, gather ingredients in original containers, and collect environmental print related to the recipe. Print simple one- or two-word clues on chart paper for some or all of the ingredients. For example, clues for flour could be "white," "wheat," and "powder." Place the ingredients (in original packaging) around the room at children's eye level. Like a treasure hunt, place clues at each ingredient for the next item. Read the clue for the first ingredient (for example, flour). Place the clue for the second ingredient (for example, salt) next to the flour. Place the clue for

(continued on the next page)

the third ingredient next to the salt, and so on. Another option is to keep the clues and read them one at a time. After children have located all the ingredients, gather them together and create a list with the children. Talk about each ingredient to help build vocabulary understanding. Invite the children to guess what they could make with the ingredients. Document their responses on chart paper. Read the recipe and talk about it in relation to their guesses. As you make the food, draw attention to the name of each ingredient as it is added to the recipe. Once completed, ask children to recall the steps they followed to make the item.

✦ Use this activity to introduce a new theme or a planned field trip. Collect environmental print related to the theme and make clues for each. Read the clues and guide the children to find each piece of environmental print described. Gather the items together. Make a list of the items, drawing attention to the print on each. Ask questions such as, "What are these items?" "What clues on the item help you tell what it is?" Document their responses. Use the responses, the environmental print, and clues to build on such areas as vocabulary and introduce or review the theme.

✦ Do this activity in connection with "Sharing Time Favorites" (see page 86). Ask the children to create drawings and word clues for their items brought from home. Use the children's clues to set up a treasure hunt. Encourage the child who brought the environmental print to share additional information about it as it is discovered along the hunt.

Variation

✦ Add a treasure box at the end of the hunt that contains one or more activities for children to do related to the theme or cooking activity. These could include a book to read together, an art activity, or an experiment.

Beach Ball Bounce

Children use environmental print to answer questions written on a beach ball.

Objectives

Phonics: Children will identify alphabet letter(s) or letter sound(s) on environmental print.

Phonological/Phonemic Awareness: Children will listen to and identify sounds in words and select environmental print according to a pre-reading skill (such as syllables, onsets, rhyming words, and so on).

Comprehension: Children will answer a question about their environment by identifying related print.

Beginning Reading: Children will locate sight words on environmental print.

Materials

packaging from various products
beach ball with solid colored
    sections
permanent marker

Theme Connections

Alphabet
Seasons
Travel and Vacations

Literacy Interactions

✦ Use this game to review concepts, such as letter and letter sound recognition, rhyming words, syllable identification, sight word recognition, and so on. Collect packaging from various products associated with learning objectives. Using a permanent marker, write questions or directions on each section of the beach ball that are specific to learning objectives. Sample directions to write on the ball include:
  - ✦ Find a product that begins with the letter (insert letter).
  - ✦ Find something that begins with same letter as your name.
  - ✦ Find something that has (insert number) syllable(s) in its name.
  - ✦ Find a product that has a name that rhymes with (insert word).
  - ✦ Find a product that contains the word (insert a sight word).

✦ Have the children sit in a circle and take turns rolling the beach ball. The child who rolls the ball answers the question that appears upright by selecting the appropriate environmental print.
✦ Bring the ball on field trips to use during a transition time or waiting period. Write questions on the ball that fit the learning environment or place. Encourage children to identify items and surrounding print that answer the questions or directions.

Variation

✦ Make dice using a plastic picture cube or square box and write questions on each side.

Rebus Lists

Children cut out and tape environmental print to compile a rebus list they can read and share.

Objectives

Oral Language/Speaking and Listening: Children will share information about themselves and their experiences using environmental print.

Print Awareness: Children will discover similarities between letters and words on environmental print with identifying word(s) or letters in print without picture clues.

Phonics: Children will create a list of words using environmental print that begins with the letters in their names.

Vocabulary: Children will obtain new vocabulary through discussion about environmental print on their lists.

Comprehension: Children will communicate understanding of events using environmental print to develop a list.

Materials

catalogs, newspaper inserts, and magazines
index cards or self-adhesive note pads
scissors
clear tape
chart paper or other large writing surface
markers

Theme Connections

All About Me
Cooking
Families
Food and Nutrition
Grocery Store
Holidays

Literacy Interactions

◆ Encourage the children to cut out pictures of their favorite things, foods, and places from catalogs, newspaper inserts, and magazines. Help them trim the environmental print and glue to index cards or

self-adhesive note pads to create rebus pictures (picture representations) of words to use in a list. Encourage children to create rebus lists of their favorite things. Demonstrate how to tape or adhere the rebus pictures on chart paper to create a list, and assist children in writing identifying words underneath the flaps on their rebus lists. (The environmental print provides a picture representation of words written underneath.) Incorporate this into an "All About Me" unit. Ask questions such as, "What do you like about this thing (food, place)?" "What do you do with it?"

✦ Encourage the children to work together to create a rebus list using restaurant-related environmental print. Encourage them to use the list as a menu board while pretending to be in a restaurant during dramatic play. Another option is to provide paper for them to create small rebus menus.

✦ Print each child's name across a large piece of paper. Ask the children to create rebus lists by finding environmental print that contains words that begin with each letter in their names. Use this activity to teach them the letters in their names and/or letter sounds. Encourage them to practice making the sounds of the letters and/or saying the name of the letter as each word in their list is read.

✦ Invite the children to create a rebus list using print gathered on a field trip. Use the print or encourage children to create and add pictures or words to depict other things or people they saw on the trip. Use this list for vocabulary discussion and review of the trip. Encourage the children to look under the flaps as they read and share their lists to associate the printed word(s) with those appearing on the environmental print. Read the list together.

Note: Incorporate this activity into "Building a Shopping List" (on page 106). For example, invite the children to help make a rebus list of materials for a cooking or art activity using environmental print. Later, incorporate the print into creating a recipe book.

Building a Shopping List

Children select environmental print word cards and use them to complete a sentence.

Objectives

Print Awareness: Children will recognize that sentences are made up of separate words by completing their own sentences using environmental print.

Oral Language/Speaking and Language: Children will share information about environmental print.

Writing Process: Children will write and/or trace environmental print words.

Beginning Reading: Children will practice reading beginning sight words and environmental print in a sentence.

Materials

small pictures of products and business logos from newspaper inserts or magazines

scissors, glue, marker

sentence strips

paper or index cards (optional)

Velcro or pocket chart

laminate or clear contact paper (optional)

Theme Connections

Community Helpers

Cultural Awareness

Grocery Store

Our Community

School

Preparation

1. Cut out environmental print (small pictures of products and business logos) from newspaper inserts or magazines.

2. Create word cards by gluing each picture on the left edge of a sentence strip, strip of paper, or index card.

3. Print the identifying word to the right of the picture. Cut strips to size of the word.

4. On long pieces of sentence strips, print sentences with blanks for environmental print words. For example, "I like to go to _____ and buy _____ ." Or, "I want to go to _____ and see _____ ." Make sure to leave adequate space for the blanks to fit word cards.

5. If you are not using a pocket chart, laminate or cover the strips with clear contact paper. Attach Velcro to blanks in sentence and to backs of word cards.

Literacy Interactions

◆ Use "building a sentence" as part of a learning center routine. Create sentence strips that encourage children to use everyday environmental print. For example, "I need to go to the _____ ," or "I need a _____ ." Children can insert word cards or photos of people into the blank (marker, tissue, playground, nurse, music teacher, and so on).

◆ Invite the children to sort the word cards into businesses or places, and things that are seen or purchased at those businesses or places. Encourage children to share stories about places they have visited in the community.

◆ Put sentence strips into a pocket chart or on a board. Invite the children to choose a place by selecting a word card. (Incorporate environmental print that contains sight words into the choice of cards.) Then, guide them to find a word card of something they would see or purchase there. Help them (as needed) to insert the cards in the sentence blanks and read it together. Encourage them to add more word cards to the end of the sentence to expand their shopping list.

Note: Put word cards in the Writing Center for children to copy or trace over. Invite them to use the cards to make their own shopping lists to use in dramatic play. (See "Environmental Print Writing Wonders" on page 163.)

Linking Environmental Print With Math

✦ In each activity in this chapter, the **objectives** are listed in order of difficulty—use them according to the skill level of the children in your class.

✦ In each activity in this chapter, the **literacy interactions** are listed in order of difficulty; use them according to the abilities and interests of the children.

Count My Cart

Children use product containers and packaging in counting, creating sets, or addition activities.

Objectives

Print Awareness: Children will use environmental print in sorting and counting activities.

Phonics: Children will count and sort environmental print associated with specific letters or letter sounds.

Phonological/Phonemic Awareness: Children will identify words that contain specific letter sounds.

Beginning Reading: Children will practice sight word identification by sorting and counting environmental print containing the same word.

Materials

product containers and
    packaging containing print
shopping cart or large box
plastic hoops, bike tires, or
    masking tape
large writing surface (chart
    paper or dry-erase board)
marker

Theme Connections

Colors
Farms
Food and Nutrition
Gardening and Plants
Grocery Store
Health and Safety
Senses
Vegetables

Literacy Interactions

✦ Gather multiples of several different product containers or packaging and place them in a cart or large box. Invite the children to examine the contents of the cart or box. Lay plastic hoops or bike tires on the floor to mark different sections, or create sections on the floor using masking tape. Ask children to help identify and locate similar items to sort into groups using the hoops or taped areas (for example, similar product boxes, things that belong in a

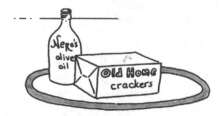 

refrigerator or in a cabinet, and so on). Direct their attention to letter or word similarities on the print as an option in the sorting process. Ask them to count and identify the number in each set. Document their responses. For example, chicken noodle soup: 5, cereal with flakes: 8, and so on. For an added challenge, ask them to divide into groups using brand names.

✦ Use all of one type of product, such as all cereal boxes or gelatin boxes. After familiarizing the children with the contents of the cart, ask them to count out items as they are named. (For example, "Find and count all the grape gelatin.") Use this opportunity to review letter identification, sounds, sight words, rhyming words, and so on. For example, "Find the *grape* gelatin. It starts with a 'g'. Can you think of words or find other items that start with the /g/ sound? Can you find any items that have words that rhyme with 'ape'?" After all the different sets have been identified and counted, ask the children to help count how many items were in the cart all together. Use this as an opportunity to give directions that review and/or introduce beginning concepts of addition using sets.

Numbers in Print

Children use environmental print containing numbers in identification, counting, and/or matching activities.

Objectives

Print Awareness: Children will examine the uses of numerals and number words within the context of print in their environment.

Beginning Reading: Children will practice recognizing number sight words using environmental print.

Writing Process: Children will dictate or write a list of places where numbers are found on print in their environment.

Materials

coupons, print containing numerals or number words
poster board, paper roll, manila folder, or index cards
scissors
glue

Theme Connections

Math
Our Community
Post Office
Sports
Transportation

Literacy Interactions:

✦ Ask children to look for and bring in environmental print that contains numerals or number words. Invite them to share their print and the number that appears on it. Discuss how numbers are used in print. Brainstorm a list of places that numbers are found in the print world, such as license plates, addresses, street signs, coupons, food labels, phone books, and so on.

✦ Start a number line around the room by adhering environmental print the children have gathered to a wall surface or paper. (Leave spaces for missing numerals.) Challenge the children to look for print containing numerals to fill in the spaces. Use the number line for numeral identification and counting games.

✦ Glue number-related environmental print on a poster board or folder to play "I Spy." Hold up a numeral, number word, or set of objects and direct the children to identify the matching environmental print on the "I Spy" collage.

✦ Create a matching game. Put environmental print containing a numeral or number word on one card and another way of symbolizing the number on another. For example, write "9 (brand name item)" on one card and the word "nine" or a set of nine stickers on the other card. Invite children to match cards.

Variation

✦ Gather supermarket advertisements. Ask the children to locate a number and/or a series of numbers and circle them.

Shape of My Box

Children use environmental print to practice shape identification and recognition.

Objectives

Print Awareness: Children will learn about and identify basic two-dimensional shapes.

Writing Process: Children will record shapes and letters.

Vocabulary: Children will learn new words associated with two- and three-dimensional shapes.

Materials

product boxes and containers:
    three-dimensional
    containers such as boxes or
    cans, and/or print that
    contains shapes as part of
    the label

paper

pencils

masking tape

plastic or wooden blocks in
    various shapes

Theme Connections

Boxes

Grocery Store

Our Community

Literacy Interactions:

✦ Encourage children to look for signs and labels in the learning environment or while on a walk. Use the opportunity to discuss the words on the signs, and to introduce or review specific shapes. Invite the children to count the sides of each shape and discuss what makes it different from other shapes. Provide a notepad for them to draw the sign and print names.

✦ Adhere masking tape to the floor to create graph. Make a section for each type of shape to be sorted. Tape a paper copy of each shape or an environmental print example at the bottom of each section to create a heading, such as a triangle shape or a cheese wedge box. Encourage children to sort print into sections by shape. Together, count how many are in each section. Read the print in each section. Ask questions such as, "Does the print have anything else in common?" "Do any of the print and containers come from the same place?"

✦ Collect or cut out environmental print that contains shapes in or as part of the label. Ask children to sort by shapes, such as a star, circle, and square, and use to create individual books or collages. Glue environmental print on paper or use "It's in the Bag" books (see page 49). Let the children "read" the print and add to their pages as they discover other relevant print. Print the name of the shape on every page. For example, a circle book may contain a label or picture of vanilla wafers, oyster crackers, fruit-flavored candy, a store that has a circle in its logo, and so on.

✦ Use containers and objects of specific geometric shapes, such as a cube, wedge, and cone, to introduce new vocabulary. Encourage children to name and match the containers to wooden or plastic block shapes.

Variation

✦ Invite children to recreate shapes they find on labels and containers using craft sticks or geoboards.

Size, Shape, and Sorting Envelope Match

Children sort cards, notes, and mail and use size and shape relationships to match them to envelopes.

Objectives

Print Awareness: Children will use environmental print during a mail sorting and matching activity.

Vocabulary: Children will review and reinforce understanding of concepts related to shape words such as "rectangle" and "square," and size words such as "long" and "short."

Materials

sets of various sizes and types of cards and notes and matching envelopes containing print

boxes, baskets, or trays

mail carrier hat and mailbag

Theme Connections

Community Helpers

Holidays

Post Office

Literacy Interactions:

✦ Collect cards and notes from junk mail, birthdays, holidays, and so on. Invite children to bring in discarded cards and mail. Make sure they get their parents' permission (send home a note to make sure children do not bring in anything important). Put the cards and notes in a box, basket, or tray and ask children to think of ways to sort it. For example, sort by type (birthday cards, holiday cards, junk mail) or size/shape (rectangle, square, small, large). Use this opportunity to introduce or reinforce concepts such as "rectangle," "square," "long," and "short." Guide them to sort the items by looking at the print, size, and shape clues to identify where each piece belongs. Provide a mail carrier hat and put items in a mailbag to encourage association of the activity to the job of sorting mail.

✦ Challenge children to use sets of environmental print they have sorted and match them to envelopes. Identify examples of cards, letters, and envelopes that have print clues to use in matching. For example, a letter containing a school name and logo might have an envelope that contains the same information. Encourage the children to share their discoveries about print as they match the mail.

Variation

✦ Use this activity in combination with post office dramatic play (see "Post Office" on page 183). Provide opportunities for children to write and sign their names inside cards or on letters.

Silhouette Shape Puzzle

Children match the shape of environmental print to corresponding silhouette shapes.

Objectives

Print Awareness: Children will develop an understanding of the function of environmental print in terms of letters, words, and distinctive shapes used to convey meaning.

Vocabulary: Children will use silhouetted environmental print shapes to expand their understanding and use of shape terminology.

Materials

signs, business logos, and so on that contain recognizable or distinctive shapes such as a stop sign or restaurant logo

poster board, tagboard, or other heavy paper product

scissors

glue

dark-colored construction paper

light-colored construction paper

pencil or dowel

Theme Connections

Alphabet
Health and Safety
Restaurant
Shapes
Sports

Preparation

1. Trim signs and logos to reveal their distinctive shapes, such as a bell shape used in a restaurant logo.
2. Mount each piece to heavy paper and trim to size.
3. Trace around each shape on dark-colored paper.
4. Cut out and glue each silhouetted shape onto the light-colored paper.

Literacy Interactions

✦ Provide several sets of environmental print for children to sort by various characteristics (for example, a set of signs, restaurant logos, sports logos, all circles, all squares, and so on). Invite children to study the print pieces to identify the grouping possibilities. After they sort the sets, encourage them to match each shape to a silhouette on a piece of paper.

✦ Cut out environmental print in their distinctive shapes and tape to a pencil or dowel. Or, recreate and enlarge the distinctive shape on another piece of paper, cut it out, and tape to a stick. Hang a thin piece of white paper or sheet in front of a light source. Hold a shape behind the sheet and encourage children to identify the shape from its shadow.

Variation

✦ Use product containers, such as a drink-mix cylinder or tissue box, and trace the bottom of each to create a matching silhouette.

Patterning Products

Children use environmental print to complete, create, and explain patterns.

Objectives

Print Awareness: Children will use environmental print to identify what comes next in a pattern.

Phonics: Children will practice letter recognition while using environmental print to complete a pattern.

Beginning Reading: Children will practice reading and using sight words in patterning activities.

Oral Language/Speaking and Listening: Children will listen to a pattern sequence and identify what comes next by selecting from environmental print.

Materials

environmental print, such as soup labels, gelatin boxes, juice box fronts, and crayons
index cards or cardstock pieces
scissors
glue
chart paper
marker

Theme Connections

All About Me
Alphabet
Food and Nutrition
Grocery Store
Health and Safety
Shapes

Literacy Interactions

✦ Gather identical product containers, wrappers, labels, and boxes that have slight variations within the product, such as several boxes of each flavor of gelatin. Glue paper print to supportive backing, such as index cards or cardstock pieces, and cut fronts off box items and use as is. Create a pattern using the print (grape gelatin box/apple juice box/grape gelatin box/apple juice box/...). Ask the children to locate the next item(s) to complete the sequence. Point to the words on the environmental print as you read it together. Ask the children to "read" the pattern.

✦ Create and read a pattern using different flavors of one type or brand of product (grape juice/grape juice/apple juice/grape juice/grape juice/apple juice/ ...). Ask children to locate the next item(s) in the sequence. After the sequence is complete, create a rhythm or chant with movement to go with the sequence as it is read. Write the identifying words in sequence on chart paper to read together.

✦ Make a pattern that uses specific alphabet letter sounds or sight words. Write the identifying words or letters in a pattern on chart paper (orange/cherry/orange/cherry/ ...). Guide the children to read the sequence and identify environmental print that could be used to continue or represent the pattern. For example, the next word in the previous example would be "orange." Children choose an item from an assortment of environmental print that contains the word "orange" to represent the next word in the pattern, and continue the pattern using more environmental print.

✦ Make a pattern using letters (ABC/ABC/ABC...). Say the letter pattern together. Ask the children to identify and put in order environmental print that contain words that start with the letters represented (for example, "apple juice," "Band-Aid," "cake mix"/ "almond candy," "biscuits," "crackers"/...). Underline or circle the letters that are represented on the print as they are added to the pattern.

Lid Sort

Children categorize and sort lids containing environmental print.

Objectives

Print Awareness: Children will observe and use environmental print as a way to visually discriminate, sort, and classify lids.

Vocabulary: Children will use lids to apply understanding of words and sorting characteristics.

Phonics: Children will use environmental print on lids in activities to sort and identify letters.

Oral Language/Speaking and Listening: Children will use environmental print on sorted lids to generate sentences and stories.

Materials

assorted sizes and colors of
    clean lids containing print,
    such as metal or plastic
    from jars, Styrofoam, plastic
    from restaurant cups or
    cardboard lids from boxes
sorting tray, muffin tin, bowls, or
    baskets
tape

Theme Connections

Colors
Food and Nutrition
Opposites
Recycling
Shapes

Literacy Interactions

✦ Invite children to gather lids containing print. Encourage them to examine, "read," and manipulate them. Ask them to share all the ways they think the lids could be classified and sorted (for example, metal or plastic, color, size, print letters, numbers, or identical words). Encourage them to sort the lids according to similar characteristics into a sorting tray, muffin tin, or bowls. (If sorting equipment and muffin tins are unavailable, divide a tray, table, or other surface into a grid using tape.) Ask them to share their observations about which sets have more and less. Invite them to compare each set of lids to look for other similarities. For example, "These all start with the letter 'c'. Are there some that are also the same color? Do any have the same words?"

✦ Gather lids that are the same shape. Invite the children to sort them from biggest to smallest or smallest to biggest. Read them together in order. Invite the children to make up silly stories and sentences using the words on the lids as they appear in order.

My Choices: Bar Graphing

Children make choices on a graph using environmental print.

Objectives

Print Awareness: Children will look at and choose from environmental print in a graphing activity.

Writing Process: Children will practice writing their names and record results in a graphing activity.

Materials

containers and/or labels from pizza, dessert, sandwich toppings, or other print

chart paper or other large writing surface

glue

markers

rulers

Theme Connections

All About Me

Food and Nutrition

Grocery Store

Health and Safety

Literacy Interactions:

✦ Plan a snack or meal together that involves making choices, such as choosing pizza toppings. Divide paper or writing surface into an evenly divided grid. Collect or invite children to locate environmental print (containers and/or labels from pizza, dessert, sandwich toppings, or other print) that represents their choices, such as pepperoni, olives, and tomato sauce. Glue one item on the bottom of each column of the graph. Ask the children to write their name or color in a grid square above each item they would like as part of their snack or meal. Ask them to identify which column(s) are the tallest, shortest, or the same size. Together count the names or colored-in grids in each column. Use the results to plan and/or write a list of how much of each item is needed for the snack or meal.

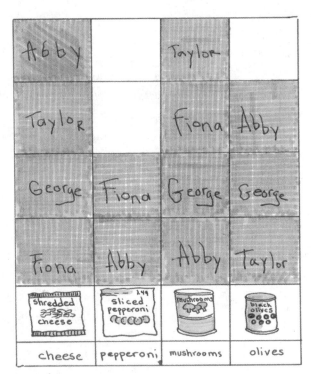

✦ Provide a grid for each child containing print from places and/or signs they see in their community. Direct them to use the grids while they are out in their community, such as on a field trip, to record how many times they see the environmental print represented. Invite them to share what they find.

My Favorites: Real Object Graphing

Children choose environmental print labels or container fronts and place in the corresponding section on a graph.

Objectives

Vocabulary: Children will learn and practice words associated with comparison such as "more," "less," "equal," "most," and "least" using environmental print.

Beginning Reading: Children will practice reading and sorting sight words in environmental print.

Phonics: Children will look at sections of environmental print and determine similarities in beginning sounds, vowel sounds, letters, and so on.

Materials

varieties of the same environmental print item, such as juice box fronts, vegetable seed packets, and so on
solid-colored shower curtain or vinyl tablecloth
permanent marker
dry-erase marker

Theme Connections

All About Me	Holidays
Colors	Our Community
Community Helpers	Opposites
Farms	Recycling
Food and Nutrition	Senses
Gardening and Plants	Sports
Grocery Store	

Literacy Interactions:

✦ Ask children to bring in environmental print associated with a specific subject matter, such as places they like to visit, favorite desserts, or favorite toys. Make graph sections on a solid-colored shower curtain or vinyl tablecloth using a permanent marker. Divide the sections into specific subcategories using a dry-erase marker. For example, dessert categories could include ice cream, cookies, pudding, fruit, and so on. Lay the graph on the floor. Put examples of print in each section as needed. Invite children to "read" their selection(s) and then place them in the section on the graph that best describes it. Count the print items in each section. Ask questions such as, "How many are in each category?" "Which categories have more (or less) items?"

✦ Pre-sort environmental print into sections on an empty graph without headings. Sort using places in the community (gas stations, grocery stores, and schools) or using a literacy skill, such as items that start with various letters divided among the sections. Invite children to look at the print, identify similarities in the sections, and explain how the sections are divided. Ask what headings they would put on the graph. Print their responses in the heading area.

✦ Use the activity to draw attention to color, safety, or other sight words. Enlist children in locating environmental print that contains specific sight words, such as "pop," "nut," or "dog." Create section headings on the graph using the sight words and invite children to read the words. Ask them to read the sight words on the environmental print ("fruit *pops*," "honey *nut*" cereal, or "*dog* treats") and place it into the section that has a matching sight word.

Measuring

Children use items or containers containing environmental print in measuring activities.

Objectives

Writing Process: Children will use environmental print as a unit in recording measurement.

Phonics: Children will reinforce letter and/or beginning letter sound recognition using environmental print in measuring activities.

Vocabulary: Children will learn and understand measuring concepts and words using environmental print.

Materials

multiples of each container or item containing environmental print, such as tissue boxes, crayons, pasta boxes, and so on

measuring units (paper clips or linking cubes)

paper

tape

marker, crayon, or pencil

Theme Connections

Colors

Farms

Grocery Store

Health and Safety

Holidays

Opposites

Shoes

Literacy Interactions

✦ Collect multiples of each container or item. Secure flaps or edges of any containers with tape, as needed. Use the activity to introduce or review the concept of measuring in terms of length. Have children use one type of container, such as pudding mix boxes, in a measuring experience. Point out that when measuring, the print on the boxes must be placed in the same direction, end to end, to get an accurate measurement. Encourage them to use several different pieces of environmental print to measure the same thing. Document their responses using the environmental print as headings. Provide ample opportunities for the children to explore measurement using the environmental print.

✦ Use one type of environmental print as a measuring tool to reinforce a literacy-related skill. For example, if discussing the beginning sound /e/, have them use egg cartons and other containers that begin with the same letter or sound to measure.

✦ Engage the children in activities involving measurement comparisons. Use familiar measurement units, such as linking cubes or rulers, or encourage them to find out how many of one type of container it takes to measure another (for example, two juice boxes = one toothpaste box). Document the children's discoveries on chart paper where they can refer to the print and length comparisons. Use discussion as an opportunity to introduce measurement vocabulary such as "inch," "foot," "centimeter," and "meter."

Estimating and Counting

Children estimate and count the amount of items that make up an ingredient amount needed for a recipe.

Objectives

Print Awareness: Children will use print on ingredients in cooking projects and estimating activities.

Vocabulary: Children will learn and apply measurement, cooking, and ingredient terms.

Materials

packaged items from snacks and lunches, and packaged ingredients for recipe

recipe

chart paper and pencil

tools for measuring and mixing

tape

Theme Connections

Bakery

Cooking

Food and Nutrition

Holidays

Literacy Interactions:

✦ Select a recipe for a cooking or snack preparation project. Collect the ingredients, keeping them in their original containers. Introduce ingredients in original containers. Discuss the name of each ingredient, its identifying print, and so on (see Recipe Books on page 53 for ideas). Identify the ingredients that are conducive to counting, such as chocolate chips or marshmallows. Invite children to estimate how many (or how many spoonfuls) of each ingredient is needed to equal the specified measurement in a recipe. For example, "How many chocolate chips will it take to fill this ½ cup?" Document their responses next to the listed ingredient on chart paper. Encourage the children to assist in counting the ingredient into the measuring tool to check their estimates. Prepare the recipe and enjoy!

✦ Locate and read various labeled packaged print items in lunches or snacks. Ask children to make estimates and then count how many items are in the package as they eat. For example, "How many chips are in your (brand name) bag?" Document responses by saving clean product containers and taping them to chart paper next to the counted amounts in each. Use this activity to compare the relationship of the size of the product containers to the size and number of contents counted.

Environmental Print Seriation

Children sort and arrange environmental print items from smallest to largest or largest to smallest.

Objectives

Print Awareness: Children will sort and arrange environmental print using picture and word clues.

Vocabulary: Children will use environmental print to demonstrate understanding of size and positional words.

Materials

print containers or print in paper form that comes in assorted sizes, such as imprinted cups and food products in varied sizes
index cards
scissors
glue

Theme Connections

Grocery Store
Health and Safety
Holidays
Opposites
Restaurant
Sports

Literacy Interactions:

✦ Collect containers and/or paper products. Cut paper products to fit on index cards and glue in place (one per card). Ask children to sort the environmental print into groups using print and picture clues. Encourage discussion about the clues that helped them to create sets. Challenge them to put sets in order from largest to smallest and smallest to largest. For example, ask them to arrange a set of cups from a popular restaurant from largest to smallest.

✦ Incorporate this activity into an introduction or review of vocabulary related to size and position. As containers or packaging is placed in order, ask children to identify which item is "smallest," "largest," "equal" to others, "first," "last," and so on. Use and point to environmental print as part of the discussion. "Which cup is smallest?"

Money Matching

Children match coin cards to cent amounts on a library pocket or envelope.

Objectives

Print Awareness: Children will use one-to-one correspondence as a way of self-assessment during a money-counting activity.

Materials

labels from products or pictures of products containing print
coin stickers, rubber stamps of various coins and a stamp pad, or coin patterns (see page 243)
marker
library pockets or envelopes
index cards

Theme Connections

Grocery Store
Math
Our Community
Restaurant

Literacy Interactions

◆ Use the activity to review coin values or counting coins and how this relates to purchasing items in a store. Glue each product label to a library pocket or envelope and print a currency amount next to it. On a blank card, print the brand name as it appears on the label and the matching coin amount using coin stickers or stamps. Pass out coin cards to a group of children. Hold up an envelope with a product label and invite the children to identify the "price." Ask them to look at their coin cards to identify the match. Once the match has been made, read the print on the envelope. Invite the child holding the matching card to verify that the words and letters match those on the environmental print. Talk about how shoppers match print on a shopping list to print on a product to identify the exact item.

◆ Make coin cards that reflect each type of coin combination for an amount on a product pocket. For example, for five cents, make one card with five pennies and one with a nickel. Print the products' identifying words on the coin cards. Put the cards in the matching pocket containing the environmental print. Encourage children to count real or play money to match amounts listed on the outside of the pockets. They can check their response by pulling out and looking at the coin cards containing the varied coin combinations.

How Much Is It Worth?

Children sort coupons and coin-amount cards into pairs.

Objectives

Print Awareness: Children will focus on and use environmental print during a coupon and coin matching activity.

Comprehension: Children will demonstrate understanding of a topic or recipe by listing related items and locating applicable coupons.

Phonics: Children will practice letter and/or sound recognition through a self-checking coupon activity.

Beginning Reading: Children will practice sight word recognition through a self-checking coupon activity.

Materials

coupons from businesses and
    newspaper inserts
money stickers, rubber stamps
    of different coins and
    stamp pad, or coin patterns
    (see page 243)
copies of coins
large note cards or other sturdy
    paper
scissors
glue

Theme Connections

Alphabet

Colors

Farms

Food and Nutrition

Gardening and Plants

Grocery Store

Health and Safety

Vegetables

Literacy Interactions

✦ Invite the children to contribute to a list of items that correspond to a unit of study (for example, a list of vegetables for a unit on gardening or nutrition). Ask them to locate and cut out coupons that correspond to the unit of study or cooking activity. Glue each coupon on one end of a note card or other heavy paper. Place money stickers or coin stamps that reflect the amount for each coupon on the opposite end of the paper, leaving space between each. Print the brand name of the coupon product on the back side of the coin portion. Cut each set of cards apart. Provide coins

(continued on the next page)

for them to count out the value for each coupon (see Coin Patterns on page 243). If possible, use some of the coupons on a shopping trip to purchase items for a project or cooking activity.

◆ Use matching cards to play a memory-type game. Turn over the coin cards to reveal the printed name as it appears on the coupon. Invite children, in turn, to choose a coin card. Read the printed name together or invite children to identify familiar words. Turn the card over and count the coin amount, for example, two dimes and a nickel. Ask children how the numbers should look on the matching coupon (25¢). Optional: Write or have them write the number. Let them turn over the coupon cards to find the matching coupon. If two coupons have the same number, the children will have to use the print clues to reveal the appropriate match. Turn coupons back over and continue until all cards are matched.

◆ Locate coupons that represent a literacy skill objective (letter recognition, sound, sight word, and so on). Print the characteristic that represents the literacy skill objective on the back of the coin card. For example, if the objective is letter recognition, print "d" for a donut coupon; if it is sight word identification, print "pop" for "pop tart." Encourage children to pair the cards using either the coin amount or the literacy skill objective.

Note: If coupons do not contain appropriate currency amounts for the skill level of the children, place blank stickers over amounts and print a different quantity.

Shopping Bag Addition

Children use environmental print to record prices of products next to matching words on a receipt, and add the numbers together to find the total amount.

Objectives

Print Awareness: Children will use environmental print in a one-to-one correspondence matching activity.

Writing Process: Children will practice letter formation by copying words.

Vocabulary: Children will learn or review vocabulary associated with shopping.

Materials

plastic fruits and vegetables
permanent marker
dot stickers
small product containers
paper lunch bags
paper
laminate or clear contact paper
pennies or other counters

Theme Connections

Bakery
Food and Nutrition
Grocery Store
Math
Our Community

Preparation

1. Print the name of the item on each piece of plastic food using a permanent marker.
2. Put numbers on each of the dot stickers to create "price" tags and adhere one per food or environmental print container.
3. Put two items in each lunch bag. (Vary the amount of items in each bag depending on the children's ability to add one or more number sets.)
4. Print the added "price" total on the bottom of the bag (for example, if one item is 10¢ and the other is 5¢, write 15¢).
5. Create a receipt for each bag by listing the name of each item in the bag on a piece of paper. Leave a blank area next to each item for children to record the price. Leave a space at the bottom to record the total. Laminate or cover with clear contact paper to make it reusable. If desired, make duplicates of each receipt so each child has a copy to write on.

(continued on the next page)

Literacy Interactions

✦ Use this activity to reinforce beginning addition. Remove two items and the receipt from a bag. Help children identify the matching items on the receipt and record the price. After they find and record the prices, ask them to them to count out that amount using pennies or other counters and then place it beside the product or food. Ask them to put coin sets together and count the total to add the numbers on the receipt. For example, if a bag contains a crayon box (5 cents) and a soap box (2 cents), children write "5" next to the word "crayon" on the receipt and "2" next to the word "soap" by using one-to-one correspondence. After they record their answer, they can check it with the number on the bottom side of the bag.

✦ Provide the children with blank paper and stickers to make their own "shopping bag" addition activity to share with each other. Let them choose or bring in two or more products (small enough to fit in a bag). Assist or encourage them to write their own price on a product. Help them copy the distinguishing words of the product container on a piece of blank paper for others to solve. If desired, place materials in the Dramatic Play area (see "Grocery Store" on page 166).

✦ Use the activity to introduce or review symbols and vocabulary related to shopping, such as "cent," "penny," and "receipt." Show them examples of these on a grocery store receipt or price tag from a familiar store.

Variation

✦ Use cards with environmental print glued to them instead of boxes or containers. Print a price on each card.

Going to the Store Story Problems

Children read, create, and solve simple story problems containing environmental print.

Objectives

Print Awareness: Children will visually track print from left to right as story problems are read.

Oral Language/Speaking and Listening: Children will share information in the form of a story problem incorporating familiar environmental print.

Writing Process: Children will observe and participate in writing story problems using environmental print.

Comprehension: Children will confirm understanding of a story problem by solving it.

Beginning Reading: Children will read story problems emergently and/or by sight.

Materials

newspaper inserts, business
    stationery, and magazines
scissors
glue
chart paper and/or note cards
    or other writing surface
markers
counters (beans, buttons,
    animals)

Theme Connections

Community Helpers
Cooking
Grocery Store
Holidays
Our Community
Restaurant
Sports
Vegetables

Literacy Interactions:

✦ Cut out environmental print from magazines, newspaper inserts, and so on. Incorporate it into written story problems (counting, addition, or subtraction) by inserting it into sentences in a rebus structure (gluing environmental print into a sentence in place of a word). Include children's names in the problems. For example, "Marcy went to the (insert name) movie theater, then to the (insert

(continued on the next page)

Marcie went to the [Northwood] movie theater, then she went to the [Fit-Rite] shoe store, and [Lucky Burger] restaurant.

How many places did she go?

name) shoe store, and (insert name) restaurant. How many places did she go?" Track the words with your finger as you read each problem together. Invite the children to read the familiar words. Let them use counters as needed to solve the problem.

✦ Ask children to select environmental print and dictate their own problems for others to solve. Ask them to glue or tape the print where it appears in sentences in the story. Invite each child to help read the problem to others. Photocopy the stories for children to bring home and read and solve with their families.

Variation

✦ Make a matching game by putting stories on one card and answers on another for children to play individually.

Linking Environmental Print With Science

✦ In each activity in this chapter, the **objectives** are listed in order of difficulty—use them according to the skill level of the children in your class.

✦ In each activity in this chapter, the **literacy interactions** are listed in order of difficulty; use them according to the abilities and interests of the children.

Taste and Tell

Children eat food during a meal or snack and later record their observations about the food contents and the packaging.

Objectives

Print Awareness: Children will recognize that environmental print on food packaging can provide information about what is inside.

Vocabulary: Children will learn new words from environmental print.

Writing Process: Children will record or view writing activities involving their observations about environmental print and food.

Oral Language/Speaking and Listening: Children will share their observations about food and its packaging.

Materials

packaging from foods served
foods to taste that contain
    multiple ingredients (cereal,
    soup, cookies)
plates, spoons, and cups
chart paper or other large
    writing surface
marker

Theme Connections

Cultural Awareness
Food and Nutrition
Holidays
Senses

Literacy Interactions

✦ Before children try a food, ask them to guess the ingredients based on the environmental print on the packaging. Draw attention to colors, pictures, and words to provide clues. Record their guesses or let them write their own. After they try the food and add more observations, read the ingredients on the label to check their guesses. Use this opportunity to introduce new vocabulary words. **Note:** Be aware of any food allergies and plan accordingly.

✦ Bring in several of one type of food for tasting during snack or a meal, such as a variety of cereals or different ice cream flavors. Point out to the children the flavor in print as you look at each package. Print the choices at the top of chart paper or other large writing surface to create columns (for example, strawberry, grape, and cherry). Incorporate environmental print from packaging, if possible. Let them taste each flavor or type and record their favorites in the appropriate column.

✦ Ask children to bring in packaged favorite foods or a food item from their particular culture. Ask the group to guess what type of food is in the package based on context clues, such as colors used, pictures, shapes, and lettering, located on the box or bag. Ask questions such as, "What color do you think it will be?" "What will it taste like?" Encourage them to use sensory words. Record their guesses. Provide an opportunity for them to try the foods, and then invite them to share their observations again. **Note:** Be aware of any food allergies. Identify changes in their observations.

Shake That Product

Children match environmental print labels and/or containers to products that produce noise when shaken.

Objectives

Print Awareness: Children will gain an understanding of how words on environmental print can describe how something sounds.

Vocabulary: Children will use environmental print to explore how words describe various sounds.

Oral Language/Speaking and Listening: Children will use listening and speaking skills to determine, describe, and match items associated with environmental print.

Writing Process: Children will dictate and document predictions about products.

Materials

product labels or containers from items that make noise when shaken

sound-producing items (dry pasta, paper clips, un-popped corn, cotton balls) that correlate with labels or containers

large, opaque plastic or paper containers with lids (dry drink mix, oatmeal)

glue or tape

poster board or construction paper (optional)

scissors

large paper bag or box

Theme Connections

Cooking

Senses

Preparation

1. Fill each plastic or paper container half full with different noise-producing items. Put only one type of item in each container.
2. Secure lids with tape or glue.
3. Save the product containers or labels for each item used. If desired, cut and glue the fronts of product labels or containers to pieces of poster board or construction paper.

Literacy Interactions

◆ In a small group, hold up a product container or label. Read the word. Ask children to take turns shaking and listening to the items in the canisters to locate its match.

◆ Put each noise-producing item, in its original packaging, into a paper bag or box. Pull one item out at a time. Ask, "I wonder how it will sound if I shake it?" Draw attention to the words on the packaging as children make predictions of how it will sound when shaken (for example, *liquid* soap or *pop*corn). Document their predictions for each product. For example, they may use words such as "quiet," "soft," "like water," and so on for liquid soap. Shake the item and encourage them to add to or remove some of their predictions. Introduce the product labels or containers and canisters with the items for them to practice matching sounds with packaging.

◆ Keep items in their original containers before doing cooking projects or other experiments. Read each label with the children. Invite them to close their eyes and shake a container. Ask them to identify which ingredient they think it is. Encourage them to find items that make similar sounds when shaken, such as salt and cornmeal. Discuss how things that are liquid, solid, soft, or hard make different sounds.

Sensory Box Match-Up

Children use their sense of touch to match environmental print labels and/or containers to tactile items.

Objectives

Print Awareness: Children will learn how words on environmental print can provide information about how things feel.

Vocabulary: Children will use environmental print from tactile items to explore and understand sense of touch words.

Writing Process: Children will dictate or write observations about environmental print and products.

Beginning Reading: Children will look at and read sight words as they appear in compound words.

Materials

containers and labels for tactile items, such as paper clip box, cotton ball bag, crayon wrappers, bar soap boxes, and aluminum foil box with sharp edge removed

tactile products (contents of each container)

empty tissue box, square box, or oatmeal container

scissors

contact paper or paint (optional)

index cards or poster board

glue

Theme Connection

Senses

Preparation

1. Collect a variety of tactile items and the environmental print containers they came in.
2. Make a hole in the top of a tissue box or oatmeal container large enough for a child's hand to fit through. If desired, cover with contact paper or paint.
3. Put a sample of tactile items in the box to make a sensory box.
4. Save containers or front labels to match with the items. Mount as needed to index cards or other sturdy paper.

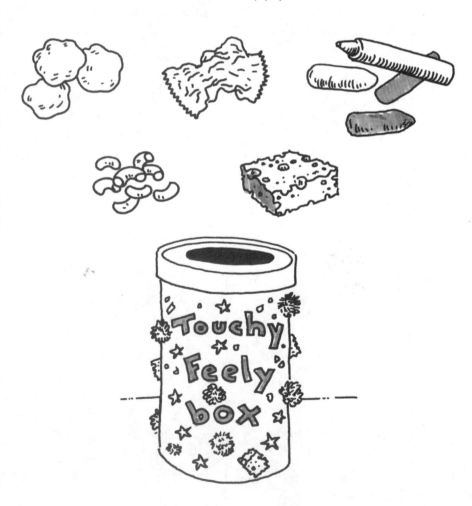

Literacy Interactions

✦ Introduce the activity to illustrate sense-of-touch vocabulary, such as "soft," "hard," "rough," "smooth," and so on. Read the labels and show each corresponding item as it is put into the sensory box. After children have become familiar with the names for each item, ask them to locate each item using their sense of touch and match each one to the corresponding labels/containers. Encourage them to share their observations about how the items felt using sense-of-touch vocabulary.

✦ After introducing the tactile items, ask children to predict and describe how each item might feel. Ask questions such as, "Do the words on the label provide clues as to how it might feel?" Document their descriptions. Put one item at a time in the sensory box. Ask the children to reach in and touch the item. Ask them to describe each item. Write the new descriptive words next to their original predictions. When they are finished, read through the words for each item so they can check their predictions. Ask, "Did any of the names of the items fool you? Did any of the names help?" (For example, cotton ball—"ball" may have led to a prediction of "round.") This can lead to a discussion about compound words, and how they can be used to describe something.

Variation

✦ Integrate this activity with other sense-of-touch activities, such as "Crayon Rubbings: Signs on the Move" (see page 215) or "Raised Label Rubbings" (see page 150). Ask children to close their eyes and feel the letters on embossed print. Invite them to identify letters, symbols, and pictures using their sense of touch.

Making Sense of Scents

Children use their sense of smell to match environmental print labels and/or original containers to scented products in canisters.

Objectives

Print Awareness: Children will understand the function of environmental print as a label to identify a scent.

Vocabulary: Children will use related environmental print to explore and develop concepts of various scents.

Comprehension: Children will retell their experiences involving awareness of scents by creating books.

Materials

containers and labels from products that have a scent, such as flavored gelatin, spices, and vanilla yogurt

scented products (oil, extract, and spices) that correspond to each piece of environmental print (**Note:** Be aware of allergies.)

container or label

cotton balls, rubber bands

film canisters or other small containers with lids

porous fabric such as nylon

glue, scissors, paper

Theme Connections

Cooking

Food and Nutrition

Gardening and Plants

Senses

Preparation

1. Put a small amount of each scented product on a cotton ball and place in a film canister or container.
2. Punch holes in the lid or stretch a square piece of porous fabric over the top and secure with a rubber band.

Literacy Interactions

✦ Introduce scented items as new vocabulary words. Point to environmental print on the labels on jars and ask children if they've seen or heard the words before. For example, "vanilla" is used in ice cream, frosting, and candles. Identify where the scents came from. "Do they come from a plant or tree?" If possible, gather some of the items in their original form (whole nutmeg, mint plant, or orange) for the children to look at and smell before identifying in canisters. Point out the name of the scent on the label.

✦ Introduce distinctive smells in canisters, three or four at a time. Invite the children to match the original containers or labels to the scented products in canisters using their sense of smell.

✦ Gather foods and environmental print that contain the same scent, such as *strawberry* gelatin, *strawberry* ice cream, *strawberry* jam, *strawberry* juice, and *strawberry* yogurt. Incorporate into a taste-testing party and encourage children to use their sense of smell to compare the items. Invite children to contribute to "sense of smell" word books containing print that pertains to a specific scent. Put in the Science Area or Book Area for children to read and discuss. Scent ideas that are contained in many products include: lemon, peppermint, cinnamon, orange, coconut, vanilla, chocolate, strawberry, banana, almond, pineapple, mint, and chili.

Variation

✦ Use ingredients for a cooking activity after the children have had an opportunity to smell and experience them (for example, cinnamon, cloves, and pumpkin for pumpkin pie).

Show and Tell Senses

Children use sensory words to describe different foods.

Objectives

Print Awareness: Children will recognize that environmental print from food packaging can provide sensory information.

Vocabulary: Children will use environmental print to explore and understand sensory words.

Oral Language/Speaking and Listening: Children will use sensory words to describe an environmental print item.

Writing Process: Children will dictate sensory words to describe products.

Materials

food packaging or picture of
    food items from grocery ads
paper
index cards
large paper grocery bag
masking tape

Theme Connections

Cooking
Food and Nutrition
Senses

Literacy Interactions

✦ With the children, create a list including the five senses and descriptive words that can be used to characterize favorite food items. Ask children to bring in environmental print packaging from one of their favorite foods. Give each child a copy of the sensory word list, a paper grocery bag, and a blank index card to bring home. Include a note to parents explaining the activity. The child will choose a food package, create clues using the word list (with parents' help), and return with the package and clues in the bag. Encourage them to share the sensory clues they have created as others guess the item in the paper bag.

✦ Integrate this activity into a unit on the five senses. Bring in familiar foods in their original packaging for a picnic or lunch, such as cereal, cheese, soup, and pickles. Use print from the packaging to make a chart to record observations. Invite the children to contribute sensory words to describe each food, such as "soft," "crunchy," or "sweet."

✦ Incorporate sensory words as new vocabulary. Ask children to bring in packaging or a picture that is a representation of a sensory word, for example, "sour," "sweet," or "smooth." Make a simple book cover by printing the word ("sour") on a piece of paper. Glue environmental print that represents the sensory word on blank pages and add to the book. Provide an opportunity to read the books.

✦ Create a bar graph on the floor with masking tape. Print key sensory vocabulary words on index cards, such as "hard," "cold," and "soft," to use as categories on the graph. Focus on one sense at a time. Read print on different food packages as children decide what sensory word best describes the contents. Ask, "Are there any words on the package that describe how it feels, smells, looks, or tastes?" Let the children place each item where it belongs on the graph. Count how many are in each section. Ask them if there are any that could be in more than one category.

The Word World of Magnets

Children use magnets containing environmental print to locate and observe things that are magnetic.

Objectives

Print Awareness: Children will learn about the function of print on magnets as they experiment with them.

Writing Process: Children will use environmental print on magnets as part of the recording process in experiments with magnets.

Oral Language/Speaking and Listening: Children will discuss, compare, and contrast the strength of magnets.

Materials

magnets containing print (from schools, doctors' offices, and restaurants)

assortment of magnetic objects (paper clips, bingo chips, metal washers, screws, and magnetic letters)

assortment of non-magnetic items (coins, Styrofoam, rubber ball, pinecone, and so on)

tray or tub

clipboard and paper or notebooks

pencils

Theme Connections

Community Helpers

Science and Nature

Tools and Machines

Literacy Interactions

✦ Put an assortment of magnetic and non-magnetic items on a tray or in a tub and show them to the children. Encourage them to use magnets with environmental print on them to locate items that are magnetic, such as paper clips and pennies. Ask, "Which items remained on the tray?" Encourage them to count the items picked up by each magnet. Provide paper and clipboards or notebooks for children to make checklists to record how many items each magnet picked up. Encourage the children to copy words on the magnets onto their paper.

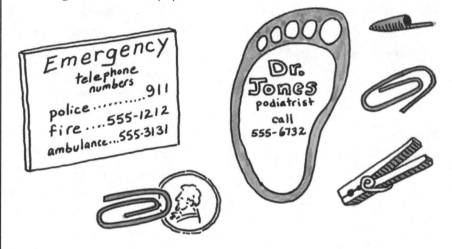

✦ Encourage the children to sort the magnets by various properties, such as size, shape, and name (school name, doctor-related, restaurants, and so on). Provide magnetic items such as paper clips or bingo chips for them to explore. Ask them to share their observations about whether size, shape, name, or other properties made a difference in the magnet's ability to pick up things. Encourage them to compare their results and conclude which magnet is the strongest. Ask, "Does size or shape make a difference in the amount of items a magnet picks up?"

Garden Markers

Children use seed packets to label and match with plants in a gardening activity.

Objectives

Print Awareness: Children will understand the function of print to label contents on seed packets.

Oral Language/Speaking and Listening: Children will share information about seeds and plants using environmental print.

Vocabulary: Children will learn and develop concepts of various plant characteristics.

Phonics: Children will use seed packets in activities involving letter and letter sound recognition.

Phonological/Phonemic Awareness: Children will practice skills such as syllable recognition, compound words, and rhyming words using seed packets in listening activities.

Materials

illustrated vegetable, flower, or fruit seed packets
self-adhesive labels
markers
clear contact paper or laminate
tongue depressors or craft sticks
clear book or packing tape
containers for planting seeds (plastic pots or cups)
potting soil
rubber bands

Theme Connections

Farms
Food and Nutrition
Gardening and Plants
Health and Safety
Science and Nature
Seasons

Preparation

1. Carefully open seed packets without tearing (so that envelope may be used for matching activity). Save seeds.
2. Write the name of the seed on a label and adhere it to the back of the seed packet.
3. Cover seed packets with clear contact paper or laminate.
4. Tape the packets to the top portion of craft sticks or tongue depressors to make plant stakes.

Literacy Interactions

✦ Encourage children to plant a variety of seeds in containers filled with potting soil. Make sure they plant each type of seed in separate containers. Guide their attention to the seed packets as they plant each type of seed. Ask them what they know about the plant while referring to the picture and word clues. Validate their responses by pointing to the print on the seed packets. For example, "Yes, that is a picture of a sunflower. It says 'sunflower' right here on the packet." Use this opportunity to expand vocabulary and learn about the care of plants. As they finish, make sure children wash their hands. Immediately label each pot with the name of the plant. Wrap a rubber band around the outside of each pot and insert a plant stake between the rubber band and pot. Put plants in a sunny location that is accessible to child observation and interaction.

✦ Encourage children to match plant stakes with planted seeds (growing plant) by looking at letter clues found on the seed packets and labels on the pots. Children can remove plant stakes by sliding the tongue depressor from the rubber bands on each pot, so that

(continued on the next page)

the soil will not be disturbed. Engage children in discussion of clues they used to match the garden stakes to the growing seeds.

✦ Put garden stakes in pocket charts or stick them into playdough and use them for repetitive sorting activities. Children can sort them by type (vegetable, flower, fruit), color, alphabet letter or sound, and so on.

✦ Give each child a plant stake to use as part of a review or introduction to hearing parts of words, such as consonants, blends, or syllables. Play music and let children march around. When the music stops, direct the children to "plant" themselves. Pronounce a plant name and say the number of syllables or a letter or sound (for example, /p/ for "pumpkin"). Ask the children to look at their plant stake and identify the match by holding up the stake.

Variations

✦ Use commercial, clean, plastic plant stakes that come with purchased plants.

✦ Put soil and plastic fruits and vegetables in the sensory table. Let children position plant stakes in the sensory table next to the appropriate fruit or vegetable growing in their "garden."

Made From Trees

Children identify, locate, and gather items (including environmental print) made from trees.

Objectives

Print Awareness: Children will learn about the functions of print (in letters, newspapers, and lists) while learning about products from trees.

Writing Process: Children will use environmental print in constructing and dictating information for a book about uses of trees and products from trees.

Phonics: Children will identify and tear out alphabet letters in newspapers.

Oral Language/Speaking and Listening: Children will share observations about uses for environmental print and products from trees.

Materials

books about trees (see Book Suggestions)
items and containers made from trees, such as paper packaging, boxes, books, magazines, newspapers, notepads, paper plates, and napkins)
wooden objects (blocks, beads, chairs, bowls, craft sticks, and pencils)
large pan or tub
blender and colander
window screen

Theme Connections

Gardening and Plants
Recycling
Science and Nature

Literacy Interactions

✦ Begin the activity by reading a book about trees to the children (see book suggestions below), under a tree outside (if possible). Take a walk around the learning environment and show the children examples of things made from trees. Encourage them to identify and gather items. Ask questions such as, "How are they alike?" "How are they different?" Use the opportunity to emphasize the many ways print is used on some items. Encourage the children to share discoveries of familiar letters and words.

✦ Invite children to bring in examples of environmental print paper products and make a collage book of tree product samples. Encourage them to draw and/or cut out pictures and dictate information about uses for trees, such as building houses, making furniture, and homes for animals.

✦ Encourage children to think of ways to conserve trees. Have them look at the print, paper, and cardboard items they have collected and brainstorm ways they can recycle and reuse these items (to conserve trees). Integrate into a language experience activity by gluing the tree product samples to a piece of paper. Add the dictated ideas the children provide. Use collected materials in a book, display, or make copies and send the information home for children to share with their families.

Book Suggestions

Hello Tree by Joanne Ryder
The Gift of the Tree by Alvin Tresselt
The Giving Tree by Shel Silverstein
A Tree Is Nice by Janice May Udry
Paper, Paper Everywhere by Gail Gibbons
Where Once There Was a Wood by Denise Fleming

Seed-to-Packet Match

Children match seed cards and plant words to the corresponding seed packet.

Objectives

Print Awareness: Children will observe and use print on seed packets in a visual discrimination activity.

Vocabulary: Children will learn about and build understanding of various plants and their seeds using environmental print.

Materials

seed packets

food and flower items in seed-producing form seeds (from seed packets)

index cards, poster board, or cardstock

glue

clear contact paper or clear packing tape

marker

magnifying glass

Theme Connections

Farms

Food and Nutrition

Gardening and Plants

Health and Safety

Science and Nature

Seasons

Preparation

1. Cut index cards, poster board, or cardstock to a size slightly smaller than seed packets.

2. Glue two or more seeds to each card. Print the name of the seed on the other side.

3. Cover each card with clear packing tape or contact paper.

4. Leave the tops of the seed packets open. Laminate or cover with clear contact paper and re-open the tops to form a pocket.

Literacy Interactions

✦ Gather several food and flower items in their natural seed-producing form to introduce the concept of seed-to-plant sequence (for example, dried corn, sunflowers, peas in pod, pumpkin, tomato, dill, peppers, and dried flowers). Cut open the items as needed to reveal the seeds. Have food items for snack. (**Note**: Be aware of any allergies.) Open up seed packets together, read the name of the item on each package, and match the seeds to the seeds found in the gathered foods or plants. Provide a magnifying glass for children to use in looking at seeds and seed packets. Encourage the children to match seeds to their seed packets.

✦ Encourage children to use the seed packets to locate the same word in other environmental print, such as supermarket advertisements (for example, "corn" in *corn* chips, *corn* syrup, and yellow *corn*). Let them circle and/or cut out words and pictures to make a collage.

✦ Use the activity to introduce the concept of food with edible seeds and those that are not edible. Use the packets to sort into these two categories. Gather edible seeds and corresponding seed packets for children to try. Use seed packets to identify distinctions between non-edible seeds and products that have edible seeds. Point out to the children that seeds used for planting are not edible.

Note: Integrate this activity with other activities such as "Garden Markers" (see page 135) and "Seed Packet Pocket Books" (see page 46).

Recycling Environmental Print

Children use recyclable items in sorting and matching activities.

Objectives

Print Awareness: Children will use environmental print in activities involving distinguishing among print letters, numbers, and symbols.

Phonics: Children will use environmental print to sort and identify alphabet letters by name and sound.

Phonological/Phonemic Awareness: Children will practice identifying parts of spoken language (such as word families and syllables) and sound units (such as onsets or rimes).

Materials

a variety of recyclable
  environmental print: plastics
  (soda bottles, milk bottles,
  shampoo), paper
  (newspaper, office paper,
  phone books), metal
  (canned food, aluminum
  soft drink cans), glass
  containers (sauces,
  condiments)
large boxes or plastic tubs
marker
masking tape

Theme Connections

Gardening and Plants
Our Community
Recycling

Literacy Interactions

✦ Invite the children to gather clean, recyclable items from home. Discuss what types of materials are safe for them to handle. Compile a list of requested items and send home to parents. Ask that the print labels remain on the containers. (**Note:** Consider leaving glass items off the list for safety reasons.) Sort out any items that are unclean or have sharp edges before allowing children to handle them. Label boxes or tubs by type (glass, metal, paper, and plastic) and put them in a safe area. Invite the children to categorize and then sort one type of recyclable item into groups (for example, plastics—soda bottles, shampoo bottles, laundry soap, and so on).

✦ Create a graph on the floor using masking tape. Ask children to put each type of recyclable into a section to create a real object graph. Count them together to see which section has more. Invite them to sort and graph again using print, such as different flavors of soda bottles.

✦ Use the collected recyclable materials as resources for examples of various literacy-related skills. Invite the children to sort items by different sounds or skills, such as by consonant ("k" in kitten chow and ketchup) or digraph ("ch" in cherry cola, chicken soup, and cheese). Read a word on the label of a recyclable and encourage children to think of other words that rhyme or have the same beginning or ending sounds.

Things That Melt Experiment

Children make predictions regarding the ability of a product to melt and record observations using environmental print.

Objectives

Print Awareness: Children will learn how words on environmental print can provide information about the physical properties (ability to melt) of its contents.

Oral Language/Speaking and Listening: Children will share observations, stories, and knowledge regarding things that melt.

Writing Process: Children will record results of an experiment on a chart.

Vocabulary: Children will demonstrate understanding of words such as "melt," "liquid," "solid," "hot," and "cold."

Materials

products that can change form
    by melting (ice cream,
    frozen fruit juice, crayons,
    chocolate, and butter)
corresponding packaging for
    products that melt
poster board or dry-erase board
clear containers with lids
markers

Theme Connections

Food and Nutrition
Opposites
Seasons

Preparation

1. Remove products from packaging and reserve for later use.
2. Create a chart by attaching the environmental print from packaging across the top of a dry-erase board or poster board.
3. Label a clear container for each product with identifying words (such as strawberry ice cream, vanilla ice cream, orange juice, and "brand name" chocolate).
4. Put a small amount of each product in the labeled containers.

Literacy Interactions

✦ Introduce or review the concept of "melting." Ask children to think of things that melt, such as snow, ice in a glass, and ice cream. Show them the chart and read the labels. Show them the containers with the products and invite them to assist in matching the product to the print on the chart. Put the containers in a sunny location. Encourage the children to observe and report changes over time, including how much time it takes for each to melt. Document their dictated observations on the chart under matching environmental print or let them write or draw their own. Provide magazines and newspaper inserts for them to locate other things they think would melt in the sun. If possible, gather some of the items and allow the children to test their predictions.

✦ Use the experiment as an opportunity to explore related concepts and vocabulary. Provide examples of solids and liquids using familiar items in a child's environment, such as lunchbox items. Invite them to gather items that are solids (cereal bar, fruit, and chips) and liquids (milk, juice, and salad dressing). Talk about the concepts of hot and cold (freezing) and how some products can change from solid to liquid and liquid to solid.

Variation

✦ Use the same methods of observation and documentation to do an experiment involving things that may or may not dissolve in liquid. (Some that dissolve are crackers, soap, and powdered pudding and some that don't are raisins, green beans, and salad oil.)

Weighing in With Environmental Print

Children use items containing environmental print in weight comparison activities.

Objectives

Print Awareness: Children will learn about the function of print in providing information about weight.

Phonics: Children will make comparisons and identify alphabet letters.

Oral Language/Speaking and Listening: Children will discuss, compare, and contrast the weight of items.

Writing Process: Children will use information on packaging as part of the recording process in weight comparisons.

Vocabulary: Children will be introduced to weight-related vocabulary, such as pounds, grams, and ounces.

Materials

small unopened containers and
    items containing print, such
    as a business card, can of
    tuna, tube of toothpaste,
    empty juice box, and full
    juice box
tape or glue
paper and pencil
clipboard or notepads
balance/scale
kitchen scale
weights or manipulatives (plastic
    counters, buttons, paper
    clips, blocks)

Theme Connections

All About Me
Food and Nutrition
Grocery Store
Math
Opposites
Post Office

Literacy Interactions

✦ Gather similar environmental print items such as products in same-size cans (soup, fruit, and juice) and encourage the children to explore them. (Secure lids on products with tape or glue as needed to avoid accidental spills.) Hold up sets of two items that are related in size, shape, or letter similarities (for example, a can of peaches and a can of peas, or chicken and stars soup and chicken noodle soup). Invite the children to predict which one will be heavier based on what they see. Record their predictions on a chart containing the identifying words or environmental print that represents each item. Give children the opportunity to pick up items and compare them again. Record their findings. Invite them to test their predictions by experimenting with a balance scale. Demonstrate and explain that the side of the balance that goes down contains the heavier product, the side that goes up contains the lighter, and if both sides remain the same level they are equal.

✦ Gather a group of four to eight products to compare, such as ingredients for a baking activity or items that all begin with the same letter. Encourage children to predict and sort the items from heaviest to lightest. Record their observations on a writing surface. Show them how to weigh each item using a balance scale and weights/manipulatives by putting an item (such as a box of tissues) on one side and weights (such as plastic bears) to the other side until the two sides are level. Help them count the number of weights used for each item and write the number next to the name of the item on a chart. Encourage them to put the items in order again from heaviest to lightest using the numbers they have recorded to guide them.

✦ Bring in a variety of scales for children to try. Ask them about their experiences using scales, such as in a grocery store, at home, or at the post office. Go on a walk to a post office or grocery store to find scales. When showing them a kitchen scale, point out the numbers on product containers that identify weight. Use the opportunity to compare the weight on the scale to the numbers that appear in print on the labels. Introduce words such as "pound," "ounce," "liter," and "gram." Show the children where these appear on product labels.

Connecting Farm to Food

Children use environmental print to learn about food ingredients that are available in several products.

Objectives

Print Awareness: Children will practice one-to-one correspondence using environmental print, and left-to-right progression by following print in recipes and books they create.

Phonics: Children will use environmental print to recognize and name alphabet letters.

Vocabulary: Children will learn, describe, and compare new foods.

Writing Process: Children will use information from environmental print to write, draw, or dictate observations.

Materials

food containers and packaging that relate to a particular ingredient or product, such as milk, corn, wheat/flour, chocolate, or eggs

food products that correspond to environmental print

index cards

marker

magnifying glasses

Theme Connections

Bakery

Cultural Awareness

Farms

Food and Nutrition

Grocery Store

Literacy Interactions

✦ Select one type of basic food, such as milk or corn. Gather products in original containers that contain the basic food as an ingredient. For example, milk is an ingredient in products such as butter, yogurt, ice cream, and cheese. Draw attention to the parts of the packaging that contain ingredient lists. Print key words on cards for children to find on the packaging. Review the letter names in the word(s). Provide magnifying glasses for them to use to locate the word(s). Ask them to tally how many times they find the word.

✦ Gather examples of food in original containers corresponding to a type of ingredient, such as corn. Ask children to locate the ingredient on the print. Invite them to look at and compare the physical properties of each item (for example, *corn* syrup, *corn* flakes, *corn*meal, *corn* tortillas, and so on). Encourage children to look at, taste, touch, and smell each item in some form. (**Note:** Be aware of any food allergies and plan accordingly.) Create a chart to record observations of the food, such as color, liquid/solid, texture, and taste. Compare and contrast the similarities and differences among them.

✦ Locate recipes that use an identical ingredient such as rice. Make several items for a meal or snack using the key ingredient in some form. Explore how people in different parts of the world use the ingredient, and gather related print from products that contain it. Incorporate recipes into a cookbook, and encourage children to add the print, record observations, and write information about how the ingredient is grown and processed. Put the cookbook in the Book Area along with other books about the ingredient.

Variation

✦ Go on a field trip to a place that processes or uses a specific food, such as a cereal factory or dairy. Look for print there that contains the key ingredient.

Food Groups Classifying Caper

Children sort environmental print by various characteristics, such as food groups or types of food.

Objectives

Print Awareness: Children will discover the function of print in identifying and categorizing food items.

Vocabulary: Children will sort environmental print as it applies to their understanding of food group-related vocabulary.

Comprehension: Children will demonstrate an understanding of food groups using environmental print to sort and retell facts.

Materials

environmental print (newspaper inserts and product boxes)
baskets or sorting trays
chart paper or bulletin board
marker
scissors
paper or blank label
tape

Theme Connections

Food and Nutrition
Gardening and Plants
Grocery Store
Restaurant

Literacy Interactions

✦ Label each section of a tray, several baskets, chart paper, or a bulletin board with a sorting/classifying characteristic, such as types of vegetables, food vs. non-food, and so on. Have children sort food-related environmental print into the trays or baskets using visual and print clues. When finished, read through the print together.

✦ Invite the children to look for similarities in product names that provide clues to where it belongs or what it contains (for example, "string *cheese*" and "cream *cheese*," "*vegetable* soup" and "*vegetable* juice," "*apple*sauce" and "*apple* juice," and so on). Assist the children in sorting the print. Discuss the similarities found among each group after sorting.

(continued on the next page)

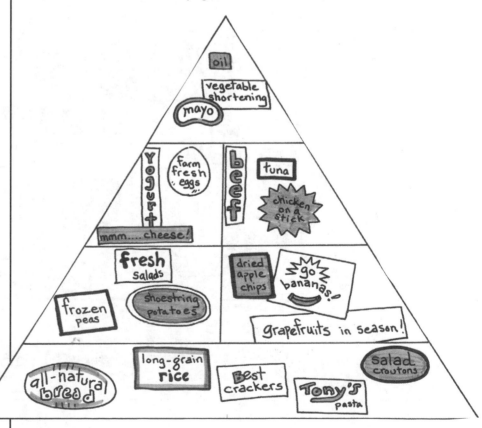

♦ Integrate this activity into a study or review of food groups. Make a list of the food groups on chart paper or use a bulletin board shaped like the food pyramid (Milk/Dairy, Fruit, Vegetables, Grains, Fats and Sweets, Meat/Protein). Ask children to select and cut out environmental print from grocery store newspaper inserts and product containers to add to the list or bulletin board. Ask them to write or dictate the name of the print as it is sorted by food group and added to the list or bulletin board.

♦ Use food-related environmental print to engage children in creating books for each food group. For example, a book on vegetables might include vegetable soup labels, canned vegetables, vegetable juices, and so on. Include dictated facts the children have learned and observations they have made.

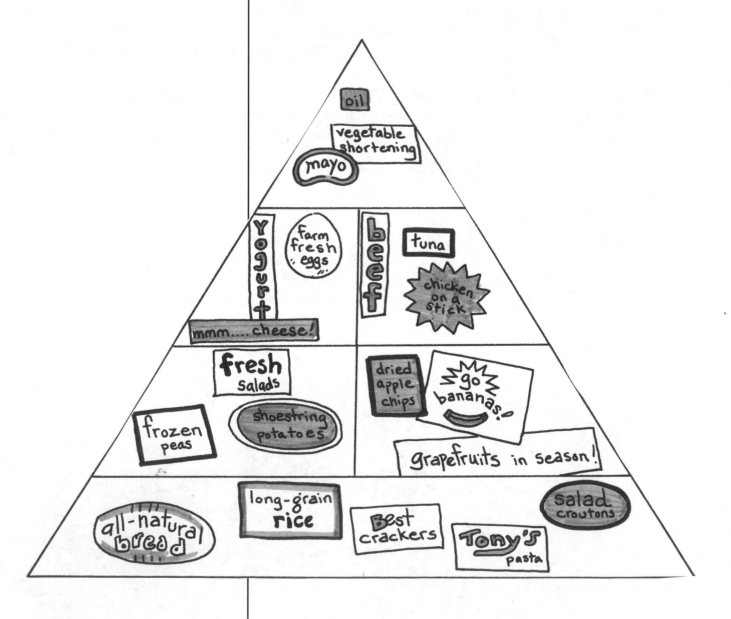

Linking Environmental Print With Small Motor Skills and Creativity

✦ In each activity in this chapter, the **objectives** are listed in order of difficulty—use them according to the skill level of the children in your class.

✦ In each activity in this chapter, the **literacy interactions** are listed in order of difficulty; use them according to the abilities and interests of the children.

All About Me Collage

Children use environmental print to create collages about themselves.

Objectives

Print Awareness: Children will use environmental print that is important or familiar to them to create a collage about themselves.

Oral Language/Speaking and Listening: Children will share stories about themselves using environmental print in a collage they create.

Writing Process: Children will add pictures and dictated or written stories to their environmental print collages.

Beginning Reading: Children will "read" familiar environmental print emergently or by recognition as it is used in a collage.

Materials

catalogs, newspaper inserts, book sale flyers, or magazines
photos of each child
scissors
glue
poster board or paper

Theme Connections

All About Me
Colors
Families
Food and Nutrition

Literacy Interactions

✦ Have a discussion with the children about their favorite things, people, and places. Gather a variety of environmental print (catalogs, newspaper inserts, or magazines) or invite the children to look for print in their homes that reflects their interests in toys, colors, foods, and places to visit.

✦ Explain that they will be making collages of their favorite things. If possible, take or ask for a photo of each child (make photocopies of the photos, if desired) and have children glue their photos to the center of their paper. Provide scissors, environmental print, and glue for the children to cut out print that is related to their favorite things or places to create a collage. When they are finished, invite them to display and "read" the stories about their choices.

Variations

✦ Have children make "What's Cooking?" collages using ingredients (print and packaging) in a favorite home recipe.

✦ Provide shoeboxes instead of poster board for children to bring home. Invite them to put things that are important to them inside the box to bring in and talk about.

Mural Town

Children create a cooperative mural using environmental print from their community.

Objectives

Oral Language/Speaking and Listening: Children will work cooperatively and share stories to create a mural about their community.

Print Awareness: Children will look for familiar environmental print to use as signs on a mural.

Writing Process: Children will use markers, crayons, and/or chalk to communicate experiences they have had in their community.

Materials

print from places in the community, including brochures, mail, paper bags, and newspaper inserts
large paper
scissors
markers, crayons, and/or chalk
paper strips or labels
glue
tape

Theme Connections

All About Me
Maps
Our Community

Literacy Interactions

✦ Before beginning, explain to the children that they will be creating a mural together about their community. Discuss how to work cooperatively, including sharing space, respecting other's drawings, and communicating needs to others. Role play solving situations that may arise from sharing drawing space. Adjust the number of children working on the mural, depending on development. For example, three-year-olds might work best with two children, while six-year-olds may work well with four children.

✦ Gather or ask parents to contribute a variety of environmental print from the children's community. Engage children in discussion about their homes, stores, friends' homes, parks, restaurants, post office, school, and other places they visit in their community. Cut paper to large size and lay or hang it on a large surface where children can access it easily. Provide materials for them to draw roads, places, signs, and so on. Invite them to cut out pictures or words of familiar places and tape or glue them on the mural. Use blank paper strips or labels to print names of places as children request. Encourage them to share stories about the places in the community they added to the mural. Expand the mural as more ideas and interest develops.

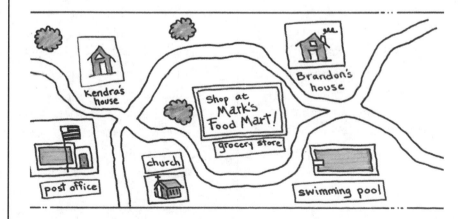

Raised Label Rubbings

Children obtain crayon rubbings from raised environmental print surfaces.

Objectives

Print Awareness: Children will recognize individual letters and words as they appear on embossed environmental print through crayon rubbings.

Writing Process: Children will practice small motor control while using crayons in obtaining rubbings.

Oral Language/Speaking and Listening: Children will share observations about their crayon rubbings.

Vocabulary: Children will learn or review vocabulary associated with special occasions using environmental print in rubbing activities.

Materials

embossed print, such as on lids of carry-out containers and plastic cups, greeting cards, signs, license plates, magnets, and so on

old crayons

muffin tin, oven, and freezer (optional)

thin white paper and tape

easel, table, or flat tray

Theme Connections

Health and Safety

Holidays

Restaurant

Transportation

Preparation

1. Trim environmental print to isolate surfaces that contain embossed (raised) print.
2. Tear paper from old crayons.
3. If desired, sort the crayons by color into a muffin tin and melt in the oven. Place in a freezer for a few minutes and pop out crayon chunks. Children can use the flat end of chunks for rubbings.

Literacy Interactions

✦ Invite children to bring in embossed environmental print to use in crayon rubbings. Demonstrate how to obtain a rubbing from the raised surface by laying paper on top of it and using a gentle stroking motion along the paper with the flat end of a crayon. Tape embossed print to an easel, table, or flat tray to keep it from moving. When children are finished, read or invite them to "read" the print they made through the rubbing process. Invite the children to share observations, comparisons, and descriptions about their rubbings.

✦ Use embossed environmental print associated with a particular holiday for children to make wrapping paper or cards from rubbings. Introduce or review related vocabulary as it appears on the environmental print. Engage the children in identifying and reading the words. Ask them to deduce what they and the associated pictures on the print mean.

Note: See "Crayon Rubbing: Signs on the Move" on page 215 for more ideas.

Variation

✦ Ask children to close their eyes and feel the letters on embossed print. Challenge them to identify letters, symbols, and pictures using their sense of touch.

Bunch of Boxes

Children use boxes containing environmental print and other items to create structures and sculptures.

Objectives

Print Awareness: Children will recognize and understand the function of print as it is used on box labels.

Phonics: Children will explore and compare alphabet letter and letter sounds while creating with environmental print.

Phonological/Phonemic Awareness: Children will engage in discussion about sounds in rhyming words, consonant blends, and digraphs found on environmental print while making box creations.

Writing Process: Children will write or dictate stories about their box creations.

Oral Language/Speaking and Listening: Children will share stories and information about their box creations.

Beginning Reading: Children will "read" and recognize familiar words on environmental print.

Materials

boxes from various items, such as food products, toys, and shoes
scrap paper, construction paper, stickers, feathers, and so on
empty paper towel tubes
yarn, ribbon, and string
wiggle eyes
tape
glue
scissors

Theme Connections

Alphabet	Recycling
Boxes	Zoo
Construction	

Literacy Interactions

✦ Provide a variety of environmental print (boxes) and collage materials for children to use to create structures or sculptures, such as robots or vehicles. Invite the children to build and create names and descriptions for their creations. Assist them in cutting, as needed. Encourage them to integrate the familiar print they have discovered on their structures into the names and stories. Write the names and stories about the creations on cards for reading and display. Invite other children, friends, and family to visit the "gallery" of sculptures.

✦ Invite the children to bring in or gather empty boxes of familiar cereals. Provide assorted materials including yarn, wiggle eyes, empty paper towel tubes, scissors, glue, and tape for children to invent, create, and construct a "cereal person" or "cereal animal." Engage them in discussions about such literacy relationships as familiar letters, similarities to their names, words that rhyme with the name of the cereal, and sight words on the boxes as they are creating. Ask the children to name their finished creatures. Provide opportunities for children to write, dictate, or draw about their creatures' adventures. Encourage them to share their creatures and stories.

Recycled Cards and Wrapping Paper

Children recycle greeting cards and comics to create wrapping paper, invitations, thank-you notes, and so on.

Objectives

Print Awareness: Children will associate words on greeting cards with familiar holidays and special occasions.

Writing Process: Children will use cards, comics, writing utensils, and scissors in cutting, writing, and drawing activities.

Oral Languages/Speaking and Listening: Children will listen to comic strips read to them.

Materials

holiday, birthday, thank-you, and special-occasion cards and comics from newspapers

scissors (straight edge and decorative, if possible)

tape

markers or crayons

Theme Connections

Holidays

Post Office

Recycling

Literacy Interactions

✦ Encourage children to use comics, scissors, and tape to wrap gifts they have made for family or friends. (Ideas for gifts include a papier-mâché treasure box or a collage picture frame). Volunteer to read the comics to them as they wrap. Provide markers or crayons for them to color in black and white comics. Add a note with the gift encouraging the recipient and the child to spend some time together reading the comics before opening the gift. Children will have fun turning the package as they read.

✦ Ask children to collect and bring in greeting cards after holidays and special occasions. Cut off the back portions of cards, or keep the back portion and trim off signatures. Ask the children to help read the cards and sort by subject, such as birthday, thank-you, Christmas, and Mother's Day. Provide cards, markers, and crayons in the Writing Center for children to write, draw, or dictate messages to loved ones and friends. Save cards from year to year for the children to create their own invitations for a special party or event. For example, use old Mother's Day cards for a "Lady in Your Life Tea." Provide decorative scissors and stickers for children to decorate the cards.

Note: Incorporate this activity into "Post Office" dramatic play (see page 183).

Cutting Coupons and Cartoons

Children will tear and/or cut environmental print to create collections of coupons or cartoons.

Objectives

Print Awareness: Children will look for familiar letters, pictures, symbols, and words on environmental print.

Writing Process: Children will strengthen small motor skills by cutting, tearing, and drawing on environmental print.

Phonics: Children will hunt for various alphabet letters and/or letter sounds in environmental print.

Beginning Reading: Children will search through environmental print to look for sight words and word family combinations.

Materials

newspaper inserts and cartoon
    strips
large tub or box
zipper-closure plastic bags or
    brown paper lunch bags
yarn
scissors
glue
paper

Theme Connections

Alphabet
Grocery Store
Recycling

Literacy Interactions

✦ Put environmental print (newspaper inserts, cartoon strips, and magazines) in a large tub or box. Encourage children to tear and/or cut out environmental print and put into plastic or paper bags. Encourage them to hunt for pictures and print of favorite toys, foods, places they recognize, and so on. Provide space for them to dump, sort, and trade their accumulated pieces. Offer staplers or paper clips for them to "organize" their collections.

✦ Provide crayons and markers for children to circle, color, or highlight their favorite pictures and/or words they recognize on the coupons, cartoons, or other environmental print they cut out. Ask questions about what they find such as, "Tell me about the cartoon you are coloring." Encourage their efforts to "read" the pictures and words. Offer notebooks or journals for them to glue favorites.

✦ As the children cut, specify several letters, words, or other criteria for their searches. For example, ask them to look for something that has a "B" at the beginning, hunt for the word "orange," or find words that are in the "all" word family.

Variation

✦ Designate a bulletin board, wall space, or other place for children to place the "treasures" they find among the cutout environmental print. Call it the "Look What I Found!" wall. Invite them to add additional discoveries they make, as well.

Cereal Lacing

Children use environmental print in lacing activities.

Objectives

Print Awareness: Children will follow words from left to right using environmental print in lacing activities.

Writing Process: Children will use lacing activities to exercise small motor skills needed for grasping tools for writing and in letter formation.

Phonics: Children will select environmental print that contains familiar letters or letter sounds such as those in their names.

Materials

cereal boxes or other product boxes containing large print

hole punch, or hammer, golf tees, and piece of wood

yarn, string, or ribbon

plastic sewing needles (optional)

permanent marker

paper

colored pencils or fine-tip markers

Theme Connections

Alphabet

Boxes

Recycling

Preparation

1. Gather a variety of cereal, cookie, and cracker boxes and cut off the fronts.
2. Punch holes around the edges of each box front using a hole punch, or place a piece of wood under the box front, place a tee on top, and hammer the tee to punch holes along the lettering.
3. Cut yarn, string, or ribbon to manageable length.
4. Wind a piece of tape around one end of each piece of yarn or string to create a "needle." Apply a flat piece on the other end to keep the string from pulling out of the holes.

Literacy Interactions

✦ To review a literacy-related skill, ask children to assist in selecting box fronts that fit criteria such as matching the beginning letter of their name, containing a color word, or an example of a blend. Encourage them to share their findings. Provide a hole punch for children to use, or assist as needed to put holes around the outside of the box fronts to create weaving cards. Demonstrate how to use the yarn "needles" to follow the holes around the edge, moving from right to left. The cards can be used again and again.

✦ Create dot-to-dot templates by placing box fronts with punched holes in the letters on top of pieces of paper. Encourage the children to use colored pencils or fine-tip markers to make a mark through each hole in the letters. When they finish, they can remove the box front and connect the dots to form the letters for the word(s) on the box front. Encourage them to add illustrations to the paper.

Box Front Weaving

Children isolate parts of words such as alphabet letters, consonant blends, onsets, and rimes while engaging in weaving activities using environmental print.

Objectives

Phonics: Children will isolate alphabet letters and sounds using environmental print in a weaving activity.

Phonological/Phonemic Awareness: Children will isolate and recognize sounds (such as consonant blends, rimes, and rhyming words) in a weaving activity.

Writing Process: Children will practice fine motor skills needed in writing and drawing through weaving.

Materials

mixture of large cereal boxes, cracker boxes, shoebox lids, or any boxes that contain large print at least 3" in size
construction paper strips, crepe paper streamers, and/or ribbon
scissors
tape

Theme Connections

Food and Nutrition
Grocery Store
Shoes

Preparation

1. To make an environmental print weaving board, cut off the fronts (or print portions) of boxes containing large lettering, such as cereal boxes, shoebox lids, or frozen pizza boxes, to create a flat surface. (Optional: Use smaller boxes as appropriate to challenge fine motor development.)

2. Cut three to six slits in the middle of each box, parallel to the identifying words. Make the slits the approximate height of the large lettering along the top and bottom of letters.

3. Leave a one-inch (or more) border around the box.

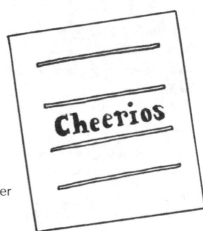

Literacy Interactions

✦ Let each child choose an environmental print weaving board. Invite the children to "read" and share what they know about their selections. Demonstrate how to alternate weaving in an over/under pattern using various paper strips. Encourage children to use paper strips, crepe paper, and ribbon the same width as lettering. Show the children as they weave how to isolate letters and other units of speech by sliding the strips over portions of the word(s). Draw attention to the letters and isolated sounds formed. For example, blocking out the "u" in "blue" isolates the blend "bl", and weaving through the "l" and "e" isolates the "u" sound. Because the weaving boards are made out of cardboard, they lend themselves to reuse. If desired, let children take them home to experiment with.

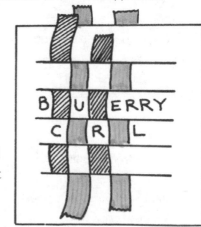

Box Label Puzzles

Children put puzzles together using matching box fronts as patterns.

Objectives

Print Awareness: Children will use environmental print clues and visual discrimination to put a puzzle back together.

Beginning Reading: Children will "read" familiar environmental print as it is used in a puzzle.

Materials

product box fronts, two of each
scissors
marker
large zipper-closure plastic bags

Theme Connections

Food and Nutrition
Grocery Store
Shoes

Preparation

1. Gather pairs of boxes (cereal, cracker, cookie, shoeboxes, and so on) containing environmental print and cut off the fronts of each.

2. Cut one of each set of fronts into puzzle pieces (the number of pieces depends on children's abilities). Store puzzle pieces and matching intact box fronts in zipper-closure bags.

Literacy Interactions

✦ Show the children the intact box fronts. Together, read and identify the words on each one. Ask, "What picture clues and letters tell you what product this is?" Put intact box fronts on a table with their matching puzzle pieces. Encourage the children to put each puzzle together on top of its matching box using the visual picture, letters, and word clues.

✦ Print identifying word(s) on the back of each intact front in the same lettering and size as appears on the front. Encourage the children to put the puzzle together using only the letter clues as they appear on the back of the box.

✦ Cut out the identifying word(s) from the middle of each box front as a puzzle piece. Invite children to "read" the words and then place them back into the matching box front using context clues.

Variations

✦ Cut letters out of one box front and encourage children to put them back in order using the intact box front as a guide. This works especially well with large letters on cereal and cracker boxes.

✦ Make floor-size puzzles using posters gathered from travel agencies, restaurants, and theaters.

Magnificent Mobiles

Children collect and use a variety of environmental print to create mobiles.

Objectives

Print Awareness: Children will seek environmental print that is familiar to them or represents a topic to create a mobile.

Comprehension: Children will demonstrate understanding of a topic by selecting corresponding environmental print to put on a mobile.

Oral Language/Speaking and Listening: Children will tell about a topic and share stories using environmental print.

Beginning Reading: Children will "read" familiar environmental print emergently or by recognition as it is used on a mobile.

Materials

a variety of environmental print, such as paper, Styrofoam, plastic, and cardboard packaging, cups, and plates; catalogs and magazines; container lids; and so on
discarded or junk CD's (optional)
hole punch
scissors
string or yarn
wooden dowels, clothes hangers, or long spaghetti boxes

Theme Connections

All About Me	Grocery Store
Community Helpers	Health and Safety
Cooking	Our Community
Food and Nutrition	Sports

Preparation

1. Cut and punch holes in plastic and heavy cardboard environmental print as needed.
2. Pound out or sand any rough edges left by holes.
3. Cut yarn or string to varied lengths, about 12" to 18".

Literacy Interactions

♦ Begin a discussion with the children about a topic that can be represented through environmental print, such as toys, colors, food groups, or shapes. Gather a variety of environmental print, or invite the children to look for print in their homes and communities that reflects the topic. Explain what a mobile is and tell them they will be making their own mobiles using environmental print. Provide assistance as needed as children cut out, punch holes, and attach string to the print they want to include in their mobiles. Offer other items, such as junk CD's, construction paper scraps, foam pieces, and aluminum foil, for them to add to their mobiles. Let children assist in hanging print items on a dowel, hanger, or long box (with holes punched in it). When they are finished, invite them to display and "read" the print and share stories about their mobiles.

Newspaper Art

Children create collages, shapes, hats, "clothing," and paintbrushes using newspapers in a variety of activities.

Objectives

Print Awareness: Children will have exposure to letters, words, symbols, and pictures by using newspaper in creative activities.

Vocabulary: Children will learn about parts of newspapers, such as sports, comics, and entertainment, during a creative activity.

Writing Process: Children will use newspaper in tearing, cutting, and painting activities to strengthen small motor skills.

Oral Language/Speaking and Listening: Children will share information about their newspaper creations.

Materials

newspapers
Liquid Watercolors and/or
    tempera paint
paint and paintbrushes
plain paper
construction paper
colored tissue paper
scissors, glue, and tape

Theme Connections

Alphabet
Cultural Awareness
Newspaper
Recycling
Science and Nature
Sports

Literacy Interactions

✦ Before beginning, show the children various sections of a newspaper and ask them to share their experiences with newspapers. Read portions of the newspaper that might interest the children, such as the comics or weather. Use the following activities as an opportunity to introduce various parts of the newspaper.

✦ Encourage children to tear or use scissors to clip words, letters, and pictures from the newspaper. Also provide construction paper scraps for them to tear and cut. Encourage them to make collages on paper by gluing the pieces to form designs, pictures, and patterns. Ask questions and encourage them to share elements of their creations. For example, "Marie, tell me about the 'a' you cut out and put on the head you created."

✦ Show children how to make paintbrushes out of newspaper. Fold a piece of newspaper in half. Cut or tear approximately 5 or 10 slits in the unfolded part about ¾ of the way down to the fold. Cutting a few slits will make big, thick brush prints, while cutting many slits will make finer, feathery prints. Roll the newspaper and wrap tape around the top portion to create a handle. Allow the cut ends to hang freely. Make various sizes of brushes. Encourage children to paint with the brushes on flat pieces of newspaper using Liquid Watercolors and tempera paints. The words and letters will still be visible through diluted Liquid Watercolors.

✦ Use newspaper pulp or "soup" saved from "Made From Trees" activity (see page 137) for children to create paper shapes and sculptures. Show children how to squish and roll the pulp into a shape. Add a little water and/or liquid starch to the mixture if it is

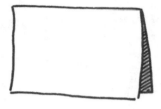

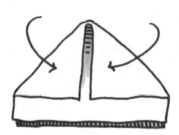

too dry. Provide newspapers and tissue paper scraps for children to cut out letters and pictures to press into their creations. Let the creations dry on screens or cooling racks.

✦ Have a "Walking Newspaper" day! Show children how to make simple newspaper hats by folding a piece of newspaper in half along the folds. Fold top corners to meet in the middle, forming a triangle shape. Make corners meet about ¾ of the way from the bottom ends of the newspaper. Fold each bottom flap outward to create a brim. Staple or tape the bottom edge to fit. Show children how to cut and tape newspaper to create shirts, sleeves, pants, skirts, shoes, and so on. Encourage them to associate certain print with a type of clothing, such as a clown costume made from comics, a helmet made from the sports pages, a coat made from weather page, and so on. Provide collage materials for them to decorate their hats and clothing. Invite them to have a parade in their costumes.

news shoes!

Variation

✦ Cut newspaper into smaller pieces, approximately 8" x 11". Encourage the children to fold, bend, twist, and roll the newspaper to make animals, people, and other sculptures. Use this activity to introduce Origami. Locate related books for the children to look at and read.

Suggested Book

Newspapers by David Petersen

Newspaper Letters

Children cut out and use letters or words from newspapers and other environmental print in several activities.

Objectives

Print Awareness: Children will recognize print properties by cutting out letters and words from newspapers, magazines, and so on.

Writing Process: Children will strengthen small motor skills by cutting out letters and words from environmental print.

Phonics: Children will use environmental print to locate and spell words such as their names.

Beginning Reading: Children will collect and "read" print that is meaningful to them.

Materials

newspapers, newspaper inserts, magazines, and catalogs

scissors

paper

glue

colored bowls

tub

markers, crayons, or colored pencils

Theme Connections

Alphabet

Newspaper

Recycling

Sports

Literacy Interactions

✦ Encourage children to cut out or tear letters and words from environmental print (newspapers, newspaper inserts, magazines, and catalogs). Engage them in conversations about what they find. Provide paper and glue for them to paste the print they want to save. Put out colored bowls for them to sort letters in. Put extra letters and words in a tub to save for other activities.

✦ Ask children to use markers, crayons, or colored pencils to trace over large lettering on newspapers, magazines, newspaper inserts, and so on. Challenge them to look for letters in their names or key letters they are learning to write.

✦ Put cut-out letters and words gathered from environmental print in the Writing Center. Provide glue and paper or blank journals for children to arrange the letters to form their name, friends' names, sight words, and so on. They may want to add whole words that they recognize, such as the name of a favorite sports team, snack, or even the name of someone they know. Encourage them to add to their collections by keeping a supply of newspaper, magazines, and so on accessible.

Papier-Mâché Print

Children tear environmental print and use it with a glue/water mixture to create sculptures.

Objectives

Print Awareness: Children will examine environmental print and distinguish between alphabet letters while creating papier-mâché.

Phonics: Children will identify words that begin with the same letters in their names.

Oral Language/Speaking and Listening: Children will listen to and follow oral directions regarding the use of environmental print and other materials to create a sculpture.

Materials

newspapers and newspaper inserts
white glue
water
bowls
extra newspaper or vinyl table covering
sponges
paper or Styrofoam bowls

Theme Connections

All About Me
Newspaper
Recycling

Literacy Interactions

✦ Invite children to bring in environmental print (newspapers and inserts). Show them how to tear the paper into strips. As they are working, encourage them to look for and identify familiar print, such as favorite places, food, toys, and movies; sight words; or letters in their names. Invite them to share their discoveries with each other. Explain that they will be making papier-mâché sculptures. Prepare a glue/water mixture by diluting white glue with water until it is a creamy consistency. Cover the work surface with newspaper or vinyl covering. Provide paper or Styrofoam bowls or other form for children to use as a support. Demonstrate how to dip the paper strips into the mixture and overlap them onto the bowl or other form. Take time to recognize the relationships with letters and familiar print as the children work. For example, "Sam, I see that you put (brand name) toy on your sculpture. Is that something you like to play with?" Or, "Which words on your sculpture start with the same letter as your name?" After the sculptures dry, remove them from the form. The children can use the papier-mâché containers for storing treasures.

Name in Lights

Children use various tools to punch holes in lettering on environmental print to create illuminated signs.

Objectives

Print Awareness: Children will use, recognize, and create print.
Writing Process: Children will exercise small motor skills needed for writing by using tools to punch holes in print.
Phonics: Children will review letter names in familiar environmental print and their names.

Materials

cardboard or heavy paper signs, labels from restaurants and stores, or other print with large lettering
scrap wood and/or Styrofoam sheets
dark-colored poster board, thin cardboard, or tagboard
golf tees
plastic or wooden mallets or small hammers
light-colored markers or crayons
scissors
tape
colored cellophane or tissue paper
flashlights

Theme Connections

All About Me
Health and Safety
Our Community

Literacy Interactions

✦ Provide poster board or cardboard for children to make signs of their names. Encourage children to print their names in large letters on the poster board. For children who are still learning to recognize or write their name, print their names for them. Invite them to punch holes along the letters using golf tees and mallets. Demonstrate how to tape a piece of cellophane or tissue paper on one side of the poster board. Encourage them to hold their signs up to a light or use a flashlight in a darkened room to illuminate their names like neon signs!

✦ Involve children in gathering environmental print with large print lettering. Trim print as needed from boxes, containers, and so on. If desired, select print to fit a specific criteria, such as all beginning with the letter "t", or related to safety signs ("Stop," "Danger," "Exit"). Prepare the print so that it lays flat and place Styrofoam or wood underneath to protect the work surface. Demonstrate how to punch holes along the lettering by pounding a golf tee with a mallet or small hammer. Introduce or review letter names and sounds as the children work.

Variation

✦ Let children add their signs to the Block Area. Turn off the lights and use flashlights to illuminate the signs.

Writing Wonders

Children use environmental print to practice forming letters and in writing activities.

Objectives

Writing Process: Children will use environmental print as a way to practice letter formation and spelling.

Phonics: Children will use environmental print writing activities as a way to practice recognition of alphabet letter and/or letter sounds.

Beginning Reading: Children will locate and use beginning sight words in environmental print for spelling activities.

Materials

newspaper inserts, package labels, business logos, and so on

sentence strips

scissors

glue

washable marker, dry-erase marker, or crayon

clear contact paper or laminate

Theme Connections

Alphabet	Gardening and Plants
Babies	Grocery Store
Camping	Health and Safety
Colors	Holidays
Community Helpers	Sports
Cultural Awareness	Transportation

Preparation

1. Create word cards by gluing each environmental print item (from newspaper inserts, package labels, and business logos) on a sentence strip on the left edge.
2. Print the identifying words to the right of the environmental print using a light-colored marker. Write upper- and lowercase letters as they appear on the environmental print.
3. Show letter formation directions as needed by adding arrows beside printed letters.
4. Cover the cards with clear contact paper or laminate them.

(continued on the next page)

Literacy Interactions

✦ Choose simple environmental print cards, such as those containing three or four letters in the word. Guide the children to trace over the top of the printed words on the sentence strips using a darker washable writing utensil. Wipe the surface with a damp sponge or paper towel to reuse.

✦ Provide environmental print cards to introduce new words for journal writing, thematic units, and/or alphabet letter or letter sound concepts. Place the cards in the Writing Area for children to use in self-directed writing activities.

✦ Show the children how environmental print can be used to determine how to spell a word. Draw attention to environmental print that contains alternative forms of spelling for a familiar word (for example, "cheez" instead of "cheese"). Invite them to locate environmental print that contains beginning sight words. Use these to create cards to practice spelling.

Linking Environmental Print With Dramatic Play

♦ In each activity in this chapter, the **objectives** are listed in order of difficulty—use them according to the skill level of the children in your class.

♦ In each activity in this chapter, the **literacy interactions** are listed in order of difficulty; use them according to the abilities and interests of the children.

Grocery Store

Children interact and pretend using environmental print and props related to supermarkets/grocery stores.

Objectives

Print Awareness: Children will look at and use environmental print in sorting activities.

Vocabulary: Children will learn and use new words related to food and grocery departments in imaginative play.

Phonics: Children will sort food-related environmental print by alphabet letter during imaginative play.

Writing Process: Children will create lists and signs related to grocery stores during imaginative play.

Materials and Props

environmental print:
brown paper bags (imprinted with store names)
clip-on name badges
coupons
empty food containers (cereal and cracker boxes, plastic condiment bottles, egg cartons, ice cream containers, plastic juice bottles, and so on)
food labels
grocery store advertisements
grocery store discount cards or gift cards
imprinted shirts or aprons
labels for departments (cereal, dairy, meat)

Materials and Props (continued)

magazines and newspapers
price tags or labels
plastic grocery carts and plastic baskets with handles
boxes of food products
large boxes
plastic food
blank stickers
box lids for sorting
permanent markers
cash register
credit cards, checks, and play money
copies of coins (see page 243)
notepads
pencils and markers

Theme Connections

Community Helpers
Cultural Awareness
Food and Nutrition
Grocery Store
Holidays

Things to Make

◆ **Box Display Cases:** Collect boxes in a variety of sizes and remove box tops. Cut out environmental print from various grocery departments, such as dairy, meat, and bread/cereal. If desired, use print that represents a type of product, such as paper goods, cookies, and canned fruit, or that represents a letter of the alphabet (for example, "apple juice" and "animal cookies" for the letter "A"). Sort the print and glue inside

label pasted
inside bottom

Book Suggestions

At the Supermarket by David
　　Hautzig
Don't Forget the Bacon! by Pat
　　Hutchins
Let's Go the Supermarket! by
　　Lorraine Gallacher
The Shopping Basket by John
　　Burningham
Signs at the Store by Mary Hill
Supermarket by Kathleen Krull
Supermarket (Who Works Here)
　　by Lola M. Schaefer
The Supermarket by Gail
　　Saunders-Smith
Teddy Bears Go Shopping by S.
　　Gretz
When We Go Shopping by Nick
　　Butterworth

the bottom of each box. Create boxes for each department in a grocery store and place them on their sides. Put in the Dramatic Play area. If desired, children can paint or glue paper scraps to the box.

✦ **Plastic Food Labels:** Create labels for simple plastic food items by writing the identifying name either on a blank self-adhesive label or directly on the plastic food using a non-toxic permanent marker. For example, print "grapes" on a bunch of plastic grapes, "beans" on plastic green beans, and so on. Put in the Dramatic Play area.

Literacy Interactions

✦ Gather empty food and product containers and plastic food. Use display cases (see "Things to Make" above) for children to sort the food and containers. Talk about the names used for each department. Encourage the children to look at picture and word clues to help them identify where the food product should go.

✦ Ask children to cut out print and pictures of food from grocery store advertisements. Talk about the various departments that are in a grocery store and the words used to identify them, such as "produce," "dairy," and "frozen foods." Show examples of what types of foods would go in these areas. Make a sign for each department in a grocery store ("Produce," "Bakery," Frozen Foods," and so on). Encourage the children to sort the environmental print and glue to the corresponding department sign. Put signs in the Dramatic Play area for children to use in organizing the store.

✦ Let children help prepare a shopping list based on the items that are available in the "grocery store" (see Shopping List Sample on page 237. Write the list on chart paper or a dry-erase board or children can write their own, if able. Transfer the list to a smaller piece of paper and make copies for each child. They can use this list to check off items they put into their cart during imaginative play. Encourage them to sort the items, for example, by food group (such as dairy, meat, and bread/cereal) by type (such as paper goods, cereal, and canned vegetables), or by beginning letter. Incorporate this idea with "My Shopping List" on page 204 (see Shopping List on page 237).

Variation

✦ Prepare items for "Count My Cart" on page 108. After the children have learned and practiced this sorting activity several times, place the items and bags in the Dramatic Play area for them to continue sorting during imaginative play.

Bakery Shop

Children interact and pretend using environmental print and props related to a bakery.

Objectives

Print Awareness: Children will be exposed to print related to bakeries and have an opportunity to use it in imaginative play.

Writing/Grammar: Children will write and draw to create signs, orders, and so on.

Vocabulary: Children will learn new vocabulary related to bakeries.

Oral Language/Speaking and Listening: Children will listen to information and ask questions regarding bakeries.

Comprehension: Children will demonstrate understanding of events and information from baker visits or bakery field trip through imaginative play.

Materials and Props

environmental print:

aprons with name of bakery or other related print

bags and boxes for baked items (such as clean, empty donut boxes)

books about cookies, cakes, and bread

cake decorating books

clip-on name badges

cookbooks (purchased and child-made)

empty ingredient containers (flour, sugar, salt, frosting, baking soda)

menus

pictures of bakery products from magazines and newspaper inserts

pre-printed napkins

spoons, measuring spoons, spatulas, bowls, beaters, rolling pin, and hand mixer

cake pans, muffin tins, and cookie sheets

cookie cutters

timer

cake decorating tools and reusable decorations

playdough

plastic food

magnetic board or felt board

cash register

play money, credit cards, and checks

copies of coins (see page 243)

note cards and recipe box

pencils

order pads

paper

Theme Connections

Bakery

Community Helpers

Cooking

Food and Nutrition

Things to Make

✦ **Cookies and Donuts:** Cut out pictures of cookies, donuts, and bread from magazines and newspaper inserts. Laminate them for durability. Or, cut felt or craft foam into cookie and donut shapes. Decorate with markers or fabric paint. Children can use these in pretend play.

✦ **Cake or Cookie Order Book:** Ask children to cut out pictures of cakes, cookies, and other bakery-related environmental print. Glue to paper and print identifying names under each, such as "chocolate chip cookie." Attach the pages together.

Literacy Interactions

✦ Follow a recipe to make an item found in a bakery. Use the same type of tools and recipes that are in the Dramatic Play area. Invite parents and others to visit the "bakery" to "buy" the baked goods.

✦ Introduce tools and products from a bakery as new vocabulary words before placing them in bakery dramatic play. Demonstrate how the tools work and provide an opportunity for the children to share what they know about each item.

✦ Invite a person that works at a bakery to visit the classroom and demonstrate some of what they do. Compile questions to ask before the visit. Encourage the visitor to bring in environmental print related to the bakery, such as recipe books, ingredients, order books, and so on. Provide these as additions to the Dramatic Play area. Invite the visitor to stay and "bake" with the children in dramatic play.

✦ Incorporate print obtained from a field trip to a bakery into the bakery props. Invite the children to recall what kinds of print they saw at the bakery and make their own signs. Provide paper, poster board, tape, and writing utensils.

Book Suggestions

Bakers Make Many Things by Carol Greene
Bread, Bread, Bread by Ann Morris
Cook-a-Doodle-Doo! by Janet Stevens and Susan Stevens
Mr. Cookie Baker by Monica Wellington
Ruth's Bake Shop by Kate Spohn

Ice Cream Store

Children interact and pretend using environmental print and props related to ice cream stores in the Dramatic Play or Block areas.

Objectives

Print Awareness: Children will develop understanding of the function of print used in an ice cream store.

Writing Process: Children will participate in drawing and/or writing activities using ice cream-related environmental print.

Phonics: Children will gain awareness of specific alphabet letters or sounds using environmental print in imaginative play.

Materials and Props

environmental print:
books about ice cream
empty ice cream, Popsicle and
    ice cream sandwich boxes
empty ingredient containers to
    make ice cream (flour,
    sugar, salt, cream cartons,
    egg carton, and milk jug)
empty topping packaging
    (sprinkles, flavored syrup,
    whipped cream)
ice cream signs and posters
ice cream store hats and aprons
menus

Materials and Props (continued)

pictures of ice cream products from magazines and newspaper inserts
plastic ice cream buckets
pre-printed napkins, cups, coupons, and sales flyers from local shop
spoons, measuring spoons, spatulas, bowls, and hand mixers
plastic ice cream dishes
ice cream scoops
hand-crank ice cream maker
cash register
play money, credit cards, and checks
copies of coins (see page 243)
playdough, yarn pompoms, or colored balls for ice cream
cardboard cones (made from cardstock, tagboard, or empty cone-
    shaped thread spools)
order pads
paper
magnetic board or felt board
note cards
pencils

Theme Connections

Community Helpers
Farms
Food and Nutrition
Grocery Store

Things to Make

✦ **Ice Cream Menu Board:** Cut out ice cream-related environmental print. Glue each piece on the left edge of a sentence strip or piece of paper and print the name on the right. Laminate or cover with clear contact paper, and adhere Velcro or magnet tape to the back of each piece to use on a felt or magnetic board.

✦ **Boxes of Ice Cream:** Cut off fronts of ice cream boxes and tape them to plastic containers. Make playdough in various "ice cream" colors (see recipes on page 241). Put each color of playdough in a matching container, for example, pink playdough in a strawberry ice cream container. Provide ice cream scoops for each container.

◆ **Ice Cream Popsicles:** Cut Styrofoam scraps into Popsicle shapes. Paint them various colors using non-toxic tempera paint or cover with contact or construction paper. Push craft sticks into the bottom of each. Insert them into empty Popsicle boxes.

Literacy Interactions

◆ Visit an ice cream store or factory. Prepare a list of items to look for before visiting, such as flavors of ice cream, ingredients, and signs. Give each child a copy of the list or check off items as they are discovered as a group. Add new words to the list, such as flavors of ice cream or signs, and add them to the props in the dramatic play ice cream store (for example, by making the signs). Use this list as part of a discussion of dairy products. Sample some of the items on the list at snack time. (**Note:** Be aware of any food allergies.)

◆ Use environmental print to create a book of ice cream recipes and ideas. Prepare ice cream recipes with the children (see recipes on page 241). Offer a variety of toppings for children to choose from. Provide paper for them to draw pictures of their dessert and dictate their own recipe (including toppings!) to put in the book. Encourage children to use the books during imaginative play.

◆ Introduce the Ice Cream Menu Board (see "Things to Make" above). Invite the children to use the print on the board to indicate the items they would like to order. Create a literacy skill "feature" box on the board by sectioning off an area with masking tape. Write or place a letter, letter sound, or word family that the children are focusing on that day or week. Place environmental print items in the "feature box" that are examples of the letter, letter sound, and so on. For example, if the children are focusing on the letter "s", examples may include "strawberry ice cream" and "swirl Popsicles." Emphasize the features in discussion about the letter or sounds.

◆ Create a set of "Missing Letter Labels" (see page 39) related to ice cream products to use on the Ice Cream Menu Board (magnetic version). Let children use magnetic letters on a magnetic board to fill in missing letters in each word. Incorporate letter sounds the children are studying.

Book Suggestions

Curious George Goes to an Ice Cream Shop by Margaret and H.A. Rey

From Cow to Ice Cream by Bertram T. Knight

From Milk to Ice Cream by Stacy Taus-Bolstad

Ice Cream by Elisha Cooper

Ice Cream Cones for Sale by Elaine Greenstein

I Like Ice Cream by Robin Pickering

Let's Find Out About Ice Cream by Mary Ebeltoft Reid

Restaurant

Children interact and pretend using environmental print and props related to a type of restaurant.

Objectives

Print Awareness: Children will learn about the function of print in restaurants through various activities and by using related environmental print in imaginative play.

Oral Language/Speaking and Listening: Children will listen to and share information using restaurant-related environmental print.

Writing Process: Children will participate in drawing and/or writing activities using print associated with restaurants in imaginative play.

Vocabulary: Children will learn and use new vocabulary related to restaurants through observation, listening, and participating in activities during imaginative play.

Materials and Props

environmental print:
aprons, shirts, and hats with
  restaurant name printed on
  them
cookbooks
food, ketchup, mustard, dressing,
  and so on)
ingredient containers (rice,
  croutons, pasta, spices,
  canned
menus from restaurants
order pads
pre-printed paper bags
pre-printed placemats and
  napkins
pre-printed Styrofoam, cardboard,
  and plastic food containers
restaurant coupons and
  advertisements
restaurant posters
restaurant sale receipts and
  receipt book

restaurant-related signs
cash register
play money, checks, and credit
  cards
copies of coins (see page 243)
serving trays
plates, bowls, cups, and utensils
cooking utensils, spatulas, tongs,
  and spoons
measuring spoons and cups
pretend microwave, stove, and
  sink
plastic food
pots and fry pans
oven mitts and pot holders
pencils
paper
felt or magnetic board
laminate or clear contact paper
scissors

Theme Connections

Community Helpers
Cooking
Cultural Awareness

Food and Nutrition
Restaurant
Travel and Vacations

Things to Make

✦ **Menu Board:** Cut out environmental print related to the type of food served, such as Chinese, Italian, or seafood. Glue the pictures to cards or paper and print or type the names under the item (lasagna, lo mein noodles, and so on). Laminate or cover with clear contact paper. Adhere Velcro or magnet tape to the back to use on felt or magnet board.

◆ **Drive-Through Window:** Use a puppet stage, or make a drive-through window using a large appliance box. Cut out a large window on the top end of one side of the box. Cut out a door on the opposite side of the box. Ask children to cut out and glue or tape restaurant-related environmental print to the outside of the box to create menus, signs, and so on. Use a tissue box or cardboard gift wrap tube to make a speaker.

Literacy Interactions

◆ As part of introducing restaurant dramatic play, invite children to put on items associated with restaurants such as hats, aprons, smocks, buttons, and so on. Role play taking food orders at a restaurant using a big writing tablet or several large pieces of paper stapled together. Encourage children to use a menu board or drive-up window (see Things to Make) to make selections. Print each child's dictated menu choices on the paper. Invite them to assist in spelling simple words. Put order pads and the menu board in the Dramatic Play area.

(continued on the next page)

- Ask children to cut out several favorite food items from magazines, newspapers, and product containers. Encourage them to glue the pictures to paper plates to create a meal. Print the name of each item next to it around the edge of the plate. Use this activity as opportunity to talk about nutrition and food groups.

- Visit an ethnic restaurant or invite a chef from an ethnic restaurant to come in and create a food item with the children. Ask the chef to talk about tools and ingredients used, and the way print is used (instructions and labels). Introduce new vocabulary words and talk about various cultures, letters, symbols, and languages. Ask for print items (ingredient containers, take-out containers, menus) to use in restaurant dramatic play. Use the new vocabulary in conversations with the children as they play.

- Invite children to bring in take-out menus from the restaurants they visit. Use the menus to introduce how food is categorized. Let children create their own menus by cutting out environmental print and gluing it under categories such as beverages, sandwiches, vegetables, and desserts. Have children dictate or write the names of their favorite items on their menus. Compile the menus together in a book (photo album) for children to use in the Dramatic Play Area (see "My Menu" on page 202).

- Incorporate a tasting party into the restaurant play area. Invite children to bring in items (and ingredient or original food containers, if possible) from their culture, traditions, and favorite restaurants. Read and talk about the food names and their meanings as children try them. Use the empty, clean food containers in imaginative play. **Note**: Be aware of any food allergies.

Book Suggestions

Dinner at the Panda Palace by Stephanie Calmenson

Eating Out by Helen Oxenbury

Friday Night at Hodges' Cafe by Tim Egan

Froggy Eats Out by Jonathan London

In Enzo's Splendid Gardens by Patricia Polacco

Sheep Out to Eat by Nancy Shaw

Toad Eats Out by Susan Schade

Pizza Shop

Children interact and pretend using environmental print and props related to a pizza parlor in the Dramatic Play area.

Objectives

Print Awareness: Children will use environmental print related to a pizza shop in imaginative play.

Oral Language/Speaking and Listening: Children will listen to and share information about making a pizza.

Writing Process: Children will use environmental print in dictating and writing activities involving pizza.

Vocabulary: Children will use environmental print related to pizza toppings during imaginative play to build and practice understanding of related word meanings.

Comprehension: Children will demonstrate understanding of the sequence of creating a pizza by making and using a pizza cookbook.

Phonics: Children will gain awareness of a specific alphabet letter or sound by discovering and learning, environmental print that represents each different pizza topping.

Materials and Props

environmental print:
aprons or shirts (pre-printed with name of pizza restaurant)
clean, empty ingredient containers (tomato sauce, spices, pepperoni boxes, crust mix, four, salt, parmesan cheese, and cooking oil)
maps
menus
order pads (pre-printed with menu options)
pizza cookbook
pizza coupons and sales circulars
posters of pizzas
pre-printed napkins, cups, and boxes from pizza restaurants
receipt book
cash register
play money, credit cards, and checks
pizza pans
plastic pizza cutter
rolling pin
spoons, bowls, plates, and utensils
telephone
cardboard circles in various sizes
pencils
dry-erase or magnetic board
tablecloth

Theme Connections

Food and Nutrition
Our Community
Restaurant

Things to Make

✦ **Pizza Toppings, Pasta, and Salad:** Make pizza crusts out of cardboard circles. Cut out red felt circles for sauce and other colors of felt for pepperoni, mushrooms, cheese, and so on. Make pretend spaghetti and meatballs by cutting yarn "noodles" and adding red yarn pompoms. Create a pretend salad by cutting various colors of tissue paper into pieces. Sort the items into labeled containers and add to the Dramatic Play Area.

✦ **Name Badges:** Cut slips of paper, write each child's name on a separate slip, and slide into clear name badges. Collect stickers from pizza restaurants to put on the edges of each badge. Encourage children to wear them in their "pizza shop."

(continued on the next page)

Book Suggestions

Curious George and the Pizza
by Margret Rey

Hi, Pizza Man! by Virginia
Walter

Little Nino's Pizzeria by Karen
Barbour

Pete's a Pizza by William Steig

*The Little Red Hen (Makes a
Pizza)* by Philemon Sturges

The Pizza That We Made by
Joan Holub

Literacy Interactions

✦ Visit a pizza shop with the children. Before the field trip, ask the owner or manager if it would be possible for the children to prepare their own pizza or watch a cook prepare a pizza. When children make a pizza (or watch someone else make it), emphasize that they must follow a sequence. Ask the guide to talk about how print is used for making, selling, and buying pizzas. Invite the children to find print to include in a written log of words related to pizza. Utilize collected vocabulary words to label items in the Dramatic Play area.

✦ Encourage the children to think of pizza toppings, real or imaginary, that start with each letter of the alphabet (for example, anchovies, broccoli, cheese, donuts, and so on) and create a list on chart paper. Label each item on the list with its beginning letter. Challenge children to find environmental print that represents each pizza topping to put on the giant pizza. Use the toppings list to create order pads (see page 236). Write the list on a smaller sheet of paper and glue corresponding environmental print or clip art next to each item. Laminate a few to use repeatedly.

✦ Encourage children to save labels and packaging from pizza toppings and ingredients after making a pizza at home, in class, or while on a field trip to a pizza shop. Invite children to draw on their knowledge and experiences to help dictate and compile a pizza recipe book. Include simple recipes for making the dough and sauce (see recipes on page 241), and the sequence of how to put a pizza together. Incorporate pizza environmental print as part of the illustrations or as rebus word representations in the recipe book. Put the pizza recipe book in the Dramatic Play area for the children to use as they make "pizza."

Library

Children interact and pretend using environmental print and props related to a library.

Objectives

Print Awareness: Children will learn about the function of print in books and libraries through various activities.

Vocabulary: Children will learn about words associated with libraries and books through observation, listening, and participating in imaginative play.

Writing Process: Children will participate in drawing and/or writing activities to create books for imaginative play and storytelling.

Oral Language/Speaking and Listening: Children will listen to and tell stories using props, print, and other materials in imaginative play.

Beginning Reading: Children will read and dramatize familiar texts and distinguish between fiction and non-fiction books in imaginative play.

Materials and Props

environmental print:
blank library cards (children can add their names)
book request forms
bookmarks (imprinted with children's books and characters or library)
calendars (desk, pocket, day planner, and so on)
children's books
date stamps and stamp pad
dictionary, atlas, and encyclopedia
library signs
magazines and newspapers
name badges
pre-printed phone message pads
telephone book

video containers or sleeves
book ends
plastic crates, boxes, and shelves to organize books (use a box for book return)
in/out trays
small rolling cart
story tapes and tape recorder
flannel board stories and flannel board
paper, pens and pencils
clipboards and paper clips
beanbag chairs, pillows, and child-size rocking chair
puppets and small puppet theatre
library pockets, due-date slips, and cards

Theme Connections

Community Helpers
Fairy Tales
Nursery Rhymes

Our Community
Storytelling

Things to Make

✦ **Puppet Theater:** Obtain a large appliance box. Cut out a large window near the top end of one side of the box. Cut out a door or the entire side of the opposite end of the box. Children can cut pictures of story characters from catalogs or book order forms and glue to the box. They can also decorate the box with collage materials and markers.

✦ **Library Cards:** Use plain index cards or cardstock to make library cards. Include the name of the library, a line for the child's name (to be filled in by child), and a line for a library number. Give one to each child to fill out and decorate. If desired, laminate them for durability.

(continued on the next page)

Quiet please

hours
Monday thru Friday
9am to 7:30pm
Saturday 10 to 6
Sunday Closed

Book Suggestions

Check It Out!: The Book About Libraries by Gail Gibbons

A Day With a Librarian by Jan Kottke

I Took My Frog to the Library by Eric A. Kimmel

The Library by Sarah Stewart

Library (Who Works Here?) by Lola M. Schaefer

Literacy Interactions

✦ Visit a library with the children. During the tour, request that the librarian identify signs and symbols that can help children at the library, such as letters on book spines for alphabetizing, non-fiction labels, bathrooms, and "quiet" signs. Listen to a story time or attend an event. Go through the process of finding materials to check out together using a computer catalog, card catalog, and/or book list. Ask for print materials that can be taken and used in dramatic play, such as bookmarks, old signs and posters, stickers, and stamps. Obtain materials about the library to send home with the children to encourage families to bring their child to the library.

✦ Look at and read familiar books together with the children. Introduce and discuss vocabulary and parts of a book such as title, author, illustrator, characters, copyright, and dedication. Invite children to share what they know about books. Give each child a blank book (paper stapled together with wallpaper or construction paper cover). Encourage them to make their own books by dictating stories or writing their own. Help them add their name (author), title, copyright, dedication, and so on. Invite them to put their books in the "library" for others to "check out."

✦ Use familiar stories or books the children have produced to create puppet characters. Provide a variety of materials for children to make puppets or masks to use to tell stories. Invite children to put their finished puppets in the Dramatic Play area and use them to tell stories with a puppet theater (see "Things to Make" above). Provide other materials, such as flannel board stories and stories on tape, for storytelling.

✦ Create a class library using library book card sets. Print the name of each book in the "library" on a book pocket and on an index card. Glue pictures of books (cut out from catalogs) to the cards to assist children in the matching process. Glue or tape each pocket on the inside back cover of the matching book. Encourage children to match the book cards to the corresponding books by sliding the cards into the pockets. Show children where to write their name on the card to check out the book. Role play checking out books, using date stamps, calendars, and due date slips. Invite children to make their own library cards to use in checking out materials (see page 177).

✦ Make signs to label the sections of the library, such as Fiction, Non-fiction, Videos, Books on Tape, and Reference, or by subject matter, such as Dinosaurs, Transportation, and Winter. Cut out and glue or draw pictures on labels that describe the section. Put labels on shelves or boxes. Provide a variety of media such as books, videos (cases), tapes, magazines, and newspapers for children to sort onto labeled shelves or boxes.

Theatre: Movie or Stage

Children interact and pretend using environmental print and props related to theatrical productions or movie theaters.

Objectives

Print Awareness: Children will learn about the function of print used in theater productions, such as story characters, programs, and tickets in dramatic play.

Oral Language/Speaking and Listening: Children will use environmental print as part of dramatizing familiar stories and movies.

Comprehension: Children will recall a story read to them by creating simple narratives and through dramatic play.

Writing Process: Children will create tickets, posters, invitations, and cast lists using drawing and writing tools.

Materials and Props

environmental print:
children's movie or play posters
familiar stories, fairy tales, and
	nursery rhymes
movie and show listings from
	newspapers
newspaper inserts
old movie gift cards or gift
	certificates
popcorn boxes and empty candy
	boxes
preprinted tickets, brochures, and
	signs
chairs
old movie projector (remove
	cords), or make one out of a
	box

old cameras
tickets
cash register
play money, credit cards, and
	checks
magnetic board, dry-erase board,
	or flannel board
puppets
dress-up clothing
music source
stage (large flattened box)
flashlight for spotlight
microphone (paper towel tube
	with a slit tennis ball on the
	end)

Theme Connections

Fairy Tales
Holidays
Nursery Rhymes
Storytelling

Things to Make:

✦ **Masks:** Encourage children to create masks related to a familiar story to use in dramatic play (nursery rhyme, fairy tale, or holiday stories). Provide materials, including paper plates, paper, glue, and paint.

(continued on the next page)

✦ **Cast Lists:** Help the children write their names on a sentence strip, piece of paper, or dry-erase board. Cut out pictures of several characters in a story or movie. Laminate and add Velcro or magnet tape, if necessary. Make a cast list by asking children to put the character pictures next to their names on a magnetic board, dry-erase board, or flannel board.

Literacy Interactions

✦ Read a simple story to the children several times. Fairy tales, nursery rhymes, and stories with repetitive lines work well ("Goldilocks and the Three Bears," "The Three Little Pigs," "Three Billy Goats Gruff"). Ask the children to "read" the repetitive parts as they appear in the story. Invite them to act out parts as the story is read. Identify the parts in the story where the characters speak and where there is action. Ask children to recall the story and help create simple speaking or repetitive parts as you write it on chart paper. Invite the children to dramatize a story. Add related props to the Dramatic Play area for children to continue to dramatize.

✦ Encourage the children to create or use tickets, invitations, and flyers to advertise their show (see Ticket on page 239). Provide materials to make signs ("open," "closed," "tickets," "snacks," "exit," and "quiet"). Incorporate environmental print as appropriate. Invite parents and friends to attend. Videotape the children acting out or reading a story, singing, performing a puppet show, or participating in a special event. Have a special movie-watching day. Set up a movie theater in the Dramatic Play area to watch the video performance. Ask the children to "review" their performance. Talk about what they liked and disliked. Remind children to give constructive (not negative) comments and compliments to each other.

Book Suggestions

Angelina on Stage by Katharine Holabird
At the Movie Theater by Sandy Francis
Clap Your Hands by Lorinda Bryan Cauley
Curious George Goes to a Movie by Margaret and H.A. Rey
Lights! Camera! Action!: How a Movie Is Made by Gail Gibbons

Office

Children interact and pretend using environmental print and props related to office work.

Objectives

Print Awareness: Children will learn about office-related print (forms, telephone books, message pads) in imaginative play.

Oral Language/Speaking and Listening: Children will describe information on print during imaginative play.

Vocabulary: Children will learn about words associated with print and the machines used in an office.

Writing Process: Children will use writing and develop an understanding of print as a communication tool using computers, forms, messages, and so on.

Beginning Reading: Children will practice spelling beginning sight words using office-related machines.

Phonics: Children will use office machines with keyboards to review and create their own alphabet print.

Materials and Props

environmental print:
appointment book
brochures and pamphlets from area businesses
business and office supply catalogs and newspaper inserts
business cards (pre-printed and blank)
calendars (desk, pocket, day planner)
children's books related to office work
dictionary
forms (job applications, order forms, flowcharts, time sheets)
ledger book
pre-printed address labels, magnets, and business envelopes
pre-printed message pads (see page 238)

telephone book
paper
stapler
stamps and stamp pad
file folders
plastic crate for files
in/out trays
old computer and/or computer keyboard
clipboards
paper clips
pens and pencils
telephones
dry-erase or magnetic board
briefcase
self-adhesive notes
boxes (with sections)
binders and notebooks
hole punch
old office equipment (calculator, fax machine with cord removed, intercom, clock)

Theme Connections

Careers
Community Helpers
Families
Our Community
Tools and Machines

Things to Make

✦ **Paperwork:** Create simple forms such as a job application. Leave spaces for the child to write or draw items such as their name and age, things they do well, and what they would like to do for a job. Cut paper or cardstock in to small rectangles for children to use as business cards.

(continued on the next page)

- **Mailbox:** Obtain boxes that have partitions, cut away top flaps, and lay them on their sides with open area facing out. Print each child's name in a section. Children can use them to sort forms, paperwork, memos, and mail.

Book Suggestions

Frida's Office Day by Thomas P. Lewis

Lyle at the Office by Bernard Waber

Literacy Interactions

- Let children use office machines such as a computer or typewriter to create print. Show them how they can create the letters in their names and other familiar letters using a keyboard. Demonstrate how to use the equipment by typing phrases or stories they dictate. Print their creations and encourage them to add drawings to the text.

- Use a presentation board (magnetic board, paper, or dry-erase board) to display a simple step-by-step sequence of a process, such as a story, cooking project, or how a block creation was constructed. Go through the sequence with the children and demonstrate the process, if possible. Put the presentation board in the Dramatic Play area and invite children to use environmental print or create their own to make their own presentations of things they do (making a bed, brushing teeth, or making a sandwich).

Post Office

Children interact and pretend using environmental print and props related to a post office.

Objectives

Print Awareness: Children will identify and learn about the function of print (such as their names and addresses) in the post office.

Oral Language/Speaking and Listening: Children will listen to information and share knowledge about postal work.

Writing Process: Children will create and receive letters, notes, and cards.

Vocabulary: Children will learn about words associated with letters and other types of mail.

Beginning Reading: Children will identify familiar words such as their names, addresses, and family names and on other text such as letters, notes, and cards when reading their own mail.

Materials and Props

environmental print:
address book
boxes (mailers, cardboard shipping)
business stationery and postcards
change of address cards
envelopes (pre-printed business, express mail, airmail)
greeting cards
maps
newspaper inserts, catalogs, and magazines
postal service stickers
postal stamps and ink pad
pre-printed mailing labels
receipt books
telephone book
zip code directory
cash register
play money, checks, and credit cards
boxes with dividers
mail bags
mail scale
telephone
stickers (for stamps)
tape
blank labels
blank envelopes and stationery

Theme Connections

Community Helpers
Holidays
Post Office

Literacy Interactions

✦ Take children to visit a local post office or other type of postal facility. Provide a list of items (see Materials and Props above) for the guide to identify during the tour. Ask the children to recall types of print and mail they saw and heard about. Add environmental print from the post office to the Dramatic Play area and invite children to bring in other similar items to include.

✦ Create a mail-sorting box. Obtain boxes that contain partitions (used to pack glass jars or bottles) and cut off the top flaps. Place the box on its side with the open area facing out. Print a child's name or other sorting criteria inside each section, such as color, number, letter, and shape. Ask the children about mail sorting they have seen. If possible, look for a mailbox or sorting box in their

(continued on the next page)

learning environment or in the community. Identify how they are labeled with names or numbers to help sort the mail. Provide children with opportunities to create mail to sort into the mail-sorting box during imaginative play. Supply tools such as letter, number, and animal stamps and stamp pads for children to use to identify mail for sorting.

✦ Staple several pieces of paper together to form an address book. Print each child's name in large letters on a page. Add other information, such as an identifying letter or number, last name, name of town, street name, and zip code to create an "address" for each child. Invite the children to use the address book to dictate or write on the mail they create. Provide a bag for children to drop the mail in. Role play being a delivery person. Say the address or hold up mail for children to identify or to sort into mailboxes.

✦ Invite the children as a group to write or compose a letter to their mothers, fathers, grandparents, or friends. They can ask for information, send a greeting or thank you, and so on. During the activity, discuss the parts and purposes of a letter or card, such as date, address, salutation, and message. Provide materials for children to create and write their own letters and cards. When they are finished, walk to a mailbox or post office to mail the letters. Extend the activity by providing materials in the Dramatic Play area for children to write letters.

✦ Ask children's parents, families, and friends to write simple notes and letters to "send" or sort into mailboxes. Prepare extra notes or invite other adults in the learning environment to send notes to the mailboxes. This could include special announcements, holiday greetings, thank you notes, and congratulations. Let children "read," share, and use them during imaginative play.

Book Suggestions

Dear Daddy by John Schindel
A Letter to Amy by Ezra Jack Keats
Mailing May by Michael O. Tunnell
The Post Office Book: Mail and How It Moves by Gail Gibbons

Travel

Children interact and pretend using environmental print and props related to travel.

Objectives

Print Awareness: Children will learn about the function of print related to travel as it appears in brochures, signs, travel offices, and airports.

Vocabulary: Children will learn about and use words and print associated with travel.

Oral Language/Speaking and Listening: Children will tell about and listen to information and descriptions about travel destinations.

Writing Process: Children will create print by making itineraries, scrapbooks, and passports to use in imaginative play.

Materials and Props

environmental print:
airline brochures
airline tickets and other types of tickets (see page 239)
airline, train, and bus membership or ticket cards
children's books about various places
foreign language books
globe
itineraries
maps
money (national and foreign)
passports
postcards from different places
telephone book
travel and tourism catalogs and magazines
travel pamphlets and posters
folders
pencils
old computer
stamp pads and stamps
stapler
cash register or box
telephone

Theme Connections

Cultural Awareness
Transportation
Travel and Vacations

Literacy Interactions

✦ Introduce vocabulary associated with travel using environmental print. Incorporate words such as "itinerary," "cruise," "hotel," "motel," "museum," "airplane," "boarding pass," "luggage," and "passport."

(contnued on the next page)

◆ Visit a city travel and business office, travel agency, airport, or train station to locate print and collect brochures, discarded signs, and posters to use in dramatic play. Write letters to various national and state travel and tourism departments to obtain more brochures. Create a brochure display board using pocket charts or clear vinyl shoe racks. Use pictures and words to label the pockets by categories, such as airline, hotel, resorts, and museums. Invite the children to look at, read, and sort the brochures after discussing the categories on the display pockets. Read excerpts from the brochures as children show interest. Assist the children in dictating or writing simple itineraries or creating scrapbooks of places they would like to visit.

◆ Invite children to bring in and share print information, food, cultural items, and stories about places they have heard about, lived in, and traveled to. Plot places on a large map together. Point out familiar print such as countries, states, cities, and park names on the map. Provide passports (small pieces of paper stapled together with construction paper cover) and stickers or stamps representing other countries, gold seals, and child photos for children to record the travels they have heard about. Put the map and additional passports in the Dramatic Play area.

Variation

◆ Incorporate environmental print related to a specific culture, country, or language as an imaginary place to visit in dramatic play. Add related clothing, books, empty food containers, toys, and so on.

Book Suggestions

ABCDrive! by Naomi Howland
Arthur's Family Vacation by Marc Brown
As the Crow Flies: A First Book of Maps by Gail Hartman
Clifford Takes a Trip by Norman Bridwell
Dinosaur's Travel by Laura Krasny Brown and Marc Brown
My Family Vacation by Dayal Kaur Khalsa
My Map Book by Sara Fanelli
Round Trip by Ann Jonas
Signs on the Road by Mary Hill

Pet Store

Children interact and pretend using environmental print and props related to a pet store.

Objectives

Print Awareness: Children will learn the function of print in providing information about pet care.

Writing Process: Children will use print related to pets and pet care in writing activities.

Oral Language/Speaking and Listening: Children will share stories about pets and listen to others tell about pets and their care.

Phonological/Phonemic Awareness: Children will practice skills such as letter sound recognition, word families, and rhyming using words related to pet words.

Beginning Reading: Children will identify pet words as beginning sight words through dramatic play and matching activities.

Comprehension: Children will share what they know about pet care after listening and reading activities.

Materials and Props

environmental print:
books and magazines about pets
clean, empty pet food and treat boxes or bag
clip-on name badges
pet care brochures and books
pet catalog or price list
pet identification tags
posters of pets
sales circulars from pet stores
sealed cans of pet food
cash register
play money, checks, and credit cards
plastic pet food and water bowls
plastic bug boxes
small animal/bird cages and pet carriers
plastic crates or baskets
stuffed animals (dogs, cats, birds, rabbits)
plastic animals (insects, fish, snakes, mice)
boxes
leashes and collars
grooming brushes
ribbons

Theme Connections

Community Helpers
Families
Farms
Pets
Zoo

Literacy Interactions

✦ Create a sign for each type of pet. Print or type simple words on large paper ("dog" or "cat") and cut out pictures of the animals from magazines or brochures. Glue pictures to the signs. Children can use the signs in their "pet store." If desired, put the signs on display boxes or baskets. Give children self-adhesive labels with pet words printed on them (or let them write the words) to adhere to the pets in the store. Encourage them to match the pet to the area in the store in which it belongs using the labels and signs.

✦ Invite children to bring in stuffed or plastic "pets" from home. Write the name of each one on a self-adhesive blank label and put it on the animal. Encourage the children to share stories about their pets. Write about the adventures they have had together.

(continued on the next page)

- Collect canned pet foods to use in dramatic play, then donate them to an animal shelter or pet care clinic. Use the opportunity to talk about the responsibilities involved in taking care of various types of pets. Encourage children to create "pet menus" to use in dramatic play gluing labels and box fronts from empty pet food to cardboard or cardstock. Prepare a menu for each type of pet.
- Introduce pet words ("dog," "cat," "fish," "mice") as beginning sound recognition, word family building, rhyming, or sight words. Ask the children to think of other words that have the same characteristic of study. For example, a word family for "cat" includes the words "mat," "rat," and "sat."
- Visit a pet shop or invite a veterinarian to visit to talk about how to care for various types of pets. Ask for print information about pets. Discuss brochures and books about pet care. Make a Pet Book with the children. Collect pictures and environmental print related to various kinds of pets, such as birds, dogs, cats, or lizards. Put the print into a blank book made from paper stapled together or an empty photo album. Encourage children to dictate information about each pet and add it to the book. Put the book in the Dramatic Play area.

Variations

- Use the same activities in zoo imaginative play.
- Make a "puppy chow snack" together using a combination of cereals or some other trail mix-type recipe (see recipe on page 242).

Book Suggestions

Arthur's Pet Business by Marc Tolon Brown

Come to the Pet Shop by Ruth Tensen

Fish (All About Pets) by Helen Frost and Gail Saunders-Smith

I Need a Snake by Lynne Jonell

I Want to Be a Veterinarian by Stephanie Maze and Catherine O'Neill
    Grace

Pet Shop by Frank Endersby

Pet Show by Ezra Jack Keats

The Pet Shop Mouse by Judie Schrecker

The Puppy Who Wanted a Boy by Jane Thayer

Gardening Center

Children interact and pretend using environmental print and props related to gardening.

Objectives

Print Awareness: Children will experience plant and other garden-related print through imaginative play.

Vocabulary: Children will use garden-related environmental print to learn new vocabulary.

Writing Process: Children will make garden plans by drawing and writing.

Phonics/Decoding: Children will sort garden-related environmental print by alphabet letters.

Materials and Props

environmental print:
children's gardening, tree, and
    plant books
commercial plastic garden
    stakes that come with plants
gardening and seed catalogs
planting calendars
posters of flowers, vegetables,
    and fruit
seed packets
plastic flower pots and shovels
plastic plants, flowers, fruits,
    and vegetables
watering cans
buckets
plastic hoe and rake
artificial turf scraps or green
    door mat
tongue depressors
baskets

Materials and Props (continued)

cash register
money, credit cards, checks
aprons with pockets
garden gloves, rubber boots, and sun hats
dirt
drop cloth or tarp for floor
plastic tubs or sensory table
garden hose
notebooks
pencils

Theme Connections

Gardening and Plants
Science and Nature
Seasons

Things to Make

✦ **Seed Packets:** Laminate seed packets or cover them with clear contact paper to use in pretend planting activities.

Literacy Interactions

✦ Make playdough "dirt" using a favorite playdough recipe (see recipes on page 241); add brown food coloring to create playdough "dirt." Put in plastic trays or flowerpots for children to "plant" with. Also provide real dirt for them to experiment with. Encourage children to use plastic plant markers to identify what they planted. Ask questions such as, "What kind of plant is identified with the marker?" "What fruit, flower, or vegetable will grow in it?" Use this opportunity to review plant- and gardening-related vocabulary.

✦ Introduce the concept of planning a garden with the children. Use seed packets and catalogs to get ideas for what to put on a garden map. Discuss the types of fruits, vegetables, and flowers they like. Provide large pieces of paper for them create maps of what and where they would plant. Encourage use in imaginative play.

(continued on the next page)

✦ Make a Planting Book for each child by stapling together pieces of paper. Encourage them to use their books to map plantings, draw pictures of their plants, tape empty seed packets, and so on. Add calendar pages for children to document when they plant their seeds. Use Planting Books as an opportunity to provide letter recognition and alphabet order. Label each page with a letter. Provide seed packets and pictures from catalogs to put in the book to use as a dictionary or catalog in imaginative play. (See "Seed Packet Pocket Books" on page 46 for more ideas.)

Variation

✦ Take gardening items to an outdoor learning area for further play.

Book Suggestions

From Seed to Plant by Gail Gibbons
The Gardener by Sarah Stewart
Growing Vegetable Soup by Lois Ehlert
The Magic School Bus Plants Seeds by Joanna Cole
Planting a Rainbow by Lois Ehlert
Garden by Robert Maass

Construction Work

Children interact and pretend using environmental print and props related to construction in the Dramatic Play or Block areas.

Objectives

Print Awareness: Children will learn the function of environmental print related to construction work and use it in imaginative play.

Vocabulary: Children will use vocabulary related to construction and tools during imaginative play

Writing Process: Children will create signs, blueprints, and forms.

Materials and Props

environmental print:
    advertisements from hardware and home supply stores
    blueprints
    order forms
    pictures and books about buildings, roads, and tools
    road signs
    tool catalogs
play mobile phones
hard hats, safety goggles, work boots, and bright-colored vests
aprons or belts for carrying tools
tools and toolboxes
blocks (cardboard, wooden, boxes, foam)
plastic PVC pipe
linoleum scraps and carpet squares
toy trucks and machinery
pencils
graph paper
poster board and paint sticks for making signs
clipboards

Theme Connections

Community Helpers
Construction
Health and Safety
Tools and Machines
Transportation

Literacy Interactions

✦ Invite a contractor, road engineer, or architect to visit and bring tools, safety signs, and so on to demonstrate what he or she does. Ask the visitor to give examples of how he or she uses print at work and incorporate associated vocabulary. Incorporate new concepts and print into the Dramatic Play area.

(continued on the next page)

◆ Incorporate vocabulary related to safety signs into the center. Talk about the print and visual clues that convey messages on the signs, such as "danger," "caution," and "stop." Invite children to make their own signs for the construction area, using materials such as colored construction paper, markers, lettering, tape, and scissors.

◆ Show children how blueprints are used to provide information about how a building or road will be constructed. Provide materials for children to make their own blueprints, including blue construction paper, white chalk, and rulers. Read books and magazines about buildings to provide context. Demonstrate how they can use their blueprints to create their own structures out of blocks, wood, boxes, and so on. Provide scrap wood pieces for children to glue together to create their own structures.

Book Suggestions

Building a House by Byron Barton

A Busy Day at the Building Site by Phillippe Dupasquier

Construction Workers (Community Helpers) by Tami Deedrick

How a House Is Built by Gail Gibbons

New Road! by Gail Gibbons

The Night Worker by Kate Banks

Road Builders by B.G. Hennessy

Road Signs by Margery Cuyler

Those Building Men by Angela Johnson

Chapter

9

Connecting Home and School With Environmental Print

✦ In each activity in this chapter, the **objectives** are listed in order of difficulty—use them according to the skill level of the children in your class.

✦ In each activity in this chapter, the **literacy interactions** are listed in order of difficulty; use them according to the abilities and interests of the children.

Time Together Bags

All of the activities in this chapter require the use of "time together" bags. Periodically, children use "time together" bags to take home environmental print activities to do with family and friends.

Objectives

Oral Language/Speaking and Listening: Children will share their ideas of ways to use environmental print at home and talk about their experiences after they do the activity.

Materials

solid-colored fabric bags or
    paper bags
permanent or fabric markers
fabric paint for fabric bags
stickers
laminate or clear contact paper
paper

Literacy Interactions

✦ On each bag, write or paint the words "time together" or something similar to identify its use. Add class, center, or school identifying information as well. Encourage children to decorate the bags. All of the activities in this chapter involve children bringing home environmental print activities to work on with their parents. For each activity, give each child a "time together" bag with laminated instructions and any items needed to assist in doing the activity. (When writing instructions, leave space at the bottom to add notes.)

✦ Before sending the bags home, talk with the children about the project. Build excitement and brainstorm ideas of how to expand the activity for the week. When children return with their bags, encourage them to share their experiences and creations.

Note: It is important to contact the children's parents or caregivers at the beginning of the school year to address the value of these activities and opportunities for their input into their child's literacy development. If desired, enlist parent volunteers to help put packs together (see Parent Letter Sample on page 232).

Chalk Chat

Children take this activity home in "time together" bags and use the supplies to create their own interactive roads, trails, and signs to use in play.

Objectives

Print Awareness: Children will look at environmental print as part of a direction-following activity.

Vocabulary: Children will practice using directional vocabulary as they create chalk roads and trails.

Writing Process: Children will use chalk to create drawings, symbols, signs, and familiar words to represent familiar places and signage.

Oral Language/Speaking and Listening: Children will listen to and follow one- and two-step directions for making chalk roads or trails.

Materials

photocopied safety and traffic sign patterns (see page 240)
sidewalk chalk
toy cars, trucks, and airplanes (optional)
small boxes (see "Box Business" on page 73)
"time together" bags
paper and pen

Theme Connections

Community Helpers
Construction
Farms
Health and Safety
Maps
Our Community
Transportation

Literacy Interactions

✦ Introduce safety and traffic signs to the children by showing them photocopied safety and traffic signs. Let children use sidewalk chalk outdoors to create roads, trails, and signs for toy vehicles, tricycles, walking, and so on. Encourage them to create signs ("stop," "go," "one way") using chalk.

(continued on the next page)

♦ With the children, create a list of "time together" opportunities for children to do with family members. Put a copy of the list and sidewalk chalk in each "time together" bag for children to bring home.

Time Together Opportunities

Use these ideas to explore environmental print with your child.

♦ Use small boxes (shoeboxes) to create buildings for the roads. Provide newspaper inserts for your child to cut out and glue on the boxes to create department stores, restaurants, grocery stores, and so on. Use chalk to label places along the road or trail, such as "park," "school," and "pond."

♦ Together with your child, use sidewalk chalk to create roads, trails, and signs for toy vehicles or tricycles. Work together to add signs such as "stop" and "go."

♦ Play a direction-following game. Use directional words ("back," "forward," right," "left") to give your child directions for places to go on the chalk road ("stand on the 'stop' sign"). Let him or her move or use a toy vehicle as directions are given. Let him or her give you directions to follow, too. If desired, cut out the bottom of a large, lightweight box and decorate it to look like a vehicle using scraps of paper, collage materials, environmental print (such as brochures from car dealerships), glue, and so on. Encourage your child to step into the "vehicle," hold onto the sides, and maneuver through the chalk roads and trails as you provide directions.

Variation

♦ Instead of chalk, send home old, solid-colored shower curtains or plastic/vinyl tablecloths and permanent markers for children to make roads. Ask parents and children to tape environmental print on the tablecloths to make interactive road maps and signs.

Environmental Print Books

Children bring home environmental print books in the "time together" bags. The child and family member use other materials in the bags to create their own environmental print book.

Objectives

Print Awareness: Children will recognize the function of familiar print.

Oral Language/Speaking and Listening: Children will listen to stories and share their ideas to create their own books.

Writing Process: Children will use environmental print, drawings, familiar words, and dictated experiences to create their own books.

Comprehension: Children will connect environmental print in books to real-life experiences.

Beginning Reading: Children will practice reading familiar words.

Materials

children's books about environmental print (see Environmental Print Book List on page 230)

"time together" bags

paper

stapler

scissors

glue

markers or crayons

Theme Connections

All About Me	Holidays
Camping	School
Families	Sports
Grocery Store	Travel and Vacation

Literacy Interactions

✦ Read environmental print books (see suggestions on page xxx) to the children several times. Encourage them to fill in familiar words as they are able. Make several books by folding and stapling pieces of paper together. Put a couple of blank books and other materials (such as scissors, glue, markers, or crayons) in the "time together" bags for children to bring home. Include published environmental print books, if possible.

✦ Make a list of "time together" opportunities to send home in the bags.

Time Together Opportunities

Use these ideas to explore environmental print with your child.

✦ Read the books with your child. Encourage him or her to fill in familiar words or read as able. Talk about where print can be found in your home or community. Ask questions about what the print means and what it is used for.

✦ Encourage your child to create his or her own environmental print book. Provide catalogs, newspaper inserts, and so on for your child to cut out items of interest, such as favorite foods, toys, and movies. Help your child glue the pictures into the book. Ask your child to dictate words and stories about the pictures for you to write in the book. Read together often!

✦ Ask your child to collect environmental print from a vacation or trip to add to a travel book. Encourage your child to use the print to share stories and recollections by writing or dictating them in the book.

Looking Out for Letters

Children take home the activity in the "time together" bags and cut out environmental print that pertains to specific letters or letter sounds.

Objectives

Print Awareness: Children will look for print in their environment.

Writing Process: Children will dictate and/or write words found in environmental print.

Oral Language/Speaking and Listening: Children will tell a story or rhyme using environmental print.

Phonics: Children will practice letter and corresponding beginning sound recognition by locating related environmental print in their homes.

Materials

small lunch bags or zipper-
    closure plastic bags
scissors
markers
chart paper
"time together" bags

Theme Connections

All About Me
Alphabet
Holidays

Literacy Interactions

✦ With the children, brainstorm a list of words that begin with a specific alphabet letter or letters. Document their responses on chart paper. Encourage them to add items from the learning environment, such as signs or print on materials and games, to the list. Invite the children to bring in some of the environmental print they find at home to share and add to the list of words. Encourage them to copy the words onto the list.

✦ Write the letter or letters of study on the outside of lunch bags or plastic bags, one letter per bag. Make a list of "time together" opportunities. Put the letter bags, "time together" opportunities (see below), and scissors (optional) in the "time together" bags. Send home one of the following ideas.

Time Together Opportunities

Use these ideas to explore environmental print with your child.

✦ Go on an environmental print search in one room such as the kitchen. Encourage your child to find as many items as he or she can that begin with a specific letter. Print the words or let your child copy them on slips of paper. Read the words together and use them to make up a silly story or rhyme.

✦ Provide catalogs, newspapers, and product containers for your child to cut out print. Read the print together. Ask your child to listen for beginning or ending sounds as you read each item. Help your child sort the words by letter sound into a paper or plastic bag containing the matching letter.

    Note: Use collected items for "Ch, Ch, Cheese Train" on page 34, "I Spy" Bulletin Board on page, or "Alphabet Scrapbook" on page 47.

Variation

✦ Send home the activity before a holiday break and encourage the children to find environmental print to share as part of telling about their break.

My Own Signs

Children bring home the activity in the "time together" bags to create their own signs to use in play.

Objectives

Print Awareness: Children will understand the function of print on signs is used to identify places and provide information.

Phonics: Children will identify alphabet letters and sounds on signs they create.

Phonological/Phonemic Awareness: Children will practice identifying syllables, letter sounds, and phonemes using signs they have made.

Materials

environmental print from community businesses

safety and traffic sign patterns (see page 240)

"time together" bags

empty film canisters

straws or dowels cut into 4" to 6" lengths

squares of cardstock, construction paper, or cardboard

scissors

clear packing tape or clear contact paper

Theme Connections

Community Helpers

Construction

Farms

Health and Safety

Our Community

Transportation

Preparation

1. Make a hole in the bottom of each film canister. Turn it over and insert one dowel or straw into each film canister to create a sign holder.

2. Place several sign holders, instructions on how to make a sign, copies of safety and traffic sign patterns, ideas for use (see below), and clear packing tape or contact paper into the "time together" bags.

Literacy Interactions

◆ Discuss the meanings of safety and traffic signs. Compile a list as they dictate. Ask the children, "What places do you visit or see in your community that you could create signs for?"

◆ Create a list of "time together" opportunities to send home appropriate for the developmental level of the children.

Time Together Opportunities

Use these ideas to explore environmental print with your child.

◆ Encourage your child to locate and cut out environmental print that represents places in the community, such as grocery stores, restaurants, schools, and gas stations. Use these to make signs. Tape the signs to the sign holders by carefully folding a piece of contact paper or clear packing tape (larger than the sign) around both the dowel and sign. Or, glue the sign to a piece of

(continued on the next page)

construction paper, write the identifying name on the other side of the paper, and cover it with clear contact paper. Encourage your child to look for the signs he or she created when out in the community and get ideas to make more.

◆ Create street signs for your home address, family addresses, workplace, and so on. Add traffic and safety signs.

◆ Encourage your child to use the signs to play with blocks, cars, maps, and roads. Make roads on an old shower curtain or on your driveway with sidewalk chalk. Add signs and cars.

◆ Talk about the words on the signs during play. Ask questions and create dialogue. For example, "What is the name of the store you are building?" "Where are you driving your car next?"

◆ Encourage your child to sort signs by type of business or service offered, for example, restaurants, grocery, schools, and gas stations. Challenge him or her to sort the signs by beginning letter.

◆ Play "Guess the Sign." Put some signs where your child can see them. Describe one using such clues as beginning letter sound, syllables, and word families, along with characteristics about the sign. For example, "Can you spy signs that start with an /s/ sound? One is red and the other is a place that serves sandwiches." Encourage your child to listen and identify which one you are describing. Invite him or her to identify other environmental print or words that fit the literacy characteristics.

Note: Incorporate this activity as an extension of "Simple Signs" (see page 70).

Variation

◆ Poke a hole in a plastic cup, turn it upside down, and insert an empty paper towel tube to make a larger sign holder.

Favorite Cut-Ups

Children bring home the activity in the "time together" bags and use the supplies to cut out and use a variety of environmental print.

Objectives

Print Awareness: Children will identify and cut out familiar environmental print and pictures.

Phonological/Phonemic Awareness: Children will identify environmental print words by sounds and/or syllables.

Phonics: Children will practice letter and corresponding beginning sound recognition by cutting out related environmental print.

Beginning Reading: Children will locate and cut out sight words and compound words.

Writing Process: Children will practice fine motor skills needed for writing by cutting and circling environmental print.

Materials

newspaper inserts, catalogs, and
    magazines
"time together" bags
scissors
paper
glue
zipper-closure plastic bags

Theme Connections

Babies	Grocery Store
Colors	Health and Safety
Community Helpers	Holidays
Farms	Sports
Food and Nutrition	Transportation

Literacy Interactions

✦ Encourage the children to cut out and use environmental print of their choice as part of preparing to do the "time together" activity. Make a list of "time together" opportunities to send home. Send home the list, environmental print, child-safe scissors, glue, and zipper-closure plastic bags. Use current themes and literacy skills as guides.

Time Together Opportunities

Use these ideas to explore environmental print with your child.

✦ Encourage your child to cut out pictures and print related to a topic. For example, find many different flavors and kinds of ice cream. Use these to introduce and talk about new, related vocabulary, such as "butterscotch," "sherbet," and "frozen."

✦ Encourage your child to cut out pictures of favorite animals, healthy foods, toys, and so on. Point out the identifying words.

✦ Together, circle or underline the identifying words on the print to draw attention to it.

✦ Help your child identify and cut out environmental print that begins with a specific letter or letter sound.

✦ Encourage your child to make a collage on a piece of paper with environmental print. Use it to play "I Spy" by calling out an item by name and encouraging your child to find it on the collage.

✦ Give your child a short list of household items, such as margarine and salad dressing. Read it together and ask him or her to find and cut out coupons for them.

✦ Find environmental print that contains compound words or words with various syllables. Together with your child identify where the words should be divided or segmented. Glue to paper and cut apart at dividing points. Say each part as you put them together.

My Menu

Children take home the activity in the "time together" bags and use the supplies and environmental print to create a menu to use in family cooking projects.

Objectives

Print Awareness: Children will identify and cut out familiar foods from environmental print to create a menu.

Writing Process: Children will create and write a menu.

Phonics: Children will practice letter and corresponding beginning sound recognition.

Vocabulary: Children will use environmental print to learn about words related to food groups.

Materials

newspaper inserts from grocery stores and magazines
scissors
glue
large paper (11" x 14") or smaller paper
pencils, crayons, or markers
"time together" bags

Theme Connections

All About Me
Alphabet
Cooking
Families
Food and Nutrition
Grocery Store
Holidays

Preparation

1. Create blank menus by dividing large pieces of paper into menu sections. (See page 172.) Another option is to staple several pieces of smaller paper together to create a menu book.

Literacy Interactions

✦ Use carryout or old menus from restaurants to introduce this activity. Encourage the children to locate familiar print on the menus, such as "milk" and "pizza." Ask questions such as, "What is the same among these menus?" "What is different?"

✦ Talk about the parts of a menu. Use the menus in conjunction with discussion related to nutrition and the food groups. Ask, "What are some things on the menu that fit into the food groups?"

✦ Make snack menus with the children. Encourage the children to save and locate environmental print to put on the menu. Use for planning snacks or identifying snack choices.

✦ Make a list of "time together" opportunities. Put blank menus, "time together" opportunities (see below), environmental print (newspaper inserts from grocery stores and magazines), scissors, and glue into "time together" bags.

Time Together Opportunities

Use these ideas to explore environmental print with your child.

✦ Plan a meal for a special day together, such as a holiday or birthday. Write each item on the menu. Encourage your child to find and cut out environmental print that corresponds to the choices on the menu. Display or use the menu during the special event.

✦ Plan several meal menus using what your child knows about the food groups. Ask him or her to look through environmental print to find and cut out favorites in each group. Print identifying words under each item as it is added to "food group" sections on the menu. Use the menus as a way to involve your child in meal planning.

Fruit/Vegetable

carrot   peach   tomato

Dairy

yogurt   ice cream   cheese

Cereal & Bread

crackers   noodles   pretzel

Meat

steak   fish

chicken

Fats / Sweets

cookies   candy

butter

✦ Create a survey to poll family members about their favorite foods. Encourage your child to cut out food from environment print and glue to a piece of paper. Encourage your child to ask others about their favorites and document their responses.

✦ Create a menu with every food item starting with the same letter or letter sounds (for example, /c/ for *corn* and *cobbler* or /ch/ for *chicken* and *cheese*). Encourage your child to find pictures of food beginning with that letter using environmental print. Choose several items to fix for a fun snack or meal.

Note: Save the real take-out menus as well as the menus created in the learning environment to add to restaurant dramatic play (see "Restaurant" on page 172).

My Shopping List

Children take home the activity in the "time together" bags and use cut-out environmental print to create a shopping list.

Objectives

Print Awareness: Children will use environmental print to match with words on a shopping list.

Phonics: Children will use knowledge of alphabet letters and their sounds to create a shopping list.

Oral Language/Speaking and Listening: Children will use environmental print to dictate or share information needed for shopping lists.

Writing Process: Children will cut out environmental print and write and/or draw shopping lists to use in locating items on shopping trips.

Vocabulary: Children will learn new vocabulary words as they create shopping lists.

Materials

newspaper inserts and coupons
cardboard or poster board
paper and stapler
magnet tape
glue, scissors
"time together" bags

Theme Connections

Cooking
Families
Food and Nutrition
Grocery Store
Holidays

Preparation

1. Create blank shopping notepads by cutting pieces of paper into approximately 4" x 11" pieces. Staple the pieces of paper together. See page 237.
2. If desired, attach a piece of magnet tape to a piece of cardboard cut to the same size of each notepad. Glue the cardboard to the back of the notepad to create a magnetic pad.

Literacy Interactions

✦ To prepare the children for the take-home activity, together create a shopping list of favorite foods or foods related to a class cooking project. Write the items as they are dictated. Encourage the children to use what they know about letters, letter sounds, and so on to help in spelling the words.

✦ Create a list of "time together" opportunities to send home. Put a blank shopping notepad, "time together" ideas (see below), scissors, and a glue stick (optional) in "time together" bags.

Time Together Opportunities

Use these ideas to explore environmental print with your child.

✦ Read several favorite recipes to your child and choose one or more to make. Print or have your child copy the ingredients onto the shopping notepad. Together look through your kitchen and locate items on the list. Draw attention to the environmental print as it matches words on the list. Cross off items as they are located. Talk about new words (ingredients) that may be unfamiliar to your child. Use the list when locating remaining items while shopping. Again, draw your child's attention to the print as you work together to locate the items.

✦ Together create a list of essential household items and food that the family uses on a regular basis. Encourage your child to cut out environmental print that matches the items on this list. Glue the print next to the words on the list. Put the list in a location where your child can see it, such as the refrigerator. Guide your child to refer to it periodically to see if any of the items need to be added to the shopping list.

Signs for My Home

Children take home the activity in the "time together" bags and use the supplies to create their own labels for things around the house.

Objectives

Print Awareness: Children will learn about the function of print in their environment.

Phonics: Children will use what they know about letters and letter sounds to identify and label items.

Writing Process: Children will create and write their own signs to label items around their homes.

Beginning Reading: Children will label and read items around their homes using familiar words such as their name, family names, and sight words ("bed," "door," and "book").

Materials

sticky notes or squares of paper and tape
crayons, pencil, or markers
"time together" bags

Theme Connections

All About Me
Alphabet
Tools and Machines

Literacy Interactions

✦ Before the children take the bags home, encourage them to dictate a list of places around their homes or bedrooms to label. Use this list to create sign ideas to send home.

✦ Ask the children to write a letter on each sticky note or paper square (letters they have already learned). Put these into the bags. Ask them to use these to identify and label items around their homes that start with the same letter. Encourage them to make a list (with the help of an adult) of the items that they found for each letter.

✦ Use sight word lists that the children are working on to create a list of items for them to find around their homes to label (for example, a rug, table, clock, and can). Review the list before putting it in the bags.

Variation

✦ Ask children to make safety signs ("Stop," "Danger," "One Way") to post around their homes where they are needed. They can engage family members to follow the directions.

"Signs for My Home" Letter and Checklist

Following is a sample letter and checklist to send home to parents in "time together" bags. Put sticky notes or squares of paper, crayons or a pencil, and a photocopied list of "Signs for My Home" (see page 205) into the "time together" bags. (**Note:** Adjust the list and "time together" opportunities to fit the developmental level of the children.)

Dear Parents and Families,

This is a list of items that you and your child can look for around your house. Please print or help your child print the name of the item on the paper squares provided. Attach the signs to each item.

Bed	Cup	Stove
Book	Door	Table
Can	Lamp	Toothbrush
Chair	Rug	Toy
Clock	Sink	Wall

Time Together Opportunities

✦ If your child is learning to recognize or write his or her own name, ask him or her to label his or her belongings. Encourage your child to make a list of the items that they found for each letter.

✦ If your child is beginning to recognize letters or letter sounds, put only the beginning letter for each place or item on the label.

✦ Cut out pictures of household places or items from catalogs, magazines, or newspaper inserts. Glue them on signs with identifying words to assist pre-readers.

✦ Encourage your child to observe as you print the words on the labels. Ask him or her to attach each label to the place it belongs.

✦ Play a game of "mix up." Remove the signs from one room and challenge your child to put them back where they belong.

✦ Put signs on special toys, games, places, and so on. Encourage your child to practice using letter sounds to spell the words on the signs.

Calendar of Activities

Children take home a calendar or list of simple activities involving environmental print to do with their families.

Objectives

Print Awareness: Children will experience and learn about various uses of print in and around their home environment.

Oral Language/Speaking and Listening: Children will share and listen to stories using environmental print.

Writing Process: Children will use environmental print to write, draw, dictate, and create lists, stories, and signs.

Phonics: Children will identify letters and words that contain the same letters as those in their name.

Beginning Reading: Children will "read" familiar environmental print emergently or by sight.

Materials

environmental print (see literacy interactions at right)

blank monthly calendar or typed list of ideas for a month

Theme Connections

Alphabet
Community Helpers
Health and Safety
Our Community
Recycling
Transportation

Literacy Interactions

✦ Choose from the following ideas or create others to put on a calendar or list to send home for children to do with their families. If using a calendar, write or type one simple activity in each blank calendar square. Select activities that can be done easily by families. Invite the children to bring in and share some of the things they enjoyed doing with their families.

 ✦ Pack a picnic. "Read" all the product packaging.
 ✦ Cut out environmental print and make a book.
 ✦ Bring home environmental print from work.
 ✦ Take a field trip to a place in your community and go on a word or letter hunt.
 ✦ Use old greeting cards to make special messages for friends and family.
 ✦ Write special events, holidays, birthdays, and trips on a calendar.
 ✦ Read and follow a recipe together to make a snack.
 ✦ Create a menu of favorite foods using environmental print.
 ✦ Sort contents of a food cabinet by alphabet letters.
 ✦ Read comics from the newspaper together.
 ✦ Go on a word search in a supermarket.
 ✦ Plot where you live on a map.
 ✦ Look for your home address on your mail or your phone number in the phone book.
 ✦ Take a walk and read street signs.
 ✦ Cut out environmental print and tape on toy blocks or cars for signs.
 ✦ Play "grocery store" with clean, empty food containers.
 ✦ Make a collage using environmental print. Play "I Spy."
 ✦ Look for color words in a grocery store or department store.
 ✦ Make play signs that include the names of streets in your neighborhood.
 ✦ Trace or circle numbers or letters in newspaper advertisements.
 ✦ Cut off fronts of cereal boxes or other boxes and make puzzles.
 ✦ Go on a word or letter hunt in each room of your house.
 ✦ Visit a library and go on a word hunt there. Read lots of print!
 ✦ Make blocks and tunnels using empty boxes and pre-printed paper bags.

Cook Together

Children bring home cooking ingredients, measuring utensils (optional), "time together" bags, and a recipe book to cook something with family members.

Objectives

Print Awareness: Children will use and see the value of print to successfully follow a recipe.

Oral Language/Speaking and Listening: Children will listen to a recipe sequence containing environmental print.

Vocabulary: Children will use new vocabulary and language through cooking activities.

Comprehension: Children will make predictions of what will happen as they add the ingredients and what will happen to the mixture as they follow a recipe.

Writing Process: Children will use print as part of dictating or writing a recipe.

Materials

recipe
"time together" bags
paper and pen (for lists)

Theme Connections

Cooking
Cultural Awareness
Food and Nutrition
Holidays

Literacy Interactions

✦ Choose a healthy, simple recipe for children to make at home with their families. Read the recipe with the children several times before sending it home. Encourage them to fill in words and numbers they recognize.

✦ Talk about vocabulary words that are a part of the recipe, such as "measuring cup," "teaspoon," "mixing," and so on. Encourage children to demonstrate actions or find examples of the new vocabulary on the tools or in other recipes.

✦ Encourage children to help create a list of "time together" opportunities to bring home to parents. Place the recipe and a list of "time together" opportunities in the "time together" bags. Suggestions for parents include:

  ✦ Ask your child to identify and locate ingredients in the recipe.

  ✦ Look at the print on measuring utensils together. Match it to the terms used in the recipe. Use terms and ingredient names as they are used in the recipe.

  ✦ Before adding and mixing each ingredient, encourage your child to predict what will happen to the mixture.

  ✦ Make your own book of your favorite recipes together. Invite your child to dictate the ingredients and steps. Look for environmental print that represents the ingredients in it.

  ✦ Encourage your child to "read" the book as you prepare the recipe together.

Variations

✦ Send simple recipe books home with the children that they can keep. (Photocopy to make multiple copies.) Encourage family members to help their child make a list of items needed for the recipe of choice and then locate them together.

✦ Ask children to bring in a recipe that they have made with a family member at home. Incorporate it into a taste-testing party. Invite them to bring one or more of the ingredients in its original container to share as a new vocabulary word.

"I Spy" Search

Children bring home the activity in the "time together" bags and use the supplies to search for places in the community while walking or driving to school, a store, or doctor's office. As they find a place or sign, they circle it on their checklist.

Objectives

Print Awareness: Children will look at and focus on environmental print in their learning area and community to match with words on an "I Spy" checklist.

Phonics: Children will locate and identify print in their community that relates to alphabet letters.

Beginning Reading: Children will read environmental print words in their community by using context clues or by sight.

Materials

environmental print observed in child's environment and community
empty paper towel tubes
scissors
glue
tape
pencil or marker
yarn
clipboard or cardboard with large clip or clothespin
"time together" bags

Theme Connections

Alphabet
Community Helpers
Construction
Farms
Health and Safety
Our Community
Transportation

Preparation

1. Obtain or create clipboards. Make clipboards by attaching a large clip to sturdy cardboard. Tape a pencil or marker to a short piece of yarn and adhere to the top end of the clipboard. (illustration)
2. Make "I Spy" glasses by cutting empty paper towel tubes in half, creating tubes identical in length. Encourage children to decorate them by cutting out environmental print from the community and gluing it collage-style around the tubes. Tape the tubes together side by side to form binoculars.
3. Put a clipboard, "I Spy" glasses, and a pencil or marker into each "time together" bag.

Literacy Interactions

✦ Invite the children to talk about environmental print they recall seeing on their way to school. Print the children's ideas and use them to create the checklist used in the take-home activity.

✦ Before sending home the activity, ask the children to locate and identify places containing print in their learning setting, such as an exit sign, office, and bathroom. Give them picture clues, words, or beginning letters to use in locating the places with print.

✦ Compile a list of alphabetical letters to find or sight words that the children have been learning to send home as an "I Spy" list. Encourage the children to practice locating the items in their learning setting first and then at home.

"I Spy" Letter and Checklist

Following is a sample letter and checklist to send home to parents in "time together" bags. Create a list of specific businesses, recreational places, and signage in the community. Choose places that are observable while walking or in a car. Add the list and "time together" opportunities to the "time together" bags. If desired, glue small pictures of places in the community on the checklist next to the words. Photocopy and use for checklists.

Dear Parents and Families,

This take-home activity provides opportunities for your child to identify places and signs in the community by recognizing the associated print. Encourage your child to identify the places while traveling to school, shopping, and so on. Check off all the places as they are found.

Grocery store	Post office	Fire station
Fast food restaurant	Library	Bank
Ice cream parlor	Department store	Donut shop
Gas station	Discount store	Pharmacy

Time Together Opportunities

✦ Collect environmental print associated with these places and make a collage together.

✦ Make your own "I Spy" checklist to use during a long car trip.

✦ Play an alphabet version of "I Spy." Find environmental print while traveling that begins with every letter of the alphabet or a specific letter sound.

✦ Use a sight word list that your child is working on to create an "I Spy" list. (Sight words can include "go," "stop," "pull," "dog," "blue," "car," and "bus.") Encourage your child to tally every time he or she sees one of the words during travel time.

Camera on My World

Children bring this activity home in "time together" bags and use the supplies to take pictures of environmental print in their community.

Objectives

Print Awareness: Children will take pictures of familiar print in their community.

Writing Process: Children will use photos of environmental print to dictate or write stories.

Phonics: Children will practice letter and corresponding beginning sound recognition when locating and taking pictures of environmental print.

Phonological/Phonemic Awareness: Children will identify multi-syllable words.

Beginning Reading: Children will locate and take pictures of sight words.

Materials

camera and film or disposable
    cameras
photo album (optional)
small notepads (optional)
"time together" bags
paper and pen (for lists)

Theme Connections

All About Me
Community Helpers
Cultural Awareness
Families
Transportation

Literacy Interactions

✦ Use your current classroom theme and/or literacy skills children are learning as a guide for creating a list of pictures for children to take. Literacy skill ideas include identifying letter or letter sounds, sight words, and syllables. Let children practice finding the types of items on the list in the learning environment before taking the activity home. Along with a list of suggested pictures and how many to take, include a list of "time together" opportunities for using the pictures and a camera and film in the "time together" bags.

Time Together Opportunities

Use these ideas to explore environmental print with your child.

✦ Create a story about the area in which you and your child live using photos of such things as street signs, a local grocery store, post office, and so on. Encourage your child to share his or her observations about the places in the photos. Read it together.

✦ Take a walk in the community, and if possible, go to a mall or shopping center. Look for environmental print that fits the given recommendations. Take pictures and copy words into a small notepad. Count how many are found. Which places have more related to the objectives? Are any of the print items the same or similar?

✦ Create a scrapbook of pictures and environmental print from home as it pertains to current theme or objectives (letter recognition, sounds, and so on). Write the identifying words under each item. Add to it as more items are found. Look in the refrigerator, cabinets, garage, and so on.

✦ Enlist families to develop film to use for projects at home and/or in the learning environment, as appropriate. Use the developed pictures to create a community map together and put in the building area. **Note:** See "Town Map" on page 75.

Variations

✦ Take photos of print in other languages to integrate into a study of various cultures.

✦ Integrate this activity with "I Spy Search" on page 209.

Linking Environmental Print With My Community

◆ In each activity in this chapter, the **objectives** are listed in order of difficulty—use them according to the skill level of the children in your class.

◆ In each activity in this chapter, the **literacy interactions** are listed in order of difficulty; use them according to the abilities and interests of the children.

Signs and Safety

Children go on a walk or trip to look for and learn about traffic and safety signs.

Objectives

Print Awareness: Children will identify the function of print and color as it is used in signs.

Vocabulary: Children will learn about color relationship to the meaning of traffic and safety signs.

Materials

traffic and safety signs
pencils, markers, and crayons
paper or notebooks
traffic and safety sign patterns
    (see appendix)

Theme Connections

Community Helpers
Health and Safety
Our Community
Transportation

Literacy Interactions

✦ Create a list of traffic and safety signs that are used frequently in the child's community, such as "Stop," "Walk," "Don't Walk," "School Crossing," "Danger," "Exit," and "Poison." If desired, include images of the signs from the appendix (see page 240) or from clip art. Make copies of the checklist and give each child a copy to take along on a walk or during a trip. Each time they locate a sign, ask them to put a mark beside it on their list. Talk about where the sign is placed. Ask questions such as, "Why do you think it is there?" "What is it trying to tell us?" "What colors are used in the sign?"

✦ Talk about how colors on signs are used to convey meaning. Find signs that have the color red on them, for example, "Stop," "Danger," and "Do Not Enter." Ask what they have in common with each other. Point out that many signs that contain the color red often signify danger or to stop doing something. Explain that the color green on signs often means that it is okay to go or identifies the location of something, such as street signs and highway signs. The colors yellow or orange on signs often gives a message to convey caution or to slow down, for example, "School Crossing" or "Caution." Look for colors on signs while on a walk. Invite children to find exceptions to these "rules" and explain what other colors mean on signs as you find them.

✦ Have children match or identify signs without color clues. Use black and white traffic and safety sign patterns to match with purchased sign stickers or signs with color (see page 240).
Note: Provide children with materials to make their own traffic and safety signs (see "Simple Signs" on page 70). Play games such as "Sign Signals" on page 94 and "Stroll to the Store" on page 95 to help children practice reading and understanding the sign meanings.

Crayon Rubbings: Signs on the Move

Children obtain crayon rubbings from raised surfaces containing environmental print on walks or field trips.

Objectives

Print Awareness: Children will expand awareness of letter shapes and forms by obtaining crayon rubbings from environmental print.

Writing Process: Children will practice small motor control by making crayon rubbings.

Oral Language/Speaking and Listening: Children will share their observations, stories, and understanding of print obtained through a crayon rubbing activity.

Phonics: Children will look for specific letters in raised environmental print.

Materials

raised surfaces that contain print
    (signs, labels, symbols)
crayons
thin or transparent paper
    (8 ½" x 11")
masking tape

Theme Connections

Careers
Community Helpers
Construction
Fire Station
Grocery Store
Health and Safety
Our Community
Restaurant
Transportation
Zoo

Literacy Interactions

✦ Using a piece of paper and an unwrapped crayon, demonstrate how to obtain a crayon rubbing from a raised surface with print by laying thin paper over the item and rubbing the surface with a crayon. Bring crayons, paper, and tape along on a walk or field trip for children to use. Invite children to use their sense of touch to locate raised environmental print as they explore. Ask them to close their eyes and try to identify letters using their sense of touch. Tape paper to raised areas and guide children to take rubbings of the print. (Make sure to ask permission as needed for children to use surfaces to obtain rubbings.)

✦ Ask children to obtain rubbings from raised print containing specific alphabet letters. For example, ask them to find words that have or start with the letter "p," such as "push" on a door. Invite the children to share observations and comparisons about the letters in their rubbings. Ask them where they found the item and what information each provides. Compile the rubbings into a book or display for children to continue to look at and discuss.

Trip Through Town Travel Log

Children use travel logs to document the sequence of events while on a walk or field trip.

Objectives

Print Awareness: Children will locate and identify print while on a walk or field trip.

Writing Process: Children will use drawing, writing, and dictation to communicate observations regarding print and other experiences during a walk or field trip.

Oral Language/Speaking and Listening: Children will share information including descriptions of environmental print using their senses.

Vocabulary: Children will learn, reinforce understanding, and incorporate new words into descriptions and collected information in a travel log.

Materials

community business logos, signs, labels, and brochures gathered from a field trip or walk

notebook or paper

yarn or string

pencil

tape

Theme Connections

Community Helpers   Our Community

Cultural Awareness   Pets

Grocery Store   Post Office

Maps   Zoo

Literacy Interactions

✦ Invite children to tell about their experiences going on trips, walks, or visits to places such as zoos, museums, parks, and camping. Give them materials to draw pictures of their recollections. Give each child a small notebook (or paper stapled together) with a pencil attached (with yarn or string) to use as a travel log. Explain to the children that they can use their travel logs to draw, dictate, and write about things they see on a field trip or walk. They can also use them to tape items they find. For example, they could draw a picture of an animal at the zoo, tape a map of a museum, or copy the words labeling their favorite ice cream on a trip to the ice cream shop. When they return, encourage them to share their travel logs and any collected print. Collect and use them for further activities as in "Trip Through Town Rebus" stories (see page 61).

✦ Incorporate travel logs into a discussion about the five senses. Ask children to predict what types of things they might see, touch, smell, taste, and hear on a trip. During the field trip, engage them in drawing, dictating, or writing words and observations in their travel logs. Extend the activity by inviting the children to describe their experience in terms of their senses. Record their collective responses on a chart to compare and discuss.

Language in License Plates

Children will identify letters on license plates and use them to formulate words.

Objectives

Print Awareness: Children will distinguish between letters and numbers in environmental print found on license plates.

Phonics: Children will locate letters on license plates and other environmental print and identify words that start with the letters.

Oral Language/Speaking and Listening: Children will use words generated from letters on license plates in sentences.

Materials

license plates
paper
pencils

Theme Connections

Alphabet
Health and Safety
Our Community
Transportation

Literacy Interactions

✦ Make a reproducible checklist consisting of numbers and/or letters in columns and give one to each child. Encourage the children to check off letters and/or numbers they see on license plates and other environmental print while on a walk or on a field trip. Invite them to count and compare their results after the trip.

✦ Ask the children to identify the letters on license plates while on a walk or ride. Challenge them to make a word that begins with each letter on the license plates. For example, the letters in the license plate "TRA 390" could make the words "tree," "rabbit," and "apple." Encourage them to use the words in a sentence or silly story. "The *rabbit* jumped to get the *apple* out of the *tree*." Write the words or sentence next to a rubbing or copied license plate number.

Safety Note: Consider safety issues if doing this activity in a parking lot. Make sure it is a place with no moving vehicles where children can be monitored easily.

Variation

✦ Have the children locate and call out numbers in order as they are discovered on license plates and signs while on a walk. Encourage them to see how high they can go.

Packing Print for a Picnic

Children incorporate environmental print activities into planning and preparing food for a picnic.

Objectives

Print Awareness: Children will identify and distinguish among environmental print associated with food and supplies for a picnic.

Oral Language/Speaking and Listening: Children will use environmental print in songs and rhymes, and to generate clues and discussion.

Writing Process: Children will use writing/dictation in association with environmental print to communicate lists of supplies for a picnic.

Vocabulary: Children will demonstrate understanding of various words represented by environmental print through a sorting activity.

Materials

newspaper inserts, food
    containers, labels, and
    packaging
paper lunch bags
paper
scissors
tape
marker
picnic basket

Theme Connections

Grocery Store   Our Community

Literacy Interactions

✦ Incorporate songs and rhymes about picnics such as "Going on a Picnic" (written by Lynn Freeman Olson and performed by Raffi on *Corner Grocery Store*) or "Picnic Prance" below. Print out the words to the song or rhyme so that the children can follow along. Gather environmental print packaging from picnic items for children to include in the song. Provide a large picnic basket for children to put items in as they are added to the song.

"Picnic Prance" (tune: "Hokey Pokey")
You put the (insert product) in,
You put the (insert product) out,
You put the (insert product) in,
And PICNIC is what you shout.
Your basket's almost loaded
And when it's ready for you,
PICNIC is what you shout!

✦ Provide environmental print for children to cut out and use to create a cooperative list of what they think would be good to take on a picnic (juice box, band-aids, bug repellent) and what may not (ice cream, un-popped microwave popcorn, a videotape). Encourage them to separate the items on the list by taping them into two columns. Print the identifying name next to each item. Engage the children in discussions about their placement of the items. Use the list to prepare for a picnic or field trip. Have the children assist in bringing and/or gathering and packing items that might be on the list.

Book Suggestions

One Hundred Hungry Ants by Elinor Pinczes
Packing for a Picnic by Lorraine Long and Mary Lou Roberts
A Picnic in October by Eve Bunting
The School Picnic by Jan Steffy
The Teddy Bears' Picnic by Jimmy Kennedy

Postcard Expedition

Children generate stories, comments, and drawings about a trip or walk using postcards or stationery and envelopes.

Objectives

Print Awareness: Children will identify the function of environmental print as it is used in stationery and postcards.

Oral Language/Speaking and Listening: Children will explain events and observations made on a trip using postcards and letters they make.

Writing Process: Children will write, draw, or dictate observations made on a trip.

Comprehension: Children will retell events of a field trip or walk by writing, dictating, or drawing on postcards or stationery.

Materials

postcards or stationery and
    envelopes
pencils and/or markers
stamps

Theme Connections

Community Helpers
Fire Station
Grocery Store
Our Community
Pets
Post Office
Transportation
Zoo

Literacy Interactions

✦ If possible, obtain postcards or stationery from a place visited on a field trip or walk. Ask the children to write, dictate, or draw the observations they made while on the trip. Ask them about what they saw, smelled, heard, or liked. Write or help children write their addresses on the envelopes, add stamps, and let them put them in a mailbox to send to their families. Encourage them to "read" and recall events on the postcard or letter with their families.

✦ If preprinted postcards or stationery are not available, bring along blank postcards or stationery for children to make their own print to document events of the trip. Ask if the postcards or stationery can be stamped with ink or an impression used by the business or place visited. Children can also gather and cut out environmental print corresponding to their trip to put on the border of the stationery before writing, drawing, and dictating events of the trip.

Seeing the World: Alphabet Search

Children locate, identify, use, and record environmental print according to letter and/or letter sounds during a walk, field trip, or ride.

Objectives

Print Awareness: Children will learn about and look for alphabet letters and words used in environmental print during walks and on field trips.

Vocabulary: Children will learn word meanings through environmental print gathered during walks or field trips.

Writing Process: Children will use words gathered from a field trip or walk in dictated or writing experiences.

Phonics: Children will use environmental print to sort and build recognition of alphabet letters and sounds.

Oral Language/Speaking and Listening: Children will share stories, rhymes, or poems.

Materials

environmental print discovered
  while on a trip, walk, or
  ride
notebooks (one large or several
  small) or paper
pencils, crayons, or markers

Theme Connections

Alphabet
Community Helpers
Health and Safety
Our Community
Transportation

Literacy Interactions

✦ Gather blank notebooks or make them by compiling blank paper into folders. Prepare one or more notebooks to take while on a walk. Print one alphabet letter per page. Collect print from businesses or other places along the way. (**Note:** Make sure children stay away from trash.) Upon return, invite the children to put any collected print onto the matching alphabet page. Let children illustrate representations of what they saw next to the words. Use this activity to introduce and/or review word meanings. For example, "What does the word 'danger' mean?" or "What does the color 'red' often mean?" Invite the children to share stories about the trip using their book.

✦ Provide children with individual smaller notebooks to take with them during riding times or waiting times. Guide them to look for print that begins with various alphabet letters or to find print with the same letter sounds they are working on. As children locate environmental print that begins with various letters of the alphabet, record their findings on the corresponding letter page in the notebook(s). Ask them to identify the letters they know and print or dictate the identifying words in the notebook. Invite them to share their findings. Save the notebooks and encourage the children to add to them on additional trips.

✦ Encourage children to use the words from the notebook(s) to document events of the trip, or to make up silly stories or rhymes using words beginning with specific letters. Invite them to write or dictate their thoughts and observations as they look through the words they discovered. Encourage them to add illustrations.

Variation

✦ Challenge children to find, identify, and/or record environmental print discoveries in alphabetical order, such as finding print that starts with "a" and "b" before finding something that starts with "c".

"Are We There Yet?" Map

Children look for environmental print by using their own maps as they travel.

Objectives

Print Awareness: Children will learn about the function and relationship among environmental print such as symbols, words, signs, and maps.

Vocabulary: Children will learn about directional words such us "up," "left," "right," "north," "south," and so on while using maps.

Writing Process: Children will communicate a trip sequence by drawing and using symbols representing environmental print on a map.

Comprehension: Children will demonstrate their recollection of a sequence of events.

Materials

simple map of field trip route
paper
markers, crayons, and pencils
copy machine
small toy cars and plastic toy
        people

Theme Connections

Community Helpers
Health and Safety
Maps
Our Community
Transportation

Preparation

1. Gather maps related to the route that will be taken to a field trip destination or event. Before bringing children, travel the route or research to find out about landmarks, places, and signs along the way.

2. Use paper to draw a simple map of the route.

3. Include cutout pictures, drawings, and photocopies of signs, landmarks, or other print where it appears (approximately) on the route.

4. Make copies for each child.

(continued on the next page)

Literacy Interactions

✦ Before going on a field trip or to an event, introduce maps as pictures and representations of locations. Show examples of area maps or maps of places children visit, such as a zoo or museum. If possible, enlarge maps for group observation and discussion. Give each child or small group of children a simple map. Draw attention to the familiar print on the map, such as words or symbols that represent starting location, signs along the way, restaurants, gas stations, and final destination. Encourage the children to use the maps while on a walk or field trip to follow the route and locate environmental print. Provide the children with crayons or pencils to mark landmarks and print indicated on the map as they are encountered.

✦ Invite children to assist in interpreting print, signs, and symbols on the map. Engage the children in taking an imaginary trip using the maps. Insert traffic signs and business logos of places they may see along the way. Provide toy cars or toy people for children to move around the map while on the imaginary trip. Introduce the words "north," "south," "east," and "west" in combination with discussion about the top and bottom of the map (as appropriate to the developmental level of the children).

✦ Bring clipboards, drawing tools, and paper along for children to create their own adventure maps of the route. Invite them to insert their own symbols and copied words of familiar places on the map as they see them. Encourage them to share their recollection of their trip by using their map.

Variation

✦ Create a map of a trip while telling or reading a simple adventure story. Engage the children in creating parts of the "story" map. Look at the map together to review the story. Re-read the story and move a marker along the route to indicate to children where the characters are as the story progresses.

"Off We Go" Webbing

Children generate predictions and report their findings on a web using their knowledge of print, their observations, and environmental print collected on a field trip.

Objectives

Print Awareness: Children will use webbing to observe and recall the use of print as part of a field trip experience.

Vocabulary: Children will use environmental print gathered, observed, and documented during a field trip in discussion about word meanings.

Comprehension: Children will share predictions and knowledge about a place in their community.

Phonics: Children will use print grouped in a web to create lists of words by beginning alphabet letters.

Materials

environmental print obtained from or related to a field trip, such as brochures, labels, signs, and maps

large writing surface (chart paper or dry-erase board)

marker

paper

Theme Connections

Community Helpers

Food and Nutrition

Grocery Store

Our Community

Post Office

Tools and Machines

Zoo

Literacy Interactions

✦ Create a web (see sample web on the next page) containing things that may be seen on a trip to an unfamiliar place, such as an ice cream factory. Print the name of the place in a middle circle or cut out and use related environmental print. Draw lines from the middle circle to other circles that contain words or print to describe the major areas the children will see, such as "office," "tasting room," "freezer," and "packaging room." Ask them to make guesses as to what they will see in each area. Help the children generate a list of questions to bring along. Gather print on the trip and bring back to add to the web. Use the activity to examine the children's comprehension of what they saw as well as develop new vocabulary understanding.

✦ Prior to going on a field trip, encourage the children to discuss and list things, people, words, and signs they may see there. For example, a trip to the grocery store might generate discussion about the words "bakery," "frozen foods," "vegetables," and "cash register." Write the name of the place to be visited at the top or center of a writing surface ("grocery store"). Document the children's responses as "threads" from the center of the web. Note any similarities the children find among the list by combining them into areas using a web. For example, items could be grouped by food groups, toy types, or people. Ask what kinds of signs, labels, and symbols they might see to identify these groups. While on the trip, gather environmental print or take pictures of print to add to the web upon return. Use the expanded web and print to explore new vocabulary, recall the trip, and develop alphabet word lists that are associated with a topic. For example, "We saw words that begin with a 'b': 'bakery,' 'bread,' and 'barbecue sauce'."

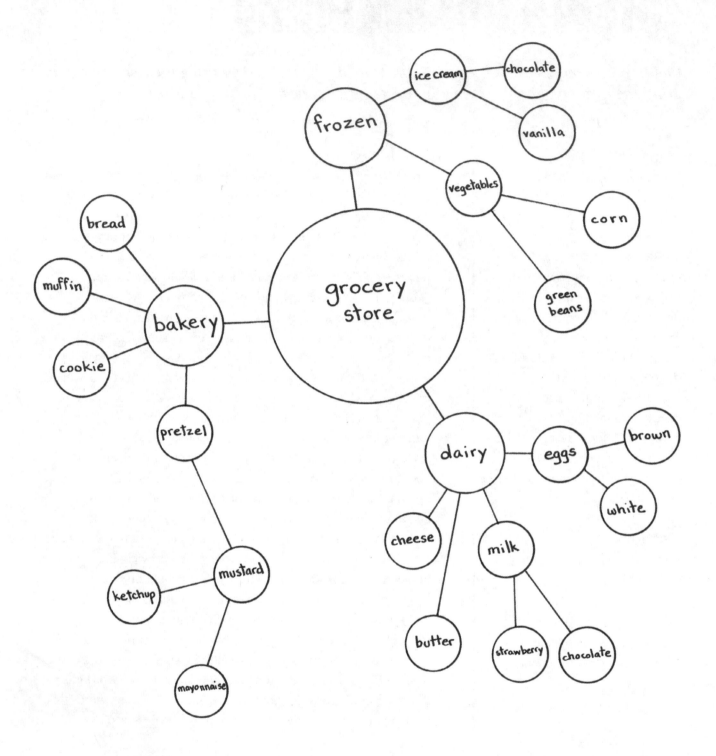

Traveling Bingo

Children match environmental print on a bingo board with places and signs they see while on a walk or a field trip.

Objectives

Print Awareness: Children will match environmental print words to identical print in a travel bingo game using one-to-one correspondence.

Vocabulary: Children will learn about sign meanings and similarities as part of playing bingo.

Phonics: Children will apply knowledge of alphabet letters and their sounds to find matching environmental print words in a bingo game.

Phonological/Phonemic Awareness: Children will demonstrate the ability to hear and identify related letter sounds in a bingo game.

Materials

small signs and logos from
　　community businesses and
　　organizations obtained from
　　stationery, newspaper
　　inserts, and photocopies
cookie sheet, magnetic boards,
　　or discarded metal CD
　　containers
permanent marker or
　　masking tape and ruler
clear packing tape or contact
　　paper
magnet tape, magnetic circles,
　　or other magnets
bingo chips, buttons, or paper
　　squares (optional)

Theme Connections

Alphabet　　　　　　　　Our Community
Community Helpers　　　Transportation
Health and Safety

Preparation

1. Draw a grid using a permanent marker on a magnetic metal surface.
2. Cut out environmental print of places, signs, and so on in the community to fit one per grid square. Tape or use contact paper to attach each picture into a square.
3. Print the identifying name of each piece of print under the corresponding picture inside the grid using a permanent marker.

(continued on the next page)

4. Cut magnet tape into pieces and adhere a bingo chip, button, or paper square to the adhesive side or use another form of magnet to create markers for the grid.

5. Optional: Make assorted sets on small surfaces such as metal CD containers so that each child has one, several larger bingo grids on cookie sheets for children to share, or photocopied assorted grids that children can mark using a crayon or pencil (see Bingo or Lotto Grid on page 244).

Literacy Interactions

◆ Introduce the environmental print the children will be looking for on the bingo boards. Encourage children to share what they know and ask questions about the signs, places, and so on. Ask them to identify similarities among the places and print, such as safety signs, restaurants, gas stations, or words and letters. Explain that they will place a magnet on each square as they find the matching sign or place on the walk or trip. Give boards to individuals or groups of children to use.

◆ Use the activity to target specific skills, such as matching alphabet letters or words on the grid with environmental print encountered. Encourage children to find and mark the spaces containing letter characteristics or words that match the print they find while on a walk or field trip.

◆ Read words from environmental print as they are encountered, and ask children to listen to and identify the sound that is represented or matches letters or words on their grid. For example, "There is a 'Shell' gas station." In this example, the children might locate the letters that represent the sound, such as /sh/, or a word that rhymes, such as "bell." These bingo boards could be used for a variety of trips, because they would not be limited to print in a specific place.

   Note: See "Alphabet Picture Bingo" on page 28 for more ideas.

Variation

◆ Provide materials such as metal CD cases, environmental print, and magnets for children to make their own magnetic bingo boards. Make the grids for them using a permanent marker. Encourage them to locate and cut out familiar print from their community to put in their grids. Send them home to use as a "time together activity" (see Chapter 9).

Photo Memories

Children identify environmental print to photograph while on a field trip or walk.

Objectives

Print Awareness: Children will identify and document print while on walks and field trips by taking photographs.

Writing Process: Children will communicate experiences and knowledge about a walk or field trip by incorporating photos of environmental print in writing, drawing, or dictating activities.

Vocabulary: Children will develop understanding of words by looking for and obtaining photographs of environmental print on walks and field trips.

Phonics: Children will identify and collect environmental print associated with specific alphabet letters and/or letter sounds through photographs.

Beginning Reading: Children will look for and collect familiar print and sight words while on walks and/or field trips.

Materials

pictures taken of print while on a field trip or walk
camera and film
notebook or photo album
paper
marker
tape or glue

Theme Connections

All About Me
Community Helpers
Cultural Awareness
Grocery Store
Our Community

Pets
Post Office
Transportation
Zoo

Literacy Interactions

✦ Show the children published books or brochures that incorporate photos and print from the community. Ask children to add their own captions or stories to the photos of environmental print they have gathered by writing, drawing, or dictation. Highlight identifying words gathered from the print in the captions or stories. Invite the children to share their understanding of messages, words, and symbols in their captions and stories. Use this as an opportunity to expand new vocabulary.

✦ Prior to the trip or walk, discuss the use of cameras with the children. Explain the criteria they should look for when taking pictures. Have the children look for items that begin or end with a specific letter sound or sight word. Engage children in seeking out environmental print during the trip, giving each child an opportunity to locate and have print photographed. (Take pictures of print that the children identify or involve them in the photo process as is feasible or age appropriate.) Put the processed photographs in a notebook or photo album and use it to review letter recognition to identify sight words, letter recognition, and so on.

Note: Ask for donations of film or disposable cameras to use on field trips. Seek parent volunteers to process film once the pictures are taken.

Variations

✦ Use this activity in conjunction with "Off We Go Webbing" on page 223.

✦ Find things that are in specific languages and lettering to integrate into a study of various cultures or to establish meaningful connections in learning a new language.

Word Hunt Wonder

Children identify and match specific simple words in environmental print found during a walk or field trip.

Objectives

Print Awareness: Children will make distinctions among print and identify functions of it while on walks or field trips.

Vocabulary: Children will look for specific words in environmental print to learn and review their meanings.

Writing Process: Children will use specific words found in print to generate written or dictated stories or drawings.

Beginning Reading: Children will look for and identify sight words among environmental print.

Materials

environmental print observed
    while on a walk or field trip
word list
paper and pencil

Theme Connections

Community Helpers
Cultural Awareness
Grocery Store
Our Community
Pets
Post Office
Transportation
Zoo

Literacy Interactions

✦ This is a great activity to introduce and/or reinforce sight words that the children are experiencing in learning, games, stories, and writing. Compile a simple word list of about five to ten sight words that children will probably see on a field trip or walk, for example, "stop," "go," "push," and "walk." Review the words and their meanings with the children before the trip and ask them to predict where they may see these words. Bring the list on the trip or walk and guide the children to mark off the words as they find them.

✦ Connect a word list from a unit to a related field trip. For example, connect a unit on pets with a trip to a pet store or veterinarian office. Invite the children to help generate a list of words they may find related to the topic, such as "dog," "cat," "food," and "pet." Bring the list along for children to search, match, and record words as they find them. Encourage the children to ask the guide to identify the words as they are used in the environment. After the trip, children can use the word hunt list to generate vocabulary for written or dictated stories and drawings about the trip. Highlight the words in the story. Post or compile stories and make them available to children to read and look at frequently.

Appendix

Suggested Books

Linking Books With My Community

ABCDrive! by Naomi Howland
Albert's Field Trip by Leslie Tryon
Around Town by Chris K. Soentpiet
Communities by Gail Saunders-Smith
Franklin's Class Trip by Paulette Bourgeois
I Read Signs by Tana Hoban
I Read Symbols by Tana Hoban
I See a Sign by Lars Klove
Miss Bindergarten Takes a Field Trip With Kindergarten by Joseph Slate
Road Signs: A Hare-y Race With a Tortoise by Margery Cuyler
Signs at School by Mary Hill
Signs by Brian Cutting
Signs by Susan Canizares

Linking Books With Science

Senses

Magic School Bus Explores the Senses by Joanna Cole
My Five Senses by Margaret Miller
Big and Little by Margaret Miller
The Spice Alphabet Book: Herbs, Spices, and Other Natural Flavors by Jerry Pallotta

Food and Nutrition

A Comer Sanamente! Eating Right by Elizabeth Vogel
Food by Sally Hewitt
El Alimento by Emma Nathan
Food Around the World by Pat Lakin
The Food Pyramid by Janine Scott
Let's Eat: Foods of Our World by Janine Scott

Recycling

Recycle!: A Handbook for Kids by Gail Gibbons
Recycle That! by Fay Robinson
Waste Not: Time to Recycle by Rebecca Weber

Trees

The Giving Tree by Shel Silverstein
A Tree Is Nice by Janice May Udry
Paper, Paper Everywhere by Gail Gibbons

Gardens and Seeds

Growing Vegetable Soup by Lois Ehlert
The Victory Garden Vegetable Alphabet Book by Jerry Pallotta
Garden by Robert Maass
A Gardener's Alphabet by Mary Azarian
Grow It Again by Elizabeth MacLeod
Growing Vegetables by Tracy Maurer
This Is Your Garden by Maggie Smith
Seeds by Gail Saunders-Smith

Suggested Environmental Print Books

Go to the library together and locate some of the other environmental print books. Read and enjoy them together. Refer to this list of environmental print books.

ABCDrive!: A Car Trip Alphabet by Naomi Howland
The Cereal Box by David McPhail
The Cheerios Counting Book (available in Spanish) by Barbara Barbieri McGrath
City Signs by Zoran Milich
The Crayon Counting Book by Pam Muñoz Ryan and Jerry Pallotta
I Read Signs by Tana Hoban
I Read Symbols by Tana Hoban
I See a Sign by Lars Klove
School Bus: For the Buses, the Riders, and the Watchers by Donald Crews

Signs by Brian Cutting

Signs by Susan Canizares

Signs at School by Mary Hill

Signs at the Airport by Mary Hill

Signs at the Pool by Mary Hill

The Story of Money by Betsy Maestro

Supermarket by Kathleen Krull

The Supermarket by Gail Saunders-Smith

Taxi: A Book of City Words by Betsy Maestro

Twizzlers: Shapes and Patterns by Jerry Pallotta

Linking Books With Building

A Busy Day at the Building Site by Phillippe
    Dupasquier

Building a House by Byron Barton

Construction Site (Who Works Here?) by Lola M.
    Schaefer

Construction Workers by Tami Deedrick

Jesse Builds a Road by Laurence Pringle

How a House Is Built by Gail Gibbons

New Road! by Gail Gibbons

Road Builders by B.G. Hennessy

Road Signs: A Hare-y Race With a Tortoise by
    Margery Cuyler

Those Building Men by Angela Johnson

Tunnels by Gail Gibbons

Up Goes the Skyscraper! by Gail Gibbons

Dear Parents,

Parents lead very busy lives. Take an inventory of your busy week and see how many of the following things you do without even thinking about it.

- ✦ write a grocery or "to do" list
- ✦ write or type a letter or email
- ✦ address or sign cards or bills
- ✦ read a book, magazine, newspaper, or note
- ✦ follow a map
- ✦ follow a recipe
- ✦ read and follow instructions (food product, equipment manual, game)
- ✦ read traffic signs
- ✦ read business signs
- ✦ read the label on a packaged food product
- ✦ read a TV guide
- ✦ read a menu in a restaurant
- ✦ look for something in alphabetical order (such as a name in a phone book)
- ✦ go to the library
- ✦ read mail
- ✦ look at newspaper inserts, catalogs, and sale flyers
- ✦ sort something by name (mail, food products)

Did you know that throughout the day these activities have the potential to help your child learn to read and write? By involving your child in the process of doing these activities and talking to them about alphabet letters, letter sounds, words, word meanings, and spelling, you can get your child off to a good start in literacy development.

The suggested activities involve using and creating print in your everyday surroundings. This print is sometimes referred to as environmental print. You may have experienced the power of this print with your child when he or she "reads" a favorite restaurant sign, toy, or food label.

We will be using environmental print often in our learning center/school by incorporating print children are familiar with into daily activities to develop literacy skills. To support this, we will be asking you to save and send in specific items throughout the year, as well as participate in activities sent home to do with your child.

Thank you,

Cereal boxes

Restaurant coupons

Grocery coupons

Store sale circulars

Boxed food labels

Canned food labels

Flavored gelatin boxes

Juice boxes

Seed packages

Signs

Restaurant food packages

Comic strips from newspapers

Newspapers

Photographs of businesses

Maps

Catalogs

Magazines

Restaurant food containers

Pizza boxes

Baking ingredient containers

Soup labels

Take-home restaurant menus

Assorted food packaging

Travel and business brochures

Voided gift cards or tickets

Junk mail

Used greeting cards and/or envelopes

Nametags, shirts, and caps with business logos

Blueprints

Travel posters

Children's movie posters

Business posters (restaurants, stores, and so on)

Alliteration: The repetition of the same initial sound, for example, "tasty, tingly toothpaste."

Comprehension: The ability to pull meaning from spoken and written words.

Consonant Blend: A combination of two or more consonants blended together where all letters are sounded, such as /bl/ in "blue."

Consonant Digraph: Two letters representing one sound, such as /ch/ in "chicken."

Context Clues: Picture, color, or shape clues that are closely matched to the words so that a "reader" can decipher the meaning of an unknown word.

Developmental or Invented Spelling: Early writing of words using known alphabet letters. Child then begins to include letters represented by understanding of sounds or phonemes to create words.

Dictated or Interactive Writing: The process in which an adult prints a child's verbal lists, stories, and thoughts.

Emergent Reader: A child in the beginning stages of learning to read. Child can identify alphabet letters and sounds, look at a book, and interpret, predict and retell familiar stories using pictures.

Environmental Print: The symbols, letters, and words encountered in one's community or life every day.

Homophones: Words that sound the same but look different, for example, "flower" and "flour."

Learning Environment: The area where children are taught, guided, and allowed to explore (for example, home, school, child care center, and camp).

Onset: All of the sounds in a word that come before the first vowel, for example /bl/ in "block."

Print Awareness: The understanding that print conveys meaning, the rules children need to know before they can learn to read. These include understanding the difference between letters and words, the left to right direction of text, and that words communicate meaning.

Phoneme: The smallest units of sound that may be used to form words, such as /b/ /a/ /t/ in "bat."

Phonemic Awareness: The awareness that spoken words are made of sounds, and the ability to identify individual sounds in spoken words.

Phonemic Blending: Blending individual sounds together to make words, for example, /d/ /o/ /g/ to make "dog."

Phonemic Segmentation: Breaking a word into its sounds by separating a word, for example, "man" into /m/ /a/ /n/.

Phonics: Relationship between alphabet letters and sounds in written words or a teaching method that stresses sound-symbol relationships.

Phonological Awareness: Awareness of speech sounds and rhythms, rhymes, sound similarities, and syllables.

Primary Language: The first language a child learns to speak.

Rime: The first vowel in a word along with all of the sounds that follow, for example, /-ock/ in "block."

Rhyming Words: Words that have the same ending sounds (for example, "pop" and "hop").

Sight Words: A word that is recognized automatically, without having to sound out.

Syllable: The smallest part that a spoken word can be broken into that includes a vowel. For example, "peanut" has two syllables, pea-nut.

Visual Tracking: Following a finger or pointer to show the correspondence of spoken and written words.

Vocabulary: The knowledge of words and their meanings.

Word Families: Words that contain the same rime. For example, the "_at" family contains words such as "cat," "pat," "hat," "mat," and "fat."

Word Wall: A chart that list words that young readers can learn to recognize and read.

Number	Item	Cost
_____	_____	$ _____
_____	_____	$ _____
_____	_____	$ _____
_____	_____	$ _____
_____	_____	$ _____
_____	_____	$ _____
_____	_____	$ _____
_____	_____	$ _____
_____	_____	$ _____

Shopping List Sample

Paper products
_____
_____
_____
_____

Dairy
_____
_____
_____
_____

Meat
_____
_____
_____
_____

Vegetables
_____
_____
_____
_____

Bread and Cereal
_____
_____
_____
_____

Fruit
_____
_____
_____
_____

Snacks and Sweets
_____
_____
_____
_____

Drinks
_____
_____
_____
_____

To: _____

From: _____

Message: _____

To: _____

From: _____

Message: _____

To: _____

From: _____

Message: _____

To: _____

From: _____

Message: _____

TICKET

Event:

Date:

Price:

Time:

TICKET

Event:

Date:

Price:

Time:

TICKET

Event:

Date:

Price:

Time:

TICKET

Event:

Date:

Price:

Time:

TICKET

Event:

Date:

Price:

Time:

TICKET

Event:

Date:

Price:

Time:

WALK

DON'T
WALK

Gryphon House, Inc. grants permission for this page to be photocopied for classroom use only.

Recipes

Safety Note: Be aware of any food allergies of children in the class before using any of these recipes.

Dirt Dough Recipe #1

2 cups flour

1 cup salt

2 tablespoons vegetable oil

brown food coloring (sold as baker's paste or gel)

1 cup water

Stir together flour and salt. Add vegetable oil. Add food coloring to water to create dark brown. Gradually add brown water to flour, salt, and oil mixture. Stir. Knead. Keep in covered container when not in use.

Dirt Dough Recipe #2

2 cups clean potting soil

2 cups sand

½ cup salt

1 to 2 cups water

Combine dry ingredients together. Add water gradually to form dough. Store in covered container.

Pizza Dough

2 small packages of dry yeast

⅔ cup warm water (105–115°)

2 tablespoons sugar

2 cups water

3 tablespoons cooking oil

1 teaspoon salt

7 cups flour

Pour yeast on top of warm water. Stir in a little of the sugar and let stand for five minutes. Combine remaining sugar, salt, and 3 ½ cups of flour in a separate bowl. Add 2 cups of water and oil. Stir. Add yeast mixture and stir. Gradually add remaining 3 ½ cups of flour to make a dough ball. Knead. Let rise until double in size. Punch down and form onto two round pizza pans or cookie sheets. If dough is sticky, add a little oil to the outside. Bake for 5–10 minutes at 400° to harden crust. Remove and add toppings. Bake at 400° to 450° until crust edge is golden and cheese is melted, approximately 15–20 minutes.

Pizza dough substitutes:

English muffins

canned biscuit dough (rolled or flattened)

crescent roll dough (rolled or flattened)

boxed pizza dough mix

Ice Cream Recipe #1

1 cup heavy whipping cream, milk, or half-and-half

1 tablespoon sugar

1 teaspoon vanilla extract

1 zipper-closure sandwich bag

packing tape (optional)

1 zipper-closure freezer bag (quart or gallon size)

6–8 ice cubes

4–6 tablespoons rock salt

clear plastic container with lid

1 spoon

Pour the cream, milk, or half-and-half cream into the sandwich bag. Add sugar and vanilla. Seal bag. Tape with packing tape, if desired, to ensure it doesn't leak. Place the sandwich bag inside the freezer bag. Place ice cubes and rock salt inside freezer bag. Seal the freezer bag and tape again. Shake bag. If if is too cold to hold, place it inside a clear plastic container with lid and shake some more. Shake between 5–15 minutes. Carefully remove and wipe away outer freezer bag, salt, and ice. Open sandwich bag and enjoy ice cream!

Ice Cream Recipe #2

2 small packages instant pudding (any flavor)
4 cups of cold milk
1 ½ quarts of half-and-half

Mix pudding with milk. Place in refrigerator until set. Mix pudding and half and half. Pour into ice cream freezer container. Fill to fit container. Freeze ice cream according to ice cream freezer directions. Makes approximately 3 quarts.

Chocolate "Ice Cream" Playdough

1 ¼ cups flour
½ cup cocoa powder
½ cup salt
½ tablespoon cream of tartar
1 ½ tablespoons cooking oil
1 cup boiling water

Mix dry ingredients together in a saucepan. Add oil and water and stir to mix well. Cook over low heat and stir until dough forms. Cool. Knead. Store in airtight container.

Berry "Ice Cream" Playdough

2 cups flour
1 cup salt
4 tablespoons cream of tartar
1 small package of fruit-flavored gelatin
2 cups boiling water
2 tablespoons cooking oil

Mix dry ingredients together in a saucepan. Add oil and boiling water. Stir over heat until mixture forms into a ball. Cool. Knead. Store in airtight container

Sweet Snack Mix ("Puppy Chow" for people)

1 large box of rice square cereal
1 stick of butter
1 cup peanut butter
1 (12 oz.) package chocolate chips
4 cups powdered sugar

Melt butter, peanut butter, and chocolate chips in a saucepan or microwave until smooth. Stir. Pour over cereal in large container with lid. Cover with lid and shake. Open and add powdered sugar. Cover again and shake.

Coin Patterns

Penny
Nickel
Dime
Quarter
Half dollar

Index

Book Index

Theme Connections Index